FROMMER'S
1983-84 GUIDE TO MEXICO CITY & ACAPULCO

by Tom Brosnahan

Published by Frommer/Pasmantier Publishers
A Simon & Schuster Division of
Gulf & Western Corporation
1230 Avenue of the Americas
New York, NY 10020

ISBN: 0–671–45298–3

Manufactured in the United States of America

Motif drawings by Ken Weiner

*Although every effort was made to ensure the accuracy
of price information appearing in this book,
it should be kept in mind that prices
can and do fluctuate in the course of time.*

CONTENTS

MAPS

A Word About Prices

You're liable to get your first unpleasant shock in Mexico when you sit down to survey a restaurant menu and see "Hamburger—$100." The wave of relief comes as you realize that the dollar sign "$" is used to indicate *pesos* in Mexico, and that your 100-dollar hamburger actually only costs 100 pesos, or about two dollars. To avoid confusion in this book, we use the dollar sign *only* to indicate U.S. dollars; peso amounts are written as just figures alone, or are qualified by the word "pesos."

Sometimes Mexican establishments will quote prices in U.S. dollars, usually written "$2 Dlls."; for the peso price, then, they may write "$100 m.n.," meaning "100 pesos, *moneda nacional*" (that is, Mexican national currency).

Although every effort is made to ensure that the information given is accurate and up-to-date at press time, keep in mind that some transportation schedules, museum opening hours, telephone numbers, and other such data may change by the time you reach Mexico.

Note also that Mexico has a Value Added Tax, or "Impuesto de Valor Agregado." Abbreviated "IVA," (EE-bah), the 10% tax appears on most bills you'll get in Mexico: hotels, restaurants, rental cars, souvenirs, transportation tickets. Essentials such as medicines are exempt. Some modest hotels and restaurants don't bother to charge IVA. Always ask whether IVA has been included.

Converting Pesos to Dollars

As this book goes to press, the Mexican economy is in chaos. This is bad news for Mexicans but very good news for foreign tourists. You may find that you'll pay even *less* than the prices indicated in this book, in terms of dollars for rooms and meals.

With inflation in Mexico running at 100% per year and the peso fluctuating wildly, our dollar prices (figured at U.S. $1=50 pesos), may be your best guide to actual costs. The peso prices will undoubtedly be higher, but that won't really matter to you.

To help you get used to spending Mexican money, here's a blank currency exchange table. Fill in the dollar values after you change money.

Pesos	U.S. $	Pesos	U.S. $
1		75	
5		100	
10		250	
15		500	
20		1,000	
25		5,000	
50			

Chapter I

MEXICO: AN INTRODUCTION

MEXICO GREETS MILLIONS of foreign visitors every year. Most come from the United States and Canada, but there are respectable numbers coming from Europe, Japan, and Central and South America. It's surprising how many people return to Mexico again and again over the years—until one considers what the country has to offer.

Look first at the land: vast stretches of desert, mighty mountain ranges (and some peaks that are snowy all year round), thousands of miles of lush, tropical seacoast, lowland jungle, and regions of hills and valleys not unlike those of Central Europe, California, or New England. From the breathtaking canyons of Chihuahua to the flat coastal plain of Yucatán, from the Pacific sandbar of Baja California to Mexico's Caribbean islands of Cancún and Cozumel, the country stretches 2000 miles from sea to sea. The land has a varied and incredible scenic beauty, plus a fabulous array of natural resources which have made it rich through the centuries, from Aztec gold hordes to present-day Chiapan oil reserves.

Look next at the people: the original Indian inhabitants saw the rise and fall of a dozen great civilizations including the Olmec, Toltec, Maya, and Aztec, before the coming of the Spanish *conquistadores*. Africans brought as slaves escaped to the relative freedom of Spanish Mexico, and Europeans of a dozen countries came on business and stayed for generations. There is even a French influence from the ill-fated attempt by Napoleon III, emperor of France, to set up a European-style Empire of Mexico with Archduke Maximilian of Hapsburg as its first emperor. The monarchy fell, but the style of music preferred by French-influenced Mexican society lives on in the mariachis (from the French word for marriage). Mexicans are not strangers to greatness, and their flair for a colorful and exciting way of life is right there to see today, especially in and around Mexico City and Acapulco. Who can say which influence played the most important part in shaping modern Mexico—the mysterious pre-Columbian cultures, the wealth of the land, the European colonizers, or Mexico's powerful neighbor to the north? The result is a land and a way of life unique in all the world, shaped by 10,000 years of history.

And you can get more than just a glimpse of this unique land by traveling to only two cities: Mexico City and Acapulco. The capital, and in many ways the center of the Republic of Mexico, Mexico City offers not only a taste of the whole country rolled up in one place, but also a colorful mixture of Mexico's past and present—the past dramatically preserved in the glorious Spanish colonial or 19th-century Baroque-style buildings and many other gracious, historic monuments, and the present expressed in the city's exciting and experimental use of modern art and architecture.

And just as Mexico City mixes history and culture with avant-garde design and the modern business practices of a great metropolis, Acapulco provides a playground unexcelled in the Western Hemisphere. Although a major city in its own right, Acapulco has enough sun-kissed beaches, glamorous resort hotels, tiny hideaways, discos, and parties to make you forget about the rest of the world as you luxuriate in the good life.

But before we tell you the specifics about these two seemingly contrasting cities, let's look at the background they both share, which has helped make them what they are today—fascinating places to see, to live in, to enjoy, and, hopefully, to return to as many times as we have.

A Brief History

The earliest "Mexicans" were Stone Age men and women, descendants of the race which crossed the Bering Strait and reached North America prior to about 10,000 B.C. These were people who hunted mastodons, bison, and the like, and gathered other food as they could. Later (5200–1500 B.C.), signs of agriculture and domestication appeared, and by 2400 B.C. the art of potting had been discovered.

THE PRECLASSIC PERIOD: It was in the period from 2000 B.C. to A.D. 300 that the area known by archeologists as Middle

America (from the northern Mexico Valley through Guatemala) began to show signs of a farming culture, by the "slash-and-burn" method, or by constructing terraces and irrigation ducts, this latter method being the one used principally in the highlands around Mexico City, where the first large towns developed. At some time during this period, religion became an institution as certain men took the role of *shaman,* or guardian of the magical and religious secrets. These were the predecessors of the folk healers and nature priests still to be found in modern Mexico.

The most highly developed culture of this Preclassic Period was that of the Olmecs, flourishing a full millennium before that of the Mayas. From 1200 to 400 B.C. the Olmecs lived in what is today the state of Tabasco, south of Veracruz, and it was to this coastal land that they transported colossal 40-ton blocks of basalt, carved as roundish heads. Besides their achievements in sculpture, the Olmecs were the first in Mexico to use a calendar of 365 days.

THE CLASSIC PERIOD: Most of the real artistic and cultural achievement came during the Classic Period (A.D. 300–900), when life was no longer centered in the villages but rather in cities. Class distinctions, absent from village life, arose as the military and religious aristocracy took control, a class of merchants and artisans grew, and the farmer who had been independent became the serf under a landlord's control. The cultural centers of this period were the Yucatán (home of the Maya), the Mexican Highlands at Teotihuacan (outside present-day Mexico City), the Zapotec cities of Monte Alban and Mitla (near Oaxaca), and the Totonac cities of Tajin and Zempoala on the Gulf Coast.

The Mayas are at the apex of pre-Columbian cultures. Besides their superior artistic achievements, the Mayas made significant discoveries in science, including the use of the zero in mathematics and their famous, complex calendar with which their priests could predict eclipses and the movements of the stars for centuries to come. The Mayas were warlike, but their sacrifices—some of them human—were on a very small scale compared to those of their successors, the bloodthirsty Aztecs.

THE POSTCLASSIC PERIOD: In the Postclassic Period (900–1520) warlike cultures in time developed impressive societies of their own, although they never surpassed the Classic peoples. All paintings and hieroglyphs of this period show war, migration, and disruption. Somehow the glue of society became unstuck, people wandered from their homes in search of a better life, the religious hierarchy lost influence over the people.

Finally, in the 1300s, the most warlike people of all, the Aztecs, settled in the Mexico Valley on Lake Texcoco (site of Mexico City), with the island city of Tenochtitlán as their capital. In time it grew to become a huge (pop. 300,000) and impressive capital. Its high lords became fabulously rich in gold, stores of food, cotton, and perfumes; the artisans were skilled and prosperous; events of state were occasions of elaborate ceremony. But the other part of the picture was that of the victorious Aztecs returning from battle to sacrifice thousands of captives on the altars atop the pyramids, cutting their chests open with stone knives and ripping the living hearts out to offer to their gods.

THE SPANISH CONQUISTADORES: When Hernan Cortes and his men landed in 1519 in what would become Veracruz, the Aztec empire was ruled by Moctezuma (also, misspelled, Montezuma) in great splendor. Despite the fact that Moctezuma and his ministers received the *conquistadores* with full pomp and glory when they reached Mexico City, Cortes pronounced the Aztec chief to be under arrest and had him tortured. Moctezuma never did reveal where he had hidden his fabulous treasure, which had been seen by a Spaniard earlier.

The Spanish conquest had started out as an adventure by Cortes and his men, unauthorized by the Spanish Crown or its governor in Cuba, but the conquest was not to be reversed and soon Christianity was being spread through "New Spain." Guatemala and Honduras were explored and conquered, and by 1540 the territory of New Spain included Spanish possessions from Vancouver to Panama. In the two centuries that followed, Franciscan and Augustinian friars converted great numbers of Indians to Christianity, and the Spanish lords built up huge feudal estates on which the Indian farmers were little more than serfs. The silver and gold which Cortes had sought made Spain the richest country in Europe.

INDEPENDENCE: Spain ruled Mexico through a viceroy until 1821, when Mexico finally gained its independence after a decade of upheaval. The independence movement had begun in 1808 when a priest, Fr. Miguel Hidalgo, cried from his pulpit "Mexicans, long live Mexico!" The revolt soon became a revolution, and their "army" threatened Mexico City. Ultimately the revolt failed, and Hidalgo was executed, but he is honored as Mexico's earliest patriot, "the Father of Modern Mexico." When independence finally came, there was a succession of presidents and military dictators until one of the most bizarre and extraordinary episodes in modern times: the French intervention.

In the 1860s, certain factions among the Mexican upper class offered the Hapsburg Archduke Maximilian the crown of Mexico, and with the support of the ambitious French emperor, Napoleon III, the young Austrian actually came to Mexico and "ruled" for three years (1864–1867) while the country was·in a state of civil war. The French emperor finally withdrew his troops, leaving the brave but misguided Maximilian to be captured and shot in Queretaro. His adversary and successor (as president of Mexico) was a Zapotec Indian lawyer named Benito Juárez, one of the most powerful and heroic figures in Mexican history. Juárez did his best to unify and strengthen his country, but he died in 1872. His effect on the future of Mexico was profound, however, and his plans and visions continued to bear fruit for decades to come.

From 1877 to 1911 the prime role in the drama of Mexico was played by one of Juárez's generals, an emotional strongman named Porfirio Díaz. Hailed by some as a modernizer, he was a terror to his enemies and to anyone who stood in his way or challenged his absolute power. He was finally forced to step down in 1911 by Francisco Madero and the greater part of public opinion.

The turbulent era from the fall of Porfirio Díaz through the next ten years is referred to as the Mexican Revolution. Drastic reforms were proposed and carried out by the leaders in this period, and the surge of vitality and progress from this exciting if turbulent time has inspired Mexicans down to the present day. Succeeding presidents have invoked the spirit of the Revolution, and it is still studied and discussed.

MEXICO TODAY: The United Mexican States today is a democratic country headed by an elected president and a bicameral legislature. It's divided into 31 states, plus the Federal District (Mexico City). The population of about 70 million is 15% white (descendants of the Spaniards); 60% mestizo, or mixed Spanish and Indian blood; and 25% pure Indian (descendants of the

Mayas, Aztecs, and other tribes). Although Spanish is the official language, about 50 Indian languages are still spoken, mostly in the Yucatán Peninsula and the mountainous region of Oaxaca. Economically, Mexico is not by any means a poor country. Only about a sixth of the economy is in agriculture. Mining, which made the Spanish colonists and their king fabulously rich, is still fairly important. Gold and silver account for some of it, and there are many other important minerals still mined, but the big industry today is oil. In the last several years fields which promise to be very rich have been opened up in Chiapas, on the Guatemalan border, and Tabasco, supplementing Mexico's already sizable income from oil. Mexico is also well industrialized, manufacturing textiles, food products, everything from high-quality auto parts to tape cassettes.

In short, Mexico is well into the 20th century, with all the benefits and problems which contemporary life brings, and although vast sums are spent on education and public welfare (much, much more than is spent on implements of war), a high birth rate and unequal distribution of wealth show that much remains to be done.

Preparing for Your Trip

As you can see, Mexico is a special place, not at all just-like-home. And although the modern conveniences, good transportation, excellent hotels, and inviting restaurants make Mexico an easy place to get to know, there are still a number of things you must consider before you climb aboard a Mexico-bound jet. For instance, you *must* have a Tourist Card, cheaper and easier to get than a passport, but absolutely essential. Then, if you plan to visit both Mexico City *and* Acapulco, you must realize that the capital is in a mountain valley over a mile above sea level, while the jet-set resort is practically in the tropics: pack accordingly. Here's all you'll need to know:

LEGAL DOCUMENTS: Visitors to Mexico from the United States and Canada need only a Tourist Card, issued free and good for up to six months, to enter and leave the country. Tourist Cards are issued to American and Canadian citizens who can show proof of citizenship such as a passport, or a birth certificate (note that a driver's license is *not* sufficient evidence of citizenship). You can get your Tourist Card at any office of the Mexican National Tourist Council (there are offices in Atlanta, Chicago,

Dallas, Houston, Los Angeles, Miami, Montréal, New Orleans, New York, Phoenix, San Antonio, San Diego, San Francisco, Toronto, Tucson, Washington, and Vancouver), at a Mexican consulate or embassy, or at the airport when you take off for Mexico (but remember to bring your proof of citizenship). Often the travel agent will obtain a Tourist Card for you along with your airplane reservation and ticket.

When you apply for your Tourist Card, ask to have it validated for six months—the full legal time limit. Although you may not be staying that long, you don't want to get caught for any reason with your Tourist Card running out—it takes a tremendous bureaucratic hassle to get an extension. Who knows? You may find the perfect stretch of beach and not want to leave, or may fall in love, or get a new job, or break a leg, and the last thing you'll want to worry over is the expiration date on your Tourist Card.

The Tourist Card is your passport in Mexico. Hold onto it carefully. You won't be permitted to leave the country without it. If you have a valid passport, it's handy to have along for cashing travelers checks and other matters.

Young people under 18 entering Mexico alone will need a notarized statement of parental consent, signed by both parents, to get their Tourist Cards. One parent entering Mexico with a minor must have a statement of consent from the other parent.

RESERVE IN ADVANCE FOR HOLIDAYS: The end-of-the-year Christmas/New Year's holidays are very popular times to visit Mexico City and Acapulco, so be sure your flight and hotel reservations are made well in advance. Also, February is Acapulco's busiest month, and you might take similar precautions if you plan to zoom down and warm up at that time. Remember that Mexican as well as American holidays can fill up Acapulco and Mexico City hotels to capacity: check your vacation dates against Chapter XIV, "Travel Tips," under Holidays. Note also that the Mexican government lets loose its thousands of office workers during the months of May and September for staggered one- or two-week vacations. This means that during those months, hotels, particularly those in the low- and moderately priced categories, are often full. Plan accordingly, plan ahead. If you decide to dare it and come anyway without reservations during a busy time, try to arrive as early as possible in the day so you can look for a room cancellation.

WEATHER, CLOTHING, PACKING: As for your clothing needs, Mexico City is high up, and so you'll need a topcoat in winter and preferably a couple of sweaters. In summer, it gets warm during the day and cool, but not cold, at night, It also rains almost every afternoon or evening between May and October (this is common all over Mexico)—so take a raincoat, or plan to dodge the drops for an hour.

Depending on the level at which you choose to live, you may need some semiformal clothing of the jacket-and-tie class, as most of the better restaurants have dress codes. In Acapulco this is even more important as the better hotels tend to be the scene of impromptu fashion shows among the guests—you may even want to bring a change of bathing suit. It can be rainy (and thus chilly) in Acapulco any time of year, and while infrequent, these storms can come suddenly and violently. Otherwise, weather in Acapulco is hot and humid in summer (both night and day), warm and less humid in winter, with cool evenings.

Remember to buy suntan lotion and film, plus any other cosmetics you use regularly. All of these things are available in Mexico, but they tend to be much more expensive than at home.

HEALTH AND MEDICAMENTS: Of course, the very best ways to avoid illness or to mitigate its effects are to make sure that you're in top health and that you *don't overdo it.* Travel, Mexico City's altitude, strange foods, upset schedules, overambitious sightseeing and swimming tend to take more of your energy than a normal working day, and missed meals provide less of the nutrition you need. Make sure you get three good, wholesome meals a day, get *more* rest than you normally do, don't push yourself if you're not feeling in top form, and you'll be able to fight off the *turista.* This is the name given to the pervasive diarrhea, often accompanied by fever, nausea, and vomiting, which attacks so many travelers to Mexico on their first trip. Doctors say it's not just one "bug," or factor, but a combination of different food and water, upset schedules, overtiring, and the stresses that accompany travel. I get it when I'm tired and careless about what I eat.

Should you come down with *turista,* the first thing to do is go to bed, stay there, and don't move on until it runs its course. Traveling with the illness only makes it last longer, whereas you can be over it in a day or so if you take it easy. Drink lots of liquids: tea without milk or sugar, or the Mexican *te de manzanilla* (camomile tea), is best. Eat only *pan tostada* (dry toast rusks), sold in grocery stores and *panaderias* (bakeries). Keep to this diet for at least 24 hours, and you'll be well over the worst of it. If you fool yourself into thinking that a plate of enchiladas can't hurt, you'll be back at Square One as far as the *turista* is concerned.

A drug recommended by your doctor is good to have along, although you should realize that no drug can restore your digestive tract to smooth functioning in an hour or two. Only time, rest, and careful eating can do that. Many *norteamericanos* have found that Pepto-Bismol, taken when *turista* hits, or even beforehand as a preventive, is a helpful, safe, and inexpensive medicine available without prescription.

Usually a person gets this illness only once on a trip, often within the first two to four days in the country. Drink only the water which is known to be *agua potable* (drinking water) or *agua purificada* (purified water) and avoid all unprocessed milk products, especially cream. Don't hesitate to consult a doctor about any illness if it begins to worry you.

Sometimes Acapulco's less expensive hotels do not equip their rooms with screens against mosquitos. In any case, insect repellant is good to have, and a small tube of antihistamine cream (available at many drugstores at home without a prescription) will soothe the itch and reduce the swelling of any sort of bite.

THE LANGUAGE: Of course, not everyone in Mexico speaks English (this isn't as silly as it sounds; these days English is taught in most Mexican schools), so it helps tremendously to have some basic vocabulary at your fingertips. For this, the Berlitz *Latin American Spanish for Travellers* Phrase Book, available at most bookstores, cannot be recommended highly enough.

THE WAGES OF CHANGE: It might be good to put in a word about prices and inflation. Back in the halcyon days (less than two decades ago) when prices throughout the world changed at a rate of about 3% a year, a traveler could take dad's copy of a good travel book abroad and make a mental adjustment for a small price rise. But recently the inflation rate for Mexico has been in the neighborhood of 50% to 70% per annum; some businesses (hotels and restaurants included) will hold off as long as they can, perhaps two years, and then raise prices by even more than this factor, perhaps as much as 100%. Every effort is made to provide the most accurate and up-to-date information in this book, even to the point of predicting price increases which I feel are on the way and which will arrive before the book reaches the reader's hands; but changes are inevitable and uncontrollable with inflation. Keep in mind when you look at price lists that even though the price may have risen over that given in the book, *the place recommended will still be a good value for the money.*

Speaking of currency, don't forget that the dollar sign ($) is used by Mexicans to denote their own national currency, and thus a Mexican menu will have "$20" for a Coke and mean 20 pesos (44¢). To avoid confusion I will use the dollar sign in this book *only* to denote U.S. currency. Peso prices will be listed either merely with figures or with the qualifying word "pesos."

With a bit of history under your belt and the advance preparations taken care of, you're ready to begin explorations in one of the world's greatest—and largest—cities.

Skyscrapers in downtown Mexico City

Chapter II

INTRODUCING MEXICO CITY

MANY FIRST-TIME VISITORS to Mexico City don't know what to expect of this great city 7240 feet in the sky. "Third world" capital? Teeming metropolis of over 15 million souls? Much to their delight, they find an absolutely fascinating modern city reminiscent of Madrid, Paris, or London, with striking and beautiful architecture, green parks, efficient public transport, plentiful cultural opportunities, and a worldwide assortment of restaurants and nightspots.

Mexico City has been at the center of Mexican national life for more than five centuries. In fact, the first important community to build on the shores of Lake Texcoco was that of Teotihuacan in 300 B.C. The tremendous pyramids and massive altars constructed by these mysterious people still stand, silent and eerie as the Sphinx, just outside the modern city at the base of the mountains which ringed the lake. But it was the Aztecs who began the current era of the city's life by building their great capital of Tenochtitlán on an island in the middle of the lake, roughly where the colonial Zócalo stands today. The Aztec kings who chose the spot did so in obedience to a prophecy which ordered them to build where they saw an eagle with a snake in its mouth alight upon a cactus—the symbol of this prophecy is today emblazoned on the Mexican flag and on every one-peso piece that jingles in your pocket. The great city they built was worthy of the immense empire they governed, and was graced with huge temples and pyramids, and decorated with staggering amounts of gold. Massive causeways stretched from the island in the lake to the shore at Chapultepec ("Grasshopper Hill" in Nahuatl, the language of the Aztecs), and these causeways were fortified against enemy attacks and rebellions. After a tantalizing look at Tenochtitlán as guests, the Spanish *conquistadores* returned with Indian armies opposed to Aztec rule and fought ferocious, bloody battles on the causeways and in the waters of the lake to take the city. When they finally emerged victorious in 1521, the great Aztec capital was pillaged and ruined, its treasures robbed, its temples pulled down, its idols smashed. Very little remained of this city of 300,000 inhabitants. Most of what we know about it is in the writings of the *conquistadores,* especially in the books of Bernal Díaz del Castillo, who saw there "great towers and temples and buildings rising from the water— it was like the enchantments!" Today, exciting archeological discoveries are bringing to light some traces of ancient Tenochtitlán. The construction of Mexico City's Metro system revealed some Aztec works, now on view in the Pino Suarez Metro station, and in 1978 an eight-ton Aztec monolith, a serpent sculpture, and the base of a pyramid were uncovered by electric company excavations just beside the National Cathedral, near the Zócalo.

After the Aztec defeat, Mexico City became the capital of the Spanish colonial state of New Spain, and many buildings went up in the style which had been brought from Spain. Lots of these grand and ornate old structures still grace the streets around the Zócalo and the Alameda Central. Lake Texcoco was gradually filled in as this construction advanced, until in the mid-1800s Maximilian of Hapsburg could (and did) plan a grand boulevard on dry land from the older part of the city to Chapultepec Castle, where he and Empress Carlotta had established themselves. Maximilian's boulevard is now the Paseo de la Reforma, the grandest and most beautiful thoroughfare in Mexico, and perhaps in all of North America.

Today much of the wealth of Mexico is funnelled through the banks, businesses, and government offices located here, and the city has great resources to draw on for its operation and beautification. In fact, the industries and businesses of the capital area produce over a third of the nation's Gross National Product, even though only a fifth of Mexico's population lives here.

But wealth and industrialization produce problems, notably traffic jams and pollution. Of these, Mexico City has its share— some visitors say more than its share. Anyone with respiratory problems will find some days when the altitude and the smog combine to make eyes watery, noses runny, and throats scratchy. Often the smog is cleared away by fresh breezes in the afternoon or evening, however.

Traffic, although very busy, moves well, and public services are fairly efficient. Parks, fountains, and monuments both old and new are common sights, and the impressive scale and glitter of this city makes it a dream-world for every Mexican who lives somewhere else. In fact, to the Mexicans, this is not the "Ciudad de México," but simply "México."

In more ways than one, the city is a creature of its history, and today it threatens to sink into history, or at least into the soft lake bottom that was once Lake Texcoco. The massive National Cathedral and other old buildings now stand at crazy angles like the Tower of Pisa or the palaces of Venice; even a building put up as recently as the 1930s, the Palacio de las Bellas Artes, is subsiding at the rate of about an inch a year. Perhaps the Aztecs will have their revenge at last!

THE LAYOUT OF THE CITY: The center of Tenochtitlán is the center of modern Mexico City as well. The Spaniards laid out the colonial town's **Zócalo,** or central plaza, right in the heart of the Aztec city, and then built the cathedral, and later the building which is now called the National Palace. The Zócalo is thus surrounded by colonial buildings, and is one of the most striking and impressive areas in all Mexico City. The Metro (subway) stop for this central plaza is, of course, Zócalo.

Going west from the Zócalo are two main streets, **Avenida 5 (Cinco) de Mayo,** and **Avenida Francisco Madero.** Many of the capital's more interesting shops are along these two streets, and along the side streets—often closed to cars—which intersect them. The architecture is predominantly colonial, and a treat for the eye.

The old colonial section gives way to 20th-century buildings at **Avenida Lázaro Cárdenas** (formerly called Avenida San Juan de Letran), a major north-south thoroughfare at the western end of Cinco de Mayo and Madero. Here you'll find the skyscraping Torre Latinoamericano (Latin American Tower), and the white marble art-deco Palacio de las Bellas Artes (Palace of Fine Arts —that's pronounced ":BEY-ahs, ARR-tess").

Next to the Bellas Artes, to the west, is the **Alameda Central,** a beautiful and romantic park filled with benches, fountains, trees and flowers, lovers smooching, Indian women selling snacks, children gamboling, and hucksters selling trinkets. North of the Alameda is the Avenida Hidalgo; south of it is the Avenida Juárez. On the **Avenida Juárez** you find a number of Mexico City's better (if older) hotels, and many moderately priced hotels and rèstaurants fill the streets parallel to Juárez to the south. Also, this is the street for stores which specialize in gorgeous displays and bewildering collections of colorful Mexican craft items.

Avenida Juárez intersects with the **Paseo de la Reforma,** the capital's grandest boulevard, and then goes on to terminate in the **Plaza de la República** with its 1930s-massive Monument to the Revolution, a huge dome resting on four tremendous legs. At the intersection of Juárez and Reforma are two large buildings belonging to the National Lottery; in the older of the two, the magic numbers which turn a pauper into a millionaire are drawn every other day (you can sit in on the magic moment—see Chapter VII, "Mexico City After Dark").

Paseo de la Reforma, laid out by the Emperor Maximilian, is Mexico City's breathtakingly beautiful and romantic main street, and also its prestigious address: the U.S. Embassy, other embassies and legations, high-class shops and restaurants, and many major hotels are somewhere in the two-mile stretch between the intersection with Juárez and the beginning of Chapultepec Park. Midway in its course, Reforma is intersected by **Avenida Insurgentes,** the prime downtown north-south artery, divided into *Norte, Centro,* and *Sur* portions.

South of Reforma and west of Insurgentes is Mexico City's high-class shopping, dining, and hotel district, called the **Zona Rosa** ("Pink Zone"), a place set off by the city fathers to catch the distilled glitter and luxury of wealthy Mexicans and tourists alike.

Finally, at the western end of the Paseo de la Reforma is **Chapultepec Castle,** set on Chapultepec ("Grasshopper Hill") and surrounded by an enormous park of the same name, perhaps the most impressive and heavily used park in the world. Within the park, surrounding the castle, are many of the city's most important museums, galleries, and concert halls, two lakes, and a zoo. Paseo de la Reforma continues through the northern portion of Chapultepec Park to join the Anillo Periferico ("Ring Artery") at the park's western edge. North of the park is **Polanco,** one of the more exclusive and beautiful of the city's residential areas.

For getting around downtown, Reforma, Juárez, Madero, and Cinco de Mayo are the most important streets. Know these names and you can't go far off the track. Outside this downtown area, Mexico City stretches for miles in every direction, with residential quarters, factories, stadiums, schools—practically a

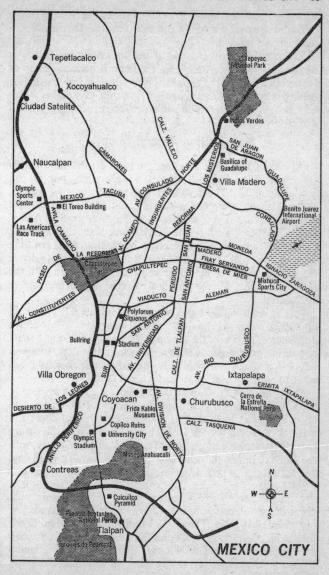

Tepetlacalco

Xocoyahualco

Ciudad Satelite

El Tepeyac
National Park

Indios Verdes

CALZ. VALLEJO

NORTE

SAN JUAN
DE ARAGON

CAMARONES

Naucalpan

Basilica of
Guadalupe

Villa Madero

GUADALUPE

Olympic
Sports
Center

MEXICO

TACUBA

AV. CONSULADO

INSURGENTES

LOS MISTERIOS

El Toreo Building

AVILA CAMACHO

REFORMA

CONSULADO

Benito Juarez
International
Airport

Las Americas
Race Track

PASEO DE LA REFORMA

M. OCAMPO

SAN JUAN

MADERO

MONEDA

Chapultepec

FRAY SERVANDO
TERESA DE MIER

IGNACIO ZARAGOZA

CHAPULTEPEC

SAN ANTONIO

Mixhuca
Sports City

AV. CONSTITUYENTES

VIADUCTO

PERDIDO

ALEMAN

Polyforum
Siquenos

SAN ANTONIO

CALZ. DE TLALPAN

Bullring

Stadium

AV. UNIVERSIDAD

AV. RIO CHURUBUSCO

Villa Obregon

SUR

Ixtapalapa

DESIERTO DE LOS LEONES

Coyoacan

AV. DIVISION DE NORTE

AV.

Churubusco

ERMITA IXTAPALAPA

Cerro de
la Estrella
National Park

Frida Kahlo
Museum

Copilco Ruins
University City

CALZ. TASQUENA

ANILLO PERIFERICO

Olympic
Stadium

Museo Anahuacalli

Contreras

N

Cuicuilco
Pyramid

W   E

Fuentes Brotantes
National Park

Tlalpan

S

Jardines de Pedregal

MEXICO CITY

nation in itself—to the borders of the *Distrito Federal* (D.F., the "Federal District," roughly equivalent to the District of Columbia) and beyond.

You can take in the whole of this incredible panorama by whisking to the observatory atop the Latin American Tower, or by taking a bus or the elevator up to Chapultepec Castle (for details on both views, see Chapter V, "Mexico City Sights"). But first, here is the information you'll need to get around this wonderful town.

Getting Around Town

ARRIVING BY PLANE: The fastest way to get downtown from the airport is to take a **cab** right from the terminal, but this can cost as much as 500 pesos ($10). You must haggle for a price, as the taxi meters can't keep up with inflation. You can cut this price sometimes if you walk toward the "Aeropuerto" Metro station and catch a cab on the street. Many of the cabs prowling the airport area have those sinister black cloth bags covering their meters, a signal that this is a "touristic" taxi—the driver can charge whatever the traffic will bear. Find a cab with the meter uncovered for the best deal, or read on for inexpensive alternatives:

Special red VW **minibuses** bearing the initials S.E.T.T.A. fill up outside the air terminal and trundle passengers to downtown hotels for a fraction of the taxi rate. Tickets are sold in a special booth; the price depends on how far you're traveling, based on a system of zones. Tell them your destination, and they'll tell you what to pay; it's usually about 99 pesos ($1.98).

Even cheaper? You can go by **city bus** for a small fraction of the S.E.T.T.A. fare if you're willing to walk for 15 minutes and change buses at least once. Go out the air terminal doors and turn left, heading for the Holiday Inn. You'll pass a six-story parking garage on your right, and come to a busy highway, with the Holiday Inn on the other side of the highway. Turn left, and down a block is a pedestrian bridge over the highway. See that PEMEX gas station near the bridge? The street beside it is "Norte 33," or "Norte Treinta y Tres." A five-minute walk down this street, on the right at Calle Oriente 184, is the starting point for no. 18 buses. The no. 18 winds through neighborhoods for a while, then shoots west down Eje 1 Norte (Avenida Rayón), a major east-west artery. You'll want to transfer to a southbound bus somewhere along this artery. The trip will take 30 minutes to an hour.

For the Zócalo, get off at Calle Carmen and take a no. 31 bus (La Villa–Xochimilco), which runs south to the east of the Zócalo.

For the Zócalo, get off at Allende and take a no. 29 or 29A (La Villa–Carrasco or La Villa–Tlalpan), which runs south along Allende and Bolívar, west of the Zócalo.

For Avenida Lázaro Cárdenas (Eje Central), get off at Lázaro Cárdenas and take a no. 27 (Reclusorio Norte–Cd. Jardín) or trolleybus south.

For the Plaza de la República, Sullivan Park, and the Zona Rosa, get off at Avenida Insurgentes and catch a no. 17 (Indios Verdes–Tlalpan) bus south along Insurgentes.

You can also take the **Metro (subway)** from the airport to downtown. Soon there will be a station right at the Terminal Aerea (airport passenger terminal), and you'll be able to board a fast train, transfer at Consulado or La Raza, and be downtown for a very low price in a very short time. Right now you must walk to the Puerto Aereo station, about a mile from the terminal, in order to pick up the Metro.

By the way, there is supposed to be a rule that no baggage is permitted on the Metro, but this rule has been ignored in many cases. Here's all you need to know about the subway system:

THE METRO: The subway system in Mexico City offers one of the smoothest rides for about the cheapest cost anywhere in the world. Six lines are either completed or nearing completion, and most of the sprawling system will be finished and operational by the time you read this.

As you enter the station, buy a *boleto* (ticket) at the glass *caja* (ticket office). Buy a booklet of tickets to save money. Insert your ticket into the slot at the turnstile and pass through; once inside you'll see two large signs designating the destination of the line (for example, for Line 1, it's Observatorio and Zaragoza). Follow the signs in the direction you want, and *know where you're going*, since there are few maps of the routes anywhere in the station. There are, however, several signs you'll see everywhere: *Salida*, which means "exit"; *Andenes*, which means "railway platforms"; and *Correspondencias*, meaning "connecting lines." Once inside the train, you'll see above each door a map of the station stops for that line, with symbols and names.

The ride is smooth, fast, and efficient (although hot and unbelievably crowded during rush hours). The stations are clean

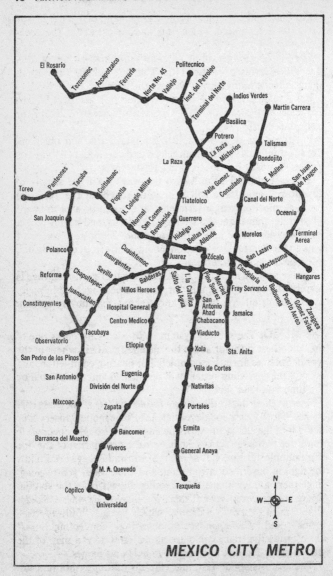

MEXICO CITY METRO

Watch for Pickpockets!

Mexico City is unique in many ways, but in one matter it resembles any big city anywhere: pickpockets. Crowded subway cars and buses provide the perfect workplace for petty thieves, as do thronged outdoor markets and bullfights, or indoor theaters. The "touch" can range from light-fingered wallet lifting or purse opening to a fairly rough shoving by two or three petty thieves. Watch out for them anyplace tourists go in numbers: on the Metro, in Ruta 100 buses, in crowded hotel elevators, at the Ballet Folklorico.

Luckily, violent muggings are pretty infrequent in Mexico City. But if you find yourself up against a handful of these guys in a crowded spot, the best thing to do is to raise a fuss—no matter whether you do it in Spanish or in English. Just a few shouts of "Robo! Robo!" ("Robbery!") or "Robador!" ("Thief!"), or anything loud, should convince the thieves that it'd be best for them to disappear.

and beautifully designed with lots of stone, tiles, piped-in music —and the added attraction of several archeological ruins unearthed during construction. There is also a subterranean passage that goes between the Pino Suarez and Zócalo stations so you can avoid the crowds and the rain along Pino Suarez. The Zócalo station has dioramas and large photographs of the different periods in the history of the Mexican Valley, and at Pino Suarez there is a small pyramid from the Aztec empire.

Important Notes: The Metro system runs between 6 a.m. and midnight *only;* it is not an all-night operation. Also, there is a rule that *no baggage* is permitted on the trains. In practice this means that bulky suitcases or backpacks sometimes make you *persona non grata,* but a large shoulderbag such as I use is not classed as luggage; nor is an attaché case, or even a case that's slightly bigger. You may be able to get away with carrying more in the evening when the Metro's less crowded. The reason for the rule is that Mexico City's Metro on an average day handles over 2,000,000 riders and that leaves precious little room for bags! You should note that Metro travel is usually very crowded, and consequently pretty hot and muggy in summer.

BUSES: Moving millions of people through this sprawling urban mass is a gargantuan task, but the city fathers do a pretty good job of it. The municipal bus system, operated by the DDF

(Departamento del Distrito Federal, or Federal District Department), is run on an enormous grid plan. Odd-numbered buses run roughly north-south, even-numbered buses go east-west, and a special express service runs along the main routes downtown. You can pick up a Spanish-language tabloid guide to the bus system in the DDF building on the south side of the Zócalo. I'll provide you with most of the routes and numbers you'll need, however.

The buses themselves are modern but they age very rapidly. They tend to be crowded or very crowded. The fare is very inexpensive. Downtown bus stops bear signs with route descriptions.

One of the most important bus routes is the **Expresso Reforma,** which runs between the Zócalo and the Auditorio (National Auditorium in Chapultepec Park) or the Observatorio Metro station. The route is via Avenida Madero or Cinco (5) de Mayo, Avenida Juárez, Paseo de la Reforma; maps of the route are posted at each bus stop.

Another important route is **no. 17, Indios Verdes–Tlalpan,** which runs along Avenida Insurgentes connecting the northern bus terminal (Terminal Norte), Buenavista Railroad Station, Reforma, the Zona Rosa, and—far to the south—San Angel and University City.

TAXIS: Mexico City is pretty easy to get around by Metro and bus, and these methods bring you few hassles. Taxis are another matter, but there are times when nothing else will do. Cabs operate under several distinct sets of rules, one of them being highway robbery. The others are as follows: The Volkswagen Beetle cabs are your best bet for low cost and good service; the larger American makes are more expensive. Avoid by all means the cabs sitting at stands before snazzy hotels with black bags over their meters. They get what the traffic will bear, and you must bargain for a price. In other cabs the meters run, and these meters are of two types. The "D" (for distance traveled) meter will show a figure, and you will pay about twice this figure. The "DT" (for distance and time) meter gives you the flat figure you pay. Decals within the cab give tables to help you figure. Both meters end up with about the same fare for similar trips—unless you ask the cab to wait while you run in somewhere, of course. Late at night there is a 10% surcharge on the fare shown by the meter. Cabs from a *sitio* (cab stand) often charge a peso or two above the meter fare. If you call a cab by phone the meter will be started when the cab begins the trip to your hotel and *not* when you get in. A normal fare for trips along our two main arteries, Juárez and Reforma, going from say, the Bellas Artes to the Zona Rosa, should be in the neighborhood of 100 pesos ($2).

PESEROS (COLLECTIVOS): Also called *taxis de rutas fijas* ("taxis with fixed routes"), these are sedans or minibuses, usually white, which run along major arteries. They pick up and discharge passengers along the route, charge fares according to distance (it usually works out to two or three times the bus fare), and provide more comfort and speed than the bus. Routes are displayed on cards in the windshield; often a Metro station will be the destination. One of the most useful routes for tourists is Ruta 2, which runs from the Zócalo along Avenida Juárez, along Reforma to Chapultepec, and back again.

Note that some of the minibuses on this route have automatic sliding doors—you don't have to shut them, a motor does.

As the driver approaches a stop, he'll put his hand out the window and hold up one or more fingers. This is the number of passengers he's willing to take on (vacant seats are difficult to see if you're outside the car).

Organized Tours

I've already mentioned that Mexico City is a great place for looking around on your own, and in general this is the cheapest way to see whatever you like. However, if your time is limited, you may wish to acclimate yourself quickly by taking a tour or two.

The most popular tours are: the four-hour city tour which includes such sites as the National Cathedral, the National Palace, and Chapultepec Park and Castle; the four- to six-hour tour of the Shrine of Guadelupe and the nearby pyramids in the Teotihuacan archeological zone; and the Sunday tour that begins with the Ballet Folklorico, moves on to the floating gardens of Xochimilco, and may or may not incorporate lunch and the afternoon bullfights. Almost as popular are the one-day and overnight tours to Cuernavaca and Taxco. There are also several popular nightclub tours.

Virtually any Mexico City hotel can help you to sign up for one of these tours, conducted by a dozen or more agencies.

Tourists have been known from time to time to return from a tour dissatisfied, and having your hotel take some responsibility in selecting the tour company is not a bad idea.

Tourism Information

The police officers in light-blue uniforms who you'll see standing on street corners along Reforma and Juárez are of an elite, English-speaking **Tourist Police** force—they wear small enameled badges with the American, Canadian, and British flags emblazoned on them. These officers are marvelously friendly, and although they may not be able to answer each and every question, they'll certainly try. However, it's only fair to warn you that since the establishment of the force some years ago, a small number of officers have discovered how easy it is to make a tidy profit by making deals with taxi drivers. If anyone tells you, for instance, that "the only way to get out to the pyramids is by cab," be suspicious. In Chapter VIII of this book you'll see exact directions for getting there by bus at a minuscule fraction of the taxi cost. Most of the time, though, you'll find the Tourist Police honest, gracious, and helpful.

If you aren't near a Tourist Policeman, the **Secretaria de Turismo** (Tourism Secretariat) has set up a special tourist "hot line" for foreign visitors: dial 250-0123 and you can ask your questions in English.

Just for the record, the offices of the Secretaria de Turismo are at Avenida Presidente Masaryk 172 in Polanco, north of Chapultepec Park. There is still (as of this writing) an information booth of sorts in the building at Juárez 92, corner of Reforma, where the Tourism Secretariat used to be located.

The **Chamber of Commerce** maintains an information office which can provide you with a detailed map of the city (or country) at least, and answer some of your questions at best. It's conveniently located at Reforma 42—look for the Camara Nacional de Comercio de la Ciudad de México, open from 9 a.m. to 2 p.m. and from 4 to 7 p.m. Monday through Thursday, to 6 p.m. on Friday; closed Saturday and Sunday.

Tourist Card Problems: Contact the consular section of your embassy if you lose your Tourist Card, or if it expires. They may be able to provide you with a document proving your citizenship which will be accepted in lieu of your Tourist Card at your port of exit from Mexico. If your card is about to expire, 15 days before this happens you'll have to contact the Tourism Secretariat, and they will then route you to the **Migración** (Immigration) officials at Juárez 92 who will see to issuing an extension. The procedure takes about two weeks. Once you've got your extension or new tourist card, you have to go through a *separate* procedure to renew or extend your car papers (if you're driving). You do this at Calzada de Tlalpan 2775, in the far southern reaches of the city: drive, or take the Metro to Taxqueña, then a taxi.

But before you get too deep into the city, you'll need a place to stay. All the necessary information is in the next chapter.

Independence ("Angel") Monument, Mexico City

Chapter III

WHERE TO STAY IN MEXICO CITY

MEXICO CITY has been fashionable, fascinating, and financially important for a long time, and so the range of hotels providing for the constant stream of visitors is great, and the number of hotels is large. There are times when hotel rooms in a particular establishment or price range may be a little hard to find, as in May when the Mexican government grants vacation leave to its armies of office workers, many of whom come in from the provinces to the capital for some good times. Also, Mexican national holidays and festivals such as Easter and Christmas tend to fill the hotels. To be sure, reserve in advance no matter what class of hotel you plan to stay in. But if you can't reserve, don't be overly alarmed—you'll find a room somewhere.

Most of Mexico City's hotels are comfortable and fully equipped in the modern style, and any double room costing 900 or 1000 pesos ($18 or $20) or more will probably have one or two double beds, a modern tile bathroom with shower or tub-shower, a telephone, wall-to-wall carpeting, piped-in music, room service, and a television set. If you pay less than this price, you will probably be without the TV, but you may find the rest of these accoutrements. Hotels renting rooms for $18 or $20 and up usually have their own private parking garages, restaurants, bars, lounges, and even sometimes a small swimming pool and/or a nightclub. The luxury hotels have all of these services, plus dozens of others.

Breakfast is not normally included in the basic room price.

All except the very cheapest hotels are air-conditioned, although this convenience is not necessary except during the hottest summer months.

All the hotels in the luxury and first-class groups, and most of the hotels in the moderate group, offer some sort of Family

Plan whereby children aged 12 or under stay free in their parents' room. Sometimes the age for children may go as high as 17—ask when you reserve. In the budget hotels, you may be able to get a discount on children; otherwise, take the built-in discount of a large room with three or four beds, always priced lower (on a per-person basis) than single or double rooms.

Mexico's ubiquitous 10% Value Added Tax, the IVA, is added to almost all hotel bills, excepting only some of the budget places. When you ask the price of a room, be sure to find out if the price quoted includes IVA. The tax will be levied on other hotel services—restaurant, bar and lounge bills, garage parking, etc.—as well.

Remember that for all but the most inexpensive hotels, reservations can be made through a travel agent at no cost to you. Many of the larger hotels have toll-free reservations numbers in the U.S. and Canada, or are represented by American firms through which reservations can be made. You should note, however, that mistakes often occur with advance reservations, even the ones made via toll-free number and computer. Keep good records of what you do, get confirmation numbers and receipts whenever possible. And don't be surprised if your "iron-clad" reservation ends up being a myth.

Here, then, are the hotels of Mexico City, arranged in my own categories according to price and degree of luxury. Prices given are for room with bath (and that is the total price for the room, *not* the price per person), *tax included*.

Deluxe Hotels
(double rooms from 3500 pesos—$70—and up)

These are Mexico City's showplaces, strikingly attractive, cosmopolitan, and expensive. Each has within it a dozen or more subestablishments for your entertainment: clubs, bars, restaurants, coffeeshops, arcades of boutiques, perhaps even a stockbroker's office.

El Presidente Chapultepec, Campos Elíseos 218, Polanco (tel. 905/250-7700, or 557-8822). The twin sleek slabs towering over the northern reaches of Chapultepec Park constitute one of the city's most prestigious places to stay. Looking for all the world like a pair of monster bookends, El Presidente Chapultepec is the latest addition to the quasi-governmental chain of hotels which includes a smaller and older Hotel El Presidente in the Pink

Zone. The new hotel was opened in 1977 by El Presidente himself, Sr. José Lopez Portillo.

Throughout the hotel you'll notice a stylized grasshopper motif, used frequently in the decor and derived from the Indian name *chapultepec*, or "Grasshopper Hill." In the lobby, a curlicue red ribbon of inch-thick steel twists and loops its way to the ceiling to form a sculpture centerpiece; mirrors on the floor and ceiling heighten the drama. Four mini-gardens at the corners of the floor mirror add a touch of verdure, and blocky leather chairs next to heavy wooden tables make this main lobby the best place to view the comings and goings of other guests. Just off the lobby is an attractive bar, with even more plants (the pampered leaves of which are cleaned daily by hand) and a grand piano.

The decor of the guest rooms is in harmony with the keynote design of the lobby: hardwood doors, blocky wood furniture, textured wall hangings, and a generally simple but bold and attractive decor. Rooms have breathtaking views of Chapultepec Park and the city.

The hotel's assortment of restaurants and nightspots can keep you busy all day. For breakfast, there's Fruitas y Floras, with tables set out café style on the mezzanine above the lobby. The grill room called La Chimenea serves breakfast, lunch, and dinner in an almost troglodytic labyrinth of white stucco paved in copper plates and dotted with wire sculptures. A glance at the menu reveals an assortment of soups, smoked salmon, and main courses such as pork chops à la Poblana (Puebla style, in a thick, rich sauce) or the specialty, New York cut sirloin. There's a decent wine list, and you sip your vintage from oversize crystal *balons*. To finish up, try the parfait Kahlua, and your total bill will be about 750 to 900 pesos ($15 to $18).

At the end of an afternoon's sightseeing, stop at the Balmoral Tea Room for afternoon tea, coffee, pastries, and candy, and then get ready for dinner at Maxim's, for El Presidente Chapultepec has its own branch of the famous French restaurant. Food, service, and prices are deluxe, and you must call a special number for reservations: 254-0033 or 254-0025. Maxim's is open for both lunch and dinner Monday through Friday from 2 to 4:30 p.m. and 8:30 p.m. to 12:30 a.m., on Saturday for dinner only; closed Sunday.

Although you'll undoubtedly want to spend a few nights wandering in the Zona Rosa, other nights you can visit the hotel's disco, called El Chapulín, or the nightclub El Mexicano. Shows at the club come at 7:30 and 9, the cover charge is a stiff 250 pesos ($5), and drinks cost about 150 pesos ($3) for local stuff, 175 to 200 pesos ($3.50 to $4) for imported liquor.

The one disadvantage of El Presidente Chapultepec is that you must go virtually everywhere by car as there's little within walking distance.

Prices for the luxurious rooms are 4000 pesos single ($80), 4250 pesos double ($85). Junior suites are available. Two children 12 or under can stay free with their folks. Call toll free to reserve a room: in the U.S., 800/854-2026 (in California, 800/542-6028); in Québec, 800/261-9300; in Toronto, 416/366-2941. Reservations can also be made through Utell International in the U.S., Canada, and the U.K. Look for the Utell number in your local telephone directory.

El Presidente Zona Rosa, Calle de Hamburgo 135 (tel. 905/525-0000, or 557-8822). Although the Hotel El Presidente in the Zona Rosa cannot compete with the flash and brilliance of its luxurious rival, the El Presidente Chapultepec, still there are many good reasons to choose the older hotel. First, it has exactly what the one in Chapultepec lacks: a cozy and unpretentious ambience, not wildly stylish but undeniably comfortable and relaxing. Second, the rooms tend to be larger than those in the newer hotel. Then, think of the location: you do not get sweeping views of Chapultepec Park from your bedroom window here, but you are within minutes—even seconds!—of the Zona Rosa's many delights.

Your room here will be done in bright solid colors and have a deep-pile rug; many rooms have interesting views of the city, and most have little triangle-shaped balconies with window boxes planted in evergreen shrubs. All come air-conditioned (of course), with servi-bar refrigerators, televisions, and telephones. The hotel has a (pay) garage. Prices for the 100 rooms are quite reasonable for what you get: in a single, the price is 3400 pesos ($68); in a double, it's 3600 pesos ($72). Two children 12 or under can stay with their parents for no extra charge.

In contrast to the tremendous proportions of the lobby at El Presidente Chapultepec, the reception area here in El Presidente Zona Rosa is smallish and low of ceiling with several big comfy sofas. Just off the lobby is the small Bar Inglés, good for a quick refresher. For more leisurely drinks and conversation, the Bar Jardín has the atmosphere of an indoor garden: potted trees and plants, and a quiet "fountain" of water slowly running down a stone wall into a large pool. Recorded music, soft and vaguely classical, fills the air in the morning, and at night there's live entertainment and music for dancing. The Grill Zafiro is here as well, and serves breakfast, lunch, and dinner, with dinner main courses costing about 400 to 500 pesos ($8 to $10), the whole meal about twice that amount, including endless trips to the salad bar. For evening entertainment, the Bar Zafiro upstairs has music and shows which change every half hour.

Like its namesake in Chapultepec, the Zona Rosa El Presidente has its own collection of elegant shops.

Maria Isabel–Sheraton Hotel, Paseo de la Reforma 325 (tel. 905/525-9060). For some years, the Maria Isabel–Sheraton was Mexico City's best hotel, and it is still one of the finest. A huge international hotel on the grand scale, it towers over Paseo de la Reforma right next to the U.S. Embassy and only a five-minute walk from the heart of the Zona Rosa. Airline offices, rental-car desks, and elegant shops including those of Cartier and Piaget are all here, of course.

As you enter the reception area, the plushness of the place surrounds you. Although the spaces are vast, you move about them easily—up the short flight of stairs to the lofty lobby bar, for instance—and the super-thick carpets preserve the hush. Everything is quite modern, although elegant bits of tradition, such as matched marble panels in the walls, add a touch of luxury, and dabs of colonial Mexican decor remind you where you are. The rooms are standard and modern, with all the conveniences, and many have an added attraction: outside the picture window, the golden angel of the Independence Monument floats over the bustle of Reforma. Rooms here cost 4400 to 6000 pesos ($88 to $120) single, 4750 to 6250 pesos ($95 to $125) double; an extra bed is 500 pesos ($10). Toll-free reservations are yours by calling 800/325-3535 in the U.S.

The Maria Isabel–Sheraton has a full selection of restaurants, of course. For a drink, the lobby bar is fine, and a normal portion of potion should cost about 150 to 200 pesos ($3 to $4). For dining, the Maria Isabel's daily luncheon buffet is a Mexico City tradition. It's served from 1 to 4 p.m. every day for about 1000 pesos ($20), and each day the menu is from a different national cuisine: Mexican, Italian, Spanish, German, American, etc. In the evenings the restaurant becomes a supper club with entertainment and a 250-peso ($5) cover charge. Main courses from the supper club menu cost between 450 and 800 pesos ($9 to $16); meals are served until 1 a.m., but the bar (which opens at 9 p.m.) serves drinks until 3 a.m. Note that the bar is closed Monday.

Mexico City's newest world-class hotel is the **Hotel Galería Plaza** (tel. 905/286-5444), in the heart of the Zona Rosa at Hamburgo 195, corner of Varsovia. The 13-story Westin hotel has 450 rooms and suites, a rooftop swimming pool and bar with a fine view of the Angel Monument and (in clear weather) of the volcanoes. Posh modern decor, air conditioning, cable TV, servibar fridges, some good city views—the rooms are top-notch, and the location is excellent. Of the half-dozen bars and restaurants, one is continental, another is open 24 hours a day, yet another is a rocking disco. Prices at the Galería Plaza are 4000 pesos ($80) single and 4625 pesos ($92.50) double. Here, you're only a few minutes' stroll from the U.S. Embassy.

Camino Real, Mariano Escobedo 700 (tel. 905/545-6960). Mexico City's most daringly designed downtown hotel is undoubtedly the Camino Real, a short stroll from the Diana Monument where Paseo de la Reforma meets Chapultepec Park, quite near Chapultepec Castle. The hotel's boldness in design and decoration is sure to strike you; whether or not you like the design, it's impossible to ignore it. As you enter from Mariano Escobedo, first you're struck by the vivid pink entryway and by the gold-and-black cape of the doorman. To one side is a "boiling" fountain—a sort of pool with a wave-maker which whips and churns the water in an unsettling way. The lobby/reception area is split level and outspokenly modern, but as you wander through the other public areas the decor becomes less daring, although always interesting and original. Next to the bar, called La Cantina, is a fountain made from a single massive block of volcanic stone. Don't let down your guard, however, for right next door to La Cantina is the coffeeshop called La Huerta, with a mural at the rear best described as Rousseau *à la Mexicana,* and with gigantic white plaster replicas of fruit (orange, plum, pear, apple, banana) next to the entrance.

Boldness is the rule in the 700 guest rooms, with one wall of each room a window and the other walls exhibiting adventurous use of patterns, solid colors, textures, and stained wood. Everything in the decor seems designed to stir you up and make your mind race rather than calm you down. (Perhaps this is why all the big and important companies have their meetings here.)

Besides its three interesting bars, the Camino Real has a culinary attraction of the first order: a branch of Fouquet's de Paris. Reservations are a must (call extensions 2517 or 3127; or from outside the hotel, dial 513-7279). There's music to dine by from 9:30 p.m. onward, and a deluxe menu. Soups are appetizing, especially the lobster bisque, while main courses include such things as New York steaks, guinea hen in sour cream sauce with apples, or tournedos of beef served three different ways. Most seafood dishes, and frogs legs, are similarly priced. The dining room overlooks a small interior garden of manicured shrubs and trees. This could be the most elegant dining in Mexico, and the bill for two people can easily be in the range of 4000 pesos ($80).

After dinner, digest. But when you're ready, head for Cero Cero, the hotel's nightclub which upholds the Camino Real's reputation for the wild and distracting. Cero Cero is open from 9 p.m. to 4 a.m. Monday through Saturday.

The Camino Real is one of the Westin Hotels chain, and you can reserve a room through their toll-free number (in the U.S., 800/228-3000; in Canada, 800/261-8383). Rooms come standard, medium, and deluxe, and cost 4350 to 6200 pesos ($87 to $124) for a single, or 5250 to 7100 pesos ($105 to $142) for a double room. Kids 17 and under stay free in a deluxe double room (two double beds).

Hotel Fiesta Palace, Paseo de la Reforma 80, at Columbus Circle (tel. 905/566-7777). The gigantic Fiesta Palace is Mexico City's number-one convention and group tour hotel, with thousands of rooms, tremendous conference chambers, and banquet halls capable of feeding small armies all at once. You're unlikely to stay here unless the arrangements are made for you by a tour operator or convention service. Room rates are much cheaper if you do come as part of a group; otherwise you pay 3850 to 5750 pesos ($77 to $115) single, 4250 to 6000 pesos ($85 to $120) double.

The place is overwhelming, with guests, bellboys and doormen, clerks, and cars swirling around in that charged atmosphere of a convention trying to get a lot done in a short time, everybody thinking efficiency and enjoying the mental speed. You can retreat to your room for quiet, however, and there you'll find a bright and unrestrained decor with lots of color, a curule chair (like the Romans used), and a small-drinks refrigerator (servi-bar) stocked with goods which you pay for (through the nose!) as you use them. Or take the elevator to the fourth floor and the Solarium, a sundeck with poolside-type lounges (although there's no pool here), tall birdcages, and a bikini-clad crew of serious tanners.

To go along with its gargantuan size, the Fiesta Palace has close to a dozen places to eat, drink, and be merry. The Villa Jardín restaurant, with international cuisine, is open all day every day from 7 in the morning until midnight. La Hacienda, the grill restaurant on the third floor, is open from 1 to 11 p.m. every day but Sunday, featuring prime rib, a flaming swordful of seafood, or red snapper filet ("filete de hauchinango á la parilla"). Dessert might be a pastry from the pastry cart, and Irish coffee—all for about 1000 pesos ($20), plus tax and tip.

Then there are the nightspots: La Azotea, the roof bar, will let you in to dance for 250 pesos ($5) cover charge. For the show at Las Sillas, the cover is 475 pesos ($9.50). Stelaris is on the 25th floor, appropriate to its name, and is open to nightclub-goers every evening but Sunday from 9 p.m. to 3 a.m. The local disco is called the Quorum, open daily except Sunday until 2 a.m., on Friday and Saturday nights until 4 a.m. It's possible to exhaust yourself, but it's not easy to exhaust the possibilities for entertainment at the Fiesta Palace.

Holiday Inn Centro (Pink Zone), corner of Liverpool and Amberes (tel. 905/533-3500). There may be places on earth where one cannot find a Holiday Inn—perhaps in Ultima Thule, for instance—but the Zona Rosa is not one of them. The Holiday Inn here offers the same dependably clean, modern, and comfortable rooms as always, with the most brightly glittering quarter of the city right outside the window. A single room costs 4400 pesos ($88); a double is 4900 pesos ($98). The bar and grill called the Holiday Pub is an artificial, but very convincing, copy of the real thing, fully equipped with stained-glass windows and British-style booths. There's even a nightclub, called El Circo, providing entertainment Monday through Saturday from 9 p.m. to 3 a.m. for a 180-peso ($3.60) per-person cover charge.

A new hotel, the **México Plaza Holiday Inn,** is scheduled to open early in 1983. Right at the intersection of Paseo de la Reforma and Avenida Juárez, the new Holiday Inn will be the city's tallest hotel, and certainly its most modern. Rooms will have one king-size or two double beds, color TV, and individual climate control. The top three floors are designated the Plaza Club, with special facilities and a slightly higher price tag. Call and find out about this one—the location is superb, and the view from higher up is sure to take your breath away.

Reservations for rooms can be made through any Holiday Inn. Be sure you specify that you want a room in the Holiday Inn "Centro" (Pink Zone) or "Plaza" (Reforma and Juárez)—there are other Holiday Inns in other parts of the city.

Hotel Aristos, Paseo de la Reforma 276, corner of Copenhague (auto entrance on Copenhague; tel. 905/533-0560). Lively

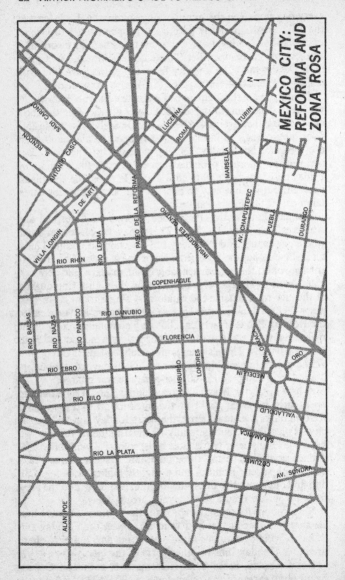

MEXICO CITY:
REFORMA AND
ZONA ROSA

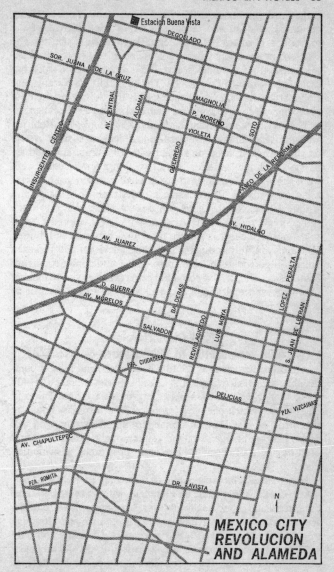

Estación Buena Vista

DEGOLLADO

SOR. JUANA I. DE LA CRUZ

MAGNOLIA

P. MORENO

AV. CENTRAL

ALDAMA

VIOLETA

SOTO

GUERRERO

INSURGENTES CENTRO

PASEO DE LA REFORMA

V. HIDALGO

AV. JUAREZ

D. GUERRA

AV. MORELOS

BALDERAS

LOPEZ PERALTA

SALVADOR

REVILLAGIGEDO

LUIS MOYA

S. JUAN DE LETRAN

PZA. CIUDADELA

DELICIAS

PZA. VIZCAINAS

AV. CHAPULTEPEC

PZA. ROMITA

DR. LAVISTA

N

**MEXICO CITY
REVOLUCION
AND ALAMEDA**

is the word that best describes the Aristos, whether one is talking about the colorful and fanciful decor, or the clientele, or the location right smack in the center of the Zona Rosa's bustle. The spacious modern lobby has a coffeeshop at one side, set off behind stained-glass windows. For drinks you have El Rincón bar and a lounge named La Mancha. The nightclub, La Naranja, has Folies-style shows, and competes with the "disco" (actually a nightspot with a live band for dancing) called La Lechuga.

The Aristos's restaurant La Mimosa overlooks the Reforma and specializes in the more hard-to-find delights such as oysters on the half shell, avocado stuffed with king crab, and cold asparagus with mayonnaise. Literally within a few seconds' walk from the Aristos's auto entrance are half a dozen more restaurants on Calle de Copenhague, a pedestrians-only street, and within a block of the hotel are dozens more places to dine.

The guest rooms at the Aristos sport lively colored fabrics, some in a bold chevron pattern for both bedspreads and drapes; all rooms are fully equipped, including television and recorded music. Single rooms cost 3000 pesos ($60), and double rooms are 3500 pesos ($70); triples cost 4200 pesos ($84). If you're looking for an upbeat hostelry right in the midst of the action, the Aristos is the place to go.

First-Class Hotels
(double rooms 2100 to 3900 pesos—$42 to $78)

Almost as luxurious as the top-class hotels, and fully as comfortable, are Mexico City's first-class hostelries. In fact, the only thing that these first-class places are missing is that flair and elegance for which one pays top price. In a first-class hotel (by the way, that classification's mine, not an official one) you will find a parking garage, bars and restaurants, a well-trained and multilingual staff eager to help, and, most times, a swimming pool.

Hotel Plaza Florencia, Calle de Florencia 61 (tel. 905/525-4800). On the pretty Calle de Florencia, with its row of graceful palm trees and many quaint old-world buildings, is the modern Hotel Plaza Florencia. Although very up-to-date and attractive in a luxurious way, the Plaza Florencia is a friendly and only semiformal place patronized heavily by well-to-do Mexican businessmen and tourists. It's a good place to escape the crowds from back home and meet Mexicans, and despite its predominantly local clientele, the staff here speaks English as well as Spanish.

Decoration is done with natural blond wood, leather and wicker furniture, chrome trim for effect, and special use of blown-up color photographs of forest scenes, both in the public rooms and the guest rooms. All rooms are modern and bright, tastefully done, and equipped with television, piped-in music, heating, and air conditioning. Rooms at the front of the hotel have a view of the Calle de Florencia with its shops catering to the carriage trade.

The Restaurant Ponte Vecchio (remember, the hotel's named after the city of Florence!) specializes in Italian dishes at lunch and dinner, but offers an unusual breakfast buffet for about 250 pesos ($5) per person. Meals are served from 7 a.m. to 1 a.m.

Prices for this amply comfortable place are 2250 pesos ($45) for a single room, 2600 pesos ($52) for a double, 450 pesos ($9) for an extra bed.

Hotel Continental, Paseo de la Reforma 166 (tel. 905/518-0700). At the intersection of Insurgentes and Reforma, the Continental has one of the best locations in the city, equidistant from the Zona Rosa and the area of the Alameda Central. Over a decade ago the hotel was part of the Hilton chain, and today it preserves the decor and amenities of this former glory. Each room has a glass wall with a view of either the Reforma or the Zona Rosa, and a television set for when you tire of the view.

Your first impression of the Continental, which you get in the lobby, is of late 1950s elegance: lots of mirrors, brass, marble, and those quaint circular sofa seats which seem to have originated in the Victorian era. Just off the lobby is the Maya Bar, boasting a large blown-up photograph of the Caracol (observatory) at Chichen-Itza, and featuring live Mexican music nightly from 8 p.m. to 1 a.m. Here is a delightful surprise, too: from the indoor bar you can step down to a small outdoor patio, shaded by a large rubber tree and hidden from the street by high walls. An unusual little fountain provides soothing background sound. Don't fail to seek out this haven away from the intense activity of Reforma for a quiet afternoon relaxant.

On the 15th floor of the hotel is the Belvedere Supper Club, with a set-price dinner which includes a show for about 2000 pesos ($40) per person, drinks, tax, and tip included. The view of the city from the dining room is very fine.

On Sunday, the Continental features a fancy and heavily laden buffet table in the Tlatelli Room, open from 1 to 6 p.m.—all you can eat for 750 pesos ($15) per person, half price for a child.

(Whether you're staying in the Continental or not, the Sunday buffet is a good thing to keep in mind.)

As with all older hotels, decor and relative modernity of the specific guest room you are given depends on the hotel's redecoration plans. Although all rooms are fine, if you don't feel completely satisfied with your room, ask to see another. The cost for a room at the Continental is 3750 pesos single ($75), 4250 pesos double ($85). By the way, you can make reservations at the Continental through Loew's Reservations, Inc., in the U.S.

Hotel Del Prado, Avenida Juárez 70 (tel. 905/518-0040). The Del Prado does not quite fit the designation of "an old, comfy downtown hotel" even though it has seen several decades of service, and it certainly is comfortable. The reason for this is the sense of innovation and modernity preserved by the management. For instance, to capitalize on the Del Prado's most famous attraction, the great two-story mural in the lobby by Diego Rivera, the hotel now sports a Solarium del Arte on the fifth floor where works of living (often young, up-and-coming) Mexican painters are exhibited. On the sixth floor is a small swimming pool, a sunning area, and a terrace overlooking Avenida Juárez and the Alameda. Many rooms look out on the Alameda as well. They're done up with modern furniture and bits of local craftwork, deep shaggy rugs, and lots of new paint. Many rooms are equipped with small refrigerators stocked with drinks (on the pay-as-you-consume plan).

In the Bar Montenegro there's live entertainment (rock or mariachi groups mostly), and in the Bar Nicte-Ha there's entertainment too, but of a more traditional nightclub style. The Vitrales Coffeeshop keeps long hours for guests' convenience. The Grill Del Prado, entered from the sidewalk of Avenida Juárez, is (and has been for years) one of Mexico City's best steak-and-chop houses, open for lunch and dinner. In addition to these attractions, the shopping arcade at sidewalk level underneath the hotel has a bookstore with foreign-language books, plus other handy shops.

The Del Prado is one of the hotels in the Nacional Hotelera group, which includes the El Presidente chain. Rates are as follows: single with bath, 2500 pesos ($50); double with bath, 2900 pesos ($58); extra persons are 400 pesos ($8) each. Remember to set aside some time to inspect the famous mural, *A Dream of a Sunday Afternoon in the Alameda Park,* and perhaps have a drink or a cup of tea, in the lobby.

Alameda Hotel, Avenida Juárez 50 (tel. 905/518-0620). The chain of Westin Hotels, which operates the Plaza in New York and the Camino Real in Mexico City, also manages the Alameda. Although it's been here on Avenida Juárez across from the Alameda Central for some time now, the rooms at the Alameda are 100% modern and up-to-date, with big, comfortable easy chairs, bright contemporary print bedspreads, thick pile carpeting, and little yellow beverage refrigerators. In the hallways and elevators, and everywhere else throughout the hotel, every trace of the building's actual age has been obliterated and only clean, attractive modernity remains.

Besides the rooms and the location, the Alameda's attractions include the famous bar called La Fería de la Música, off the mezzanine above the lobby, where four different musical groups perform each evening, switching perhaps from mariachi to marimba, but always remaining Mexican. This is one of the best spots in the city to enjoy mariachi music; open daily from 7 p.m. to 2 a.m. for a 195-peso ($3.90) cover charge. For dancing to a rock beat, ascend to El Caminchin bar on the 17th floor next to the swimming pool. Meals are served in the Alameda's restaurant, La Brasserie, 24 hours a day. The restaurant's right next to the lobby.

Single rooms at the Alameda cost 3400 to 4800 pesos ($68 to $96), and doubles are 3900 to 5600 pesos ($78 to $112), depending on the location of the room, the view, and the degree of luxury desired. To make reservations at the Alameda, call the Westin Hotels number in your city, or (in the continental U.S.) dial, toll free, 800/228-3000.

Gran Hotel Ciudad de México, Avenida 16 de Septiembre 82 (tel. 905/510-4040). While Mexico City can boast of many tremendous, splendid hotels, I can't imagine that any has more grandeur than the Gran Hotel Ciudad de México, just a few steps off the Zócalo. It is, very simply, palatial! You enter a rather unprepossessing doorway only to find yourself underneath a brilliantly glistening crystal chandelier. You ascend a short flight of stairs to the lobby, four stories high, ringed with fancy metalwork balustrades at the story levels, and crowned by a simply magnificent stained-glass canopy. At either end of the lobby are semielliptical "birdcage" elevators which glide quietly up and down. Lighting in the lobby is provided by brass-and-crystal lamps, each with milk-glass globes. Two Tiffany birdcages are filled with (stuffed) songbirds, and the chirping is electronically simulated. Take a seat on one of the circular sofas to take it all in.

The rooms are similarly elegant, with white walls enlivened by gilded trim (not real gilt, though), comfortable furnishings, large bathrooms, and lots of headroom. The hotel was completely restored and redone in 1968, and was reopened by none other than the president of the republic, Sr. Gustavo Díaz Ordaz. Cheap? Not exactly. Reasonable? Where else can you stay in a palace for 1960 pesos ($39.20) single, 2100 ($42) double, 2240 ($44.80) triple (suites cost 440 to 880—$8.80 to $17.60—more). Nowhere else will you get so much art nouveau for so little money. Even if you can't stay here, have a look, or buy a drink in the bar off the lobby. A branch of Delmonico's, called the Del Centro, serves as the Gran's restaurant.

Hotel Internacional Havre, Calle Havre 21 (tel. 905/533-2300), between Reforma and Hamburgo, is a tall, modern building of over a dozen stories on a quiet side street only steps from the action in the Zona Rosa. The weighty cultural influence of the French Embassy next door has dictated the hotel's style, and so visiting diplomats (and readers of this book) stay in Parisian style: French wallpapers and soothing oval-shaped still lifes of flowers grace the dignified lobby, and the rooms carry on in the same refined mood. Each room has piped-in FM music, a fireplace with an imitation (electric) fire, and a comfy loveseat/sofa besides the beds; the bathrooms have tub-shower combinations and a good deal of nice marble. Off the lobby and the mezzanine are several small restaurants and cozy bars, never very busy, always dignified. Prices at the Internacional Havre are 1820 pesos ($36.40) for a single, 2100 ($42) in a double, with an extra bed costing 210 pesos ($4.20). The hotel has its own garage.

The **Hotel Century Zona Rosa** (tel. 905/584-7111), Liverpool 152 at Amberes, is a dramatic, futuristic tower in the Pink Zone. Each of the 143 rooms has color TV, balcony, AM/FM radio, servi-bar, air conditioning, and marble "Roman" bath. A pool and sundeck are perched atop the hotel, 16 stories closer to the sun. Prices are the best part: for pure luxury, you pay 2750 pesos ($55), single or double; up to two children 12 or under can stay with you free (if you need two rooms, you can get a slight cut on the rate).

Right across the street from the Century is the **Hotel Krystal Zona Rosa** (tel. 905/533-3500), Liverpool 157 at Amberes, which is almost as luxurious, equally well located, and charges 2875 pesos ($57.50) single or 3125 pesos ($62.50) double, tax included.

Among Mexico City's most popular upper-bracket hotels is

the trusty **Hotel Casa Blanca** (tel. 905/566-3211), Lafragua 7, between Reforma and the Plaza de la República. A tower of metal and glass, the Casa Blanca is well kept up and shiny for its age, with dark wood and tasteful decor. There's even a nice rooftop sundeck and a tiny pool, plus a bar. For a room in this very convenient location, you pay 1875 pesos ($37.50) single, 2250 pesos ($45) double, a few hundred pesos more for a larger junior suite.

Moderately Priced Hotels
(double rooms 1000 to 1700 pesos—$20 to $34)

The surprising thing about many of Mexico City's moderately priced hotels is that they offer most of the services and conveniences of first-class hotels, but at approximately half the price. The rooms in these hotels may be a bit smaller (then again, they are oftentimes the same size) compared to first-class rooms; in these hotels, the television set in your room will be black and white rather than color, and a few hotels will not offer TV at all. In fact, it's location which makes the greatest difference between first-class and moderately priced hotels, with the moderate ones being on the fringes of, say, the Zona Rosa and downtown rather than right in the center of the Zona Rosa. But none of these hotels is a long walk from an important part of town or from a convenient bus or Metro stop.

In the three subgroups that follow you'll find, first, several older hotels with well-preserved and charming colonial ambience; then, the best of the modern, moderately priced hotels; finally, more hotels in this price range of varying ages and aspects, all good places to stay.

THE COLONIAL FAVORITES: Hotel de Cortes, Avenida Hidalgo 85, corner of Calle Dr. Mora (tel. 905/585-0322). One of Mexico City's true colonial gems is located just at the northwest corner of the Alameda Central. Built as a private home over two centuries ago and converted into an inn in 1780, the Hotel de Cortes is something of a well-kept secret among frequent visitors to the capital who enjoy colonial surroundings, modern services, and a central location. The two-floor building has its small guest rooms opening onto the inner court; the rooms would be darkish due to the old-style plan which left out windows except that the furniture is painted bright yellow, and cheerful colors have been chosen for the drapes and spreads. Gleaming tile baths are a part of every room. The one window in each room looks onto the courtyard, which is the prime reason to choose to stay at the de Cortes: café tables with umbrellas and leather "bucket" chairs are scattered among trees and shrubs populated with twittering birds, all around a central fountain. With the sun streaming into the courtyard or fluffy clouds passing overhead it's easy to dream you're actually in the country, and only the occasional muffled rumble of a passing bus reminds you that you're not. Breakfast, lunch, and dinner are served in the courtyard, as are tea, coffee, and drinks; if it rains, service takes place in the elegant but simple dining rooms. The price for a single room here is 1540 pesos ($30.80); for a double, 1680 pesos ($33.60). As the Hotel de Cortes is something special, it is often full, so reservations with a deposit are strongly recommended. The hotel is part of the Hostales de México and Best Western groups.

Hotel Maria Cristina, Río Lerma 31 between Río Neva and Río Amazonas (tel. 905/546-9880). The area north of Paseo de la Reforma, on the other side of that boulevard from the Zona Rosa, is a residential district. This accounts for the fact that the Maria Cristina is so quiet, peaceful, and serene, yet only a few minutes' walk from the battle of traffic at the intersection of Reforma and Insurgentes. A colonial mansion with a pretty green lawn, grand trees, climbing vines, little pools and fountains, this place is centuries away from the mood one finds in an ultramodern hotel tower. The lobby shows rich use of blue-and-white tiles, of leather and stained wood and wrought iron, colonial right down to the elevator doors! There's a large restaurant, always well attended. A lounge nearby exhibits such colonial detail and has such an impressive fireplace that it qualifies as baronial—this is the place to escape to when the lawn outside is soaked with rain. Many of the rooms were remodeled recently; all are priced at 840 pesos ($16.80) single, 980 pesos ($19.60) double. A small nightclub building is stuck in a front corner of the grounds.

Hotel Montejo, Paseo de la Reforma 240 (tel. 905/511-9840), at the corner of Niza, in the Zona Rosa, is in a building said to have been built by Don Francisco de Montejo, one of Cortes's officers and the founder of the city of Merida. For all that antiquity the building is comfortably up-to-date in construction, although decoration harks back to Mexico's romantic colonial era. In the lobby is an engaging statue of St. Francis, and there's even a fascinating colonial shoeshine chair (why not? didn't Montejo need his boots polished?). The rooms tend to be small but cozy with small and very clean tiled baths. Those rooms with a view of the Reforma cost 910 to 1022 pesos ($18.20 to $20.44) single, or 1190 to 1246 pesos ($23.80 to $24.92) double; those in the back of the hotel are the cheaper ones. On the top (fifth) floor of the Montejo is a restaurant-bar called Cancún, with an indoor dining area with glass walls, and several outdoor tables with thatch "umbrellas." The Montejo is a small, quiet, personal hotel at a prime location in the Pink Zone.

Hotel Majestic, Avenida Madero 73 (tel. 905/521-8600). A hotel of the Hostales de México group, the Majestic has 85 rooms which look onto Mexico City's main square (the Zócalo), the Avenida Madero, or the hotel's own inner court. The attractiveness of the hotel starts with its lobby, a place of stone arches, brilliant tiles, and warm colors, plus a pleasantly gurgling little stone fountain at the far end. On the second floor is the courtyard, with a floor of glass blocks (actually the ceiling of the lobby) set with sofas, tables, and chairs, and decorated with pots of vines and hanging plants all the way up to the glass roof six stories above. Nice touches of art and color are everywhere: each room doorway has a border of blue-and-white tiles to lighten the darkness of the heavy, colonial-style doors. Inside the rooms, however, colonialism is left behind in favor of pastel colors, simple and attractive decors, and newly redone tile bathrooms with tubs. On the lower floors facing the Avenida Madero noise from the street may be a problem, but on the upper floors and in the rooms which front on the Zócalo you needn't worry.

Finishing touch to the Majestic's offering is a rooftop café-restaurant in which you can choose a table shaded by a bright-yellow umbrella for breakfast or just a drink or a cup of tea.

For all this comfort and class, the prices are surprisingly moderate: single rooms cost 1300 pesos ($26); double rooms are 1500 pesos ($30).

SHINY AND NEW: Hotel Emporio, Paseo de la Reforma 124 (tel. 905/566-7766). The outlandish Hotel Emporio, in an excellent location on Paseo de la Reforma, might best be termed a "moderately priced Camino Real," for the dedication to ultra-daring design, brilliant colors, and unorthodox use of materials surrounds you here as it does in the luxury-class Camino Real. The Emporio's snazzy plastic facade gives way to a reception area in which you're liable to zoom right by the front "desk," because the "desk" is circular, canted, and low to the ground, a space-ship-like structure. At the rear of the reception area is a television lounge and sitting area up a flight of bright-blue carpeted steps. The ceiling in this room is of undulating ribbons, the floor and walls paved in crimson carpeting, the furniture a collection of dented-marshmallow chairs and jigsaw-puzzle tables (the small tables actually do fit together to make longer ones!). The elevators to the guest rooms have alabaster slabs as floors, translucent and lit from below. You can bet the rooms are boldly done: several different designs are used, but you will probably find shaggy carpeting going all the way up at least one wall, low and always undulant furniture, and the most striking patterns in fabrics. All in all, the Emporio is a mad designer's mad circus of color, texture, and shapes—great fun!

In the Emporio's mezzanine restaurant, the set-price lunch costs 240 to 265 pesos ($4.80 to $5.30). Below in the coffeeshop you can view the sidewalk activity through plate glass and stuff yourself at the buffet breakfast table until 10 a.m. for only 155 pesos ($3.10).

Prices for the Emporio's rooms depend on which section of the hotel you want to stay in. The original building (which is what you enter from Reforma) was built in 1943, but completely renovated and redecorated in 1977. Here rooms cost 840 pesos ($16.80) single, 1050 pesos ($21) double, 1190 pesos ($23.80) triple, or 1330 pesos ($26.60) for a room with two double beds capable of sleeping four people. All rooms come with telephone and recorded music.

In the newer section on Calle Atenas, built in 1970, rooms have extras such as color television, air conditioning, refrigerator, loudspeaker telephones, and even more daring decor than in the original building. Prices here are 1120 pesos ($22.40) single, 1330 pesos ($26.60) double, 1470 pesos ($29.40) triple. Note that you can reserve a room at the Emporio through Alexander Associates (tel., toll-free, 800/221-6509) in the U.S., or through Eastern Airlines's hotel reservation service.

Hotel Corinto, Calle Vallarta 24 at Antonio Caso (tel. 905/566-6555 or 566-9711). Mexico City is equally important to businessmen and tourists, and the Hotel Corinto welcomes both types of travelers. The modern 90-room hotel was finished just in the last few years, and so everything here is clean, shiny, and modern—not to mention comfortable, even luxurious. The guest rooms have coordinated drapes and spreads, reproductions of paintings by modern Mexican artists, tiled showers, televisions, piped-in music, and a special tap for purified water. Just off the lobby is a little restaurant, and on the ninth floor is a small swimming pool, sunning area, and sloping patch of grass. The ninth-floor bar provides service indoors or at poolside. For businessmen, the Corinto's attractions are a good location, just a block off Reforma, and a staff that's out to please. For tourists, extras include a tour desk in the lobby and an aggressive lot of drivers in the taxi rank out front. All rooms have either twin single beds or one double bed, and cost 1050 pesos ($21) single, 1232 to 1386 pesos ($24.64 to $27.72) double. Lower prices are sometimes offered if business is slack (although it seldom is).

Hotel Doral, Calle Sullivan 9 (tel. 905/592-2866), just off the intersection of Insurgentes and Reforma, is a good example of the sort of medium-priced hotels easily found throughout Mexico City. A high-rise of almost 20 stories, it overlooks the plaza (with a public parking lot beneath) at this major intersection, and from its swimming pool, sundeck, and bar on the roof one can see most of the city. Rooms are close to the standard motel or medium-priced hotel in the U.S. or Canada, with fine bathrooms. The location couldn't be better. The price isn't bad: 896 pesos ($17.92) single, 980 ($19.60) double.

Hotel Stella Maris, Calle Sullivan 69 (tel. 905/566-6088). Here the starfish motif is carried to the lengths of having a brass effigy of this sea creature attached to each room key. Other than this, though, there's little nautical about the place except the small rooftop swimming pool. The rooms in this brand-new building are sort of small and some are a bit dark, but part of this is due to the agreeable subdued colors. TV, radio, bathrooms with separate washbasin cubicle, bottles of pure water in each room, and (from front rooms) views of Sullivan Park and its Sunday art exhibitions are the extras. Prices are moderate, and you get your money's worth, for sure: single rooms cost 882 pesos ($17.64); doubles 1008 pesos ($20.16); junior suites are 1050 to 1260 pesos ($21 to $25.20). The hotel's restaurant serves an excellent set-price lunch for only 132 pesos ($2.64). This is a fine, modern hotel, not all that far from Reforma.

OTHER MODERATELY PRICED HOTELS: Hotel Palace, Calle Ignacio Ramirez 7 (tel. 905/566-2400). The Hotel Palace, just off the Plaza de la Revolución, was one of Mexico's outstanding luxury hotels only a decade or so ago. Today it retains its comfort, its good location, its experienced staff, and over 200 well-kept, bright, and modern rooms. The bustle of a large hotel surrounds you here, with tobacco kiosk and travel desk in the lobby, bag-bearing bellboys scurrying here and there, and the occasional busload of tourists. Of the rooms, over half are priced at 840 pesos ($16.80) single, 980 pesos ($19.60) double; the rest are about 100 pesos ($2) higher in price.

Hotel Viena, Calle Marsella 28 between Dinamarca and Berlin (tel. 905/566-0700). Several hotels are a short walk east of the Zona Rosa, and give you the convenience of being almost right there. The Hotel Viena is actually an older hotel but you wouldn't know it from its sleek, modern exterior. The 60 rooms are all well kept, although a bit older than the facade would indicate; some have bathrooms with tubs, and twin beds, and others have one double bed and cost 1200 pesos ($24) single, 1250 pesos ($25) double. Blown-up color photos of forest scenes and Alpine views abound. There's a parking lot beneath the hotel, and a little Swiss-style restaurant at sidewalk level. Indeed, the hotel seems to be a favorite with European visitors. The rooms at the Viena are among the quietest in the downtown area.

Hotel Bristol, Plaza Necaxa (tel. 905/533-6060). Across Reforma to the north from the Zona Rosa is the Hotel Bristol on the little Plaza Necaxa, which is at the intersection of Panuco and Sena. Although many of its rooms are filled with sedate tour groups or long-term residents, the eight-story structure usually has rooms to spare for 1680 ($33.60) double. Although bright and modern, shiny and clean, the Bristol is a fairly somnolent place. A branch of the Denny's chain restaurants is in the ground-floor level of the hotel.

Hotel Ambassador, Calle Humboldt 38, just south of Juárez (tel. 905/518-0110), specializes in tour groups, but if rooms are tight you might try here as groups often have cancellations which leave a few rooms unexpectedly available. The hotel has recently undergone extensive renovations. Prices are 868 pesos ($17.36) single, 1008 pesos ($20.16) double, with bath and piped-in music; a travel desk, garage, and multilingual staff complete the picture.

The **Hotel El Romano** (tel. 905/510-8800), at Humboldt 55, at the corner of Guerra/Articulo 123, is more up-to-date than many others in this area, with over 150 rooms going for low prices: 840 pesos ($16.80) single, 950 pesos ($19) double, 1065 pesos ($21.30) triple. The private baths here are often made of a dramatic black stone, although the rooms are kept light by bright-colored spreads, walls, and curtains. Ten of the rooms— are you ready?—have circular beds. The roof terrace or patio has grass, a tiny swimming pool, and a tremendous view, plus a rather elegant *palapa*-topped restaurant.

Hotel Principado (tel. 905/592-2211), at Calle José Ma. Iglésias 55, is just off Avenida Juárez near the intersection with Avenida Insurgentes, a stone's throw from the Monument to the Revolution. It's brand new, clean, and shiny bright, a ten-story tower with 150 fully modern rooms decorated in cheery solid colors. Standard equipment includes television sets, wall-to-wall carpeting, central air conditioning, a parking lot, a restaurant and bar. Prices as of this writing are surprisingly low, and can be expected to rise in years to come. Right now, the rooms are a real bargain at 1008 pesos ($20.16) single, 1190 pesos ($23.80) double, 1400 pesos ($28) triple; an extra person pays 175 pesos ($3.50); (a handful of rooms cost a bit less; junior suites are more expensive).

Similar to the aforementioned hostelry, although not quite so new, is the large and well-located **Hotel Purua Hidalgo** (tel. 905/585-4344), Colón 27 right at the corner with Reforma—a block north of the Reforma/Juárez intersection. Here you'll have a telephone in your room, plus FM music, and all the standard comforts. Prices are 854 pesos ($17.08) single, 994 pesos ($19.88) double, 1190 pesos ($23.80) triple; an extra bed costs 155 pesos ($3.10). The Purua Hidalgo is popular with tour groups because of its fine location.

The **Hotel Geneve Calinda Quality Inn** (tel. 905/525-1500) is very convenient to all the delights of the Pink Zone at Londres 130, near the corner of Genova. A huge old place that's recently undergone a substantial facelift, it has 378 rooms with private baths, newsstand, boutiques, a travel agency, and the famous glass-roofed, plant-filled bar called El Jardín. The rooms come in price ranges, depending on newness, size, and comforts. Singles cost 2100 pesos ($42); doubles are 2280 pesos ($45.60); an extra person pays 375 pesos ($7.50); and kids 16 and under stay free. You can reserve toll free in the U.S. by calling 800/228-5151 (in Maryland, call 800/492-2930); in Toronto, call 416/485-2600; in the rest of Canada, call 800/268-8990.

The **Hotel Mallorca,** Serapio Rendon 119 (tel. 905/566-4833), is modern and comfortable, with wall-to-wall carpeting almost everywhere, Muzak, air conditioning, a parking garage, coffeeshop, bar, and restaurant. Every room has its own TV (good for Spanish practice). If you get a *matrimoniál* (double bed) the cost is 980 pesos ($19.60); twin beds cost 1260 pesos ($25.20); singles are 840 pesos ($16.80).

Should the Hotel Mallorca be full, you can go across the street to the **Hotel Sevilla,** a similar hotel, at Sullivan and Serapio Rendon 126 (tel. 905/566-1866), with rooms and prices very similar to those at the Mallorca. Rooms come with telephone, television, FM radio, and special purified drinking-water taps in the bathrooms; a garage in the hotel's basement is served by the elevators; all rooms are air-conditioned. The hotel's restaurant-bar is at your service, either in the dining room or in your own room.

Budget Hotels
(double rooms 700 to 1250 pesos—$14 to $25)

The range of hotels in the capital follows the range of incomes among Mexicans who come here to visit. Thus, there are plenty of modest but comfortable hotels, usually ten years old or more, sometimes a bit of a walk from the center of things, but many times not that far at all from where the action is. Many budget hotels have garages or can arrange for parking; a few even have tiny swimming pools and/or televisions in their more luxurious rooms. In every one there is at least a coffeeshop, or there's one virtually next door. You should not have too much trouble with the language, either, as the desk clerk or manager will know some English. One thing is sure: few other cities in the world of the size and importance of Mexico City can boast such a good selection of low-priced, respectable, comfortable, and safe budget hotels.

A Pension

The **Casa Gonzalez** (tel. 905/514-3302), at Río Sena 69, is made up of two old city mansions which have been converted to hold guest rooms. It's a different sort of place, costing 420 to 490 pesos ($8.40 to $9.80) single, 700 to 840 pesos ($14 to $16.80) double for room and bath—your money could not be better spent. The house is beautiful, with several terraces, a big shady tree, lots of grass (for a house in the city, that is), and absolutely spotless, almost lushly furnished rooms. Meals are taken in a bright dining room, and all is cheerful, clean, and efficient. All of the rooms have private baths (some with tubs). Meals are optional, and cost 140 pesos ($2.80) for breakfast, 280 pesos ($5.60) for lunch, and 210 pesos ($4.20) for supper. Parking in the driveway. Highly recommended.

BUDGET TIPS: First, remember that Mexican budget hotels have an assortment of rooms, and that those with a view of the street may be more expensive (and noisier!) than those with windows opening onto an airshaft. Second, rooms are usually furnished with one single bed, one double bed, or two twin beds; the best buy is for two people to take the double bed—twins are almost always more expensive. To get the double bed ask for *una cama matrimoniál*. Third, although all rates are controlled by the Mexican government, these rates are the *maximum* allowable, and in many cases a desk clerk will quote you a lower price if business is slack or if you suggest a slight reduction. By the way, the room rates are required to be posted in plain view near the reception desk and as a rule they generally are, places like Acapulco being the exceptions. Ask the clerk to show you the *Tarifa*, and get to recognize the official form it's on to help you locate it in other hotels. Fourth, *test the beds* if you intend to stay any length of time. Price often has nothing to do with the comfort of the beds. Why pay good money for something that's going to give you a backache? Often the cheaper hotels will have beds bought at different times, so one room may have a bad bed but another one a good bed.

BUDGET ACCOMMODATIONS: The 17-room **Hotel Maria Angelo's,** Río Lerma 11, at Río Marne (tel. 905/546-6705), is an older place with rooms of all sizes and shapes; it's recently undergone some renovation, though many of the bathrooms remain unredeemed. The tiny lobby adjoins a small reading lounge to which departing guests sometimes contribute (you'll find English magazines, Spanish paperbacks). There is also a cheery (and cheap) café and restaurant entered from the street or lobby, which offers a full lunch for 100 pesos ($2), and stays open from 9 a.m. to 9 p.m. There's no elevator, and only one telephone per floor, but each room has a private bath with a tub, freshly painted walls, and windows so wide that the sun streams in each morning. Single rooms cost 720 pesos ($14.40), doubles are 860 pesos ($17.20), and some rooms are large enough to accommodate three or four persons; an extra bed is 200 pesos ($4) per night. In addition, there are eight suites. The suites are quite large and have their own terraces—a fine extra.

Near the Plaza de la República

For what you get, rooms at the modern **Hotel Principado** (tel. 905/592-2211) are a surprising bargain. The good-looking, tall new hotel is just off the Plaza de la República at José Maria Iglésias 55. Many rooms have fine views of the plaza and the monument, and all have TVs, clean tile baths or showers, air conditioning, and lounge chairs. A decent little restaurant is off the lobby, and a parking lot is underneath. For this comfort, the price is just 910 pesos ($18.20) single, 1025 pesos ($20.50) double, 1200 pesos ($24) triple—excellent value.

The small triangle formed by Insurgentes Centro, Antonio Caso, and Reforma has good budget hotel choices. The 40-room **Hotel Uxmal,** Madrid 13 (tel. 905/566-7044) is a modern place with a tiny lobby, cafeteria, elevator, central air conditioning, free parking lot, and tiny balconies overlooking the street from some of the rooms. It's not a big hotel, and everything is small in scale, but it is very comfortable. The hotel boasts a purified-water tap in each room, and, of course, tile bathrooms equipped with showers. Most rooms have black-and-white TV. Rates are 630 to 770 pesos ($12.60 to $15.40) single, 770 to 910 pesos ($15.40 to $18.20) double; 140 pesos ($2.80) for each extra person. Try the Uxmal, for the hotel is well run, the staff exceptionally friendly.

The Uxmal's sister hotel (same ownership) is the rather swankier **Hotel Mayaland,** half a block away at Antonio Caso 23 (tel. 905/566-6066). The 91 rooms here all have purified-water taps, huge closets (with lots of hangers!), and lots and lots of extras: parking lot under the hotel, air conditioning, elevators, beauty salon, restaurant, travel agent, sauna (for a fee). Prices reflect this opulence: the rooms cost 840 to 980 pesos ($16.80 to $19.60) single, 1050 to 1190 pesos ($21 to $23.80) double. Think of how close you'll be to everything and perhaps you'll decide it's worth it.

Another good choice, very much like the two preceding hotels although not so friendly, is the **Hotel Regente** (tel. 905/566-8933), at Paris 9, between Madrid and the three-way intersection of Antonio Caso, Insurgentes, and Paris. Over 100 rooms plus a garage fill this modern building. Bold-patterned bedspreads and flowered drapes plus wall-to-wall carpeting make the rooms lively and comfortable. Bathrooms with showers are pretty small but new and quite adequate. A restaurant and travel-agent desk are at your disposal in the lobby. Here one person pays 700 to 840 pesos ($14 to $16.80), and two pay 840 to 980 pesos ($16.80

to $19.60). Again, the location and transportation possibilities are excellent.

Another good area for budget hotels is the district just north and west of the Reforma-Juárez intersection, particularly the Calle General Jesus Teran.

Considering its appointments, the five-story **Hotel Jena** (pronounced "hena"), Jesus Teran 12 (tel. 905/566-0277), is a good budget-priced choice. From the swanky exterior, you might think it expensive, but not so. The 60 rooms, nicely furnished with "Hotel Formica," each with telephone and glistening tile bath, cost 700 to 1050 pesos ($14 to $21) single, 840 to 1260 pesos ($16.80 to $25.20) double, the higher price being for a huge room with a couch, rather like a junior suite. The hotel has a restaurant and free parking, and some of the rooms have television.

On par with the Jena but slightly less expensive, the **Hotel New York**, Edison 45 (tel. 905/566-9700), is a large four-story building, a cubist's dream of mosaic tile, grass-green paneling, and glass. The 45 rooms are equipped with telephones and tile baths, carpeting, Formica furniture, wood paneling on one wall, and hanging glass lamps. Very pleasant. Prices: 775 pesos ($15.50) single, 900 pesos ($18) double. The small restaurant off the lobby solves the breakfast problem with hotcakes, eggs, and coffee for 100 pesos ($2). It's open every day from 7 a.m. to 10 p.m. Parking in the hotel's locked garage is free.

The 100-room **Hotel Frimont**, Jesus Teran 35 (tel. 905/546-2580), stands up well when compared to the Jena and the New York. Singles here rent for 630 pesos ($12.60), doubles for 770 to 840 pesos ($15.40 to $16.80), triples for 1050 pesos ($21); four-person rooms for a low 1190 pesos ($23.80)—that's a mere $5.95 per person!—all with telephones and private baths. But it is a pleasant hotel boasting a slick marble lobby, 72 nicely decorated rooms, free parking, and a medium-priced restaurant just off the lobby, open daily from 7 a.m. to 1 a.m., featuring a 95-peso ($1.90) lunch from 1 to 5 p.m.

The **Hotel Edison** (tel. 905/566-0933), Edison 106, a block from the Revolución monument at the corner of Iglésias, is a real find. In the midst of the city's noise and bustle, its odd construction around a narrow court with grass and trees gives a sense of sanctuary. Some rooms are built in tiers overlooking the court, and even larger ones are hidden away down hallways. These latter rooms tend to be dark, but big and comfortable with huge king-size beds, and cost 560 pesos ($11.20) single, 660 pesos

($13.20) double. Of the other rooms, a few singles go for 440 pesos ($8.80), most are a bit higher; other doubles go for 770 pesos ($15.40), with a few extra-luxurious rooms costing more. Blond wood and light colors, piped-in music, and sunlight make this a cheerful place. Services include bathrooms with separate washbasin areas, and some even have bidets, plus tub-shower combinations. Location is fairly quiet and near downtown.

Another hotel choice convenient to the Monument to the Revolution is the **Hotel Arizona** (tel. 905/546-2855), Gómez Farías 20 at Avenida Insurgentes. For the very reasonable prices of 630 pesos ($12.60) single, 728 pesos ($14.56) double, 826 pesos ($16.52) triple, you get very clean rooms with tile showers, black-and-white TV sets, telephones, air conditioning, and a large covered parking garage right next door. Color TVs are yours at a small additional charge. Try not to get a room that looks onto busy Insurgentes. The Arizona is only a half block from the monument.

Off Cinco de Mayo

Bronze statuettes cradling cut-glass lamps set the tone at the entrance of the **Hotel Gillow**, Isabel la Católica 17 at the corner of Cinco de Mayo (tel. 905/518-1440). It's a dignified old establishment built during an era when space was not at a premium: nearly every room flourishes a small entrance hall. Tall French doors open onto tiny balconies from the exterior rooms. All 115 rooms are comfortably furnished in a modern style with carpeting, boldly patterned bedspreads, newish furniture, and telephones, and a good many of the bathrooms are equipped with tubs. They even follow the curious custom of putting a white paper band bearing the words "Sterilized for your Protection" across toilet and washbasin. Rooms come in several sizes and prices, from 600 to 750 pesos ($12 to $15) single, 820 to 920 pesos ($16.40 to $18.40) double. The restaurant, handy for breakfast eggs and coffee, also serves a six-course *comida corrida* featuring such delectables as oyster cocktail, enchiladas suizas, and paella à la Valenciana for a reasonable 250 pesos ($5.00), plus tax and tip.

North of the Zócalo and Alameda

Another fantastic bargain is the **Hotel Antillas,** Belisario Dominguez 34 (tel. 905/526-5674), near the corner of Allende, with rooms priced at 504 to 595 pesos ($10.08 to $11.90) single, 560 to 735 pesos ($11.20 to $14.70) double. The Antilles is rather old-world, a five-story study in burnished red lava block with huge plate-glass windows hung with rust drapes. Inside, the lobby is lit by black wrought-iron chandeliers. It has a lot of charm. The 70 rooms, all with telephones and private baths, are extraordinarily large and very clean, bright, and modern—lots of new paint and new furniture. Parking is free, making it an excellent choice if you have a car. Without, it's a short walk to a main transportation artery.

The Antillas is a top choice of Mexican families, and is one of the best hotels—for the price—anywhere in the city. Prices are low because the area is dingy—but urban renewal has already begun.

South of the Alameda Central

On the street south of Juárez with the unpronounceable name of Revillagigedo, at no. 35, is the **Hotel Fleming** (tel. 905/510-4530), a building of 100 rooms from which I've had good reports which were borne out by inspection. Although well used, the heavy service has still left the rooms quite presentable, and the bathrooms are larger than most. Elevators take you to the upper floors. Singles at the Fleming cost 505 pesos ($10.10); doubles are 558 pesos ($11.16) in a double bed, 610 pesos ($12.20) in twin beds. A blindingly colorful coffeeshop-restaurant is located next to the lobby, and offers a set-price lunch daily.

Mexico City's fine selection of hotels is rivaled by its vast number of good restaurants, descriptions of which follow directly.

University City

Chapter IV

WHERE TO DINE IN MEXICO CITY

WE HAVE ALL EATEN Mexican food, whether at inexpensive sit-down restaurants or at drive-in taco stands. But when you go to Mexico City, throw out your preconceptions of what you will find to eat and start all over. Ever heard of tortilla soup? Did you know that much of the seafood served in the U.S. and Canada—prawns, shrimp, red snapper, etc.—comes from Mexican waters? When is the last time you had a rabbit stew? Or charcoal-grilled kid? Or even a fresh (not weeks-old) corn tortilla, hot from the oven? Did you know that Mexican bakery-pastry shops sell the most delectable and impossibly good pastries and sweet rolls for practically nothing?

Mexico City, of course, is the place to go for the grandest Mexican buffet of them all: dozens of restaurants headed by chefs who have come from all over the country, bringing their skills and regional recipes to the capital. In addition, the city's cosmopolitan ambience means that one finds true French and continental restaurants, Chinese and Japanese places, even authentic hamburger joints, and prices are inexpensive to expensive-but-reasonable.

For breakfast (*desayuno*), Mexicans may just have rolls and coffee, or they may charge into an American-style repast of bacon and eggs, orange juice, coffee, tea, or chocolate, and a side order of *frijoles refritos* (refried beans). Hotcakes—called just that in Spanish here—are on almost every breakfast menu, as are corn flakes with milk. So far so good. But at lunchtime Mexicans dine very differently from their North American neighbors. The main meal of the day is taken between 1 and 4 p.m., and it is a full-course, leisurely meal, perhaps followed by a short nap or a stroll in the park. Soup, pasta, salad, meat or fish, with vegetables, dessert, and coffee make up a normal *almuerzo* or *comida* (lunch). Most restaurants offer a set-price lunch called *comida corrida* (literally, "continuous lunch"), also called a *cubierto,* in which you are brought the various courses in succession, with only a few elements of choice, perhaps in the soup and main courses. The price is always far below what the various courses would cost if ordered à la carte, and constitutes the best food buy of the day. Prices for a full *comida corrida* can be anywhere from 90 pesos ($1.80) to 500 pesos ($10), but the majority are in the range of 135 to 275 pesos ($2.70 to $5.50). The difference in price depends on the class of the restaurant, the number of courses, and the quality of the dishes (i.e., chicken soup at an inexpensive place, oyster stew at a luxury restaurant). To live *á la Mexicana,* you should try to adapt to the big meal at lunchtime; try to sit down to lunch before 3 p.m., though, as restaurants sometimes run out of one or another of the items offered.

For supper (*cena*), the custom is to eat lightly about 8 or 9 p.m., although most restaurants offer complete menus for diners, both native and foreign, who are going out for a night on the town. Watch out: it is possible to get hooked on delicious *comidas* and then to find yourself sitting down to a big meal in the evening.

In the pages which follow, you'll find the best restaurants of Mexico City in all price ranges listed according to style of cuisine or specialty. Note especially that hotel restaurants have *not* been included here, but have been described along with their parent hotels in the preceding chapter—so if you're looking for the Mexican branch of Maxim's of Paris, or of Fouquet's, turn back to the descriptions of the Hotel El Presidente Chapultepec and the Hotel Casino Real, respectively. For the better restaurants, reservations are advised; and they should be honored or cancelled.

TAXES AND TIPS: Mexico's 10% Value Added Tax (IVA) is added to most restaurant bills, the exceptions being in small, inexpensive eateries. As for tipping, ignore what you may read in other publications about "15% of the total." Norteamericanos invariably overtip south of the border, and if you watch a Mexican paying his bill you'll see what the local custom is: for inexpensive meals under 100 pesos, just leave the loose change of, say, 5 pesos; for moderately priced meals of 100 to 250 pesos, leave about 6% to 10%; above 250 pesos you're into the 10%

to 15% tipping bracket. Only in the poshest places will the staff expect the full 15%.

Unless otherwise noted, prices given below *do not* include tax or tip.

Mexico City's Top Restaurants
(meals for $18 and up)

It is generally expected that top-class restaurants will be inspired by French or continental cuisine, for the culinary arts seem to have reached a peak in France, in ingredients, preparation, and service. Special care means greater expense, and so Mexico City's top-class French and continental restaurants are not cheap, although they are considerably cheaper than similar establishments in New York, Montréal, London, or—especially —Paris. Make reservations for dining at the restaurants listed below, and observe the jacket-and-tie (at least!) dress code.

There is only one way to approach the **Rivoli**, and that is in your best clothes with a good appetite and a well-conditioned palate. Rivoli, at Hamburgo 128 (tel. 525-6862 or 528-7789), is unabashed in its elegance. Crystal sconces, velvet-backed salon chairs, and lots of mirrors set the mood for the cuisine, which is classic French and international. Last visit I enjoyed an oyster cocktail, escalopas de ternera Marsala con fettuccine (thin slices of veal cooked in Marsala, with fettuccine), and profiteroles for dessert. A summer alternative would have been vichyssoise, pescado blanco de Patzcuaro (the famous whitefish from the lake of Patzcuaro), and pastry. For all its refined service and elegant setting, the Rivoli is not wildly expensive, for either of the above meals would cost less than 1200 pesos ($24), including tax and tip, but not including the price of wine and drinks. Come to the Rivoli (preferably with a reservation) for a relaxed and refined lunch or dinner from 1 p.m. to 1 a.m. daily. Don't forget that the dress code is strictly enforced here: men are not admitted without jacket and tie, women without suitably presentable dress.

For many years the restaurant called **Ambassadeurs**, Reforma 12 (tel. 535-6495), has been one of the city's outstanding deluxe restaurants, and the staff and management are zealous in preserving this reputation. When the desire for a special celebration strikes you, call for a reservation and then get to the restaurant a little early so you can have a drink (about 85 to 125 pesos, $1.70 to $2.50) in the Bar Amba among the leather club chairs, dark

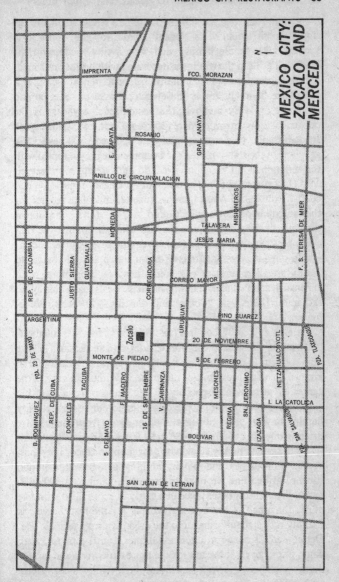

MEXICO CITY:
ZOCALO AND
MERCED

wood, and stained glass. When your table's ready, stroll into the dining room to enjoy its elegant, classic touches: those little sconces with candle lamps, each with a tiny shade, and the ironwork grills in the windows, decorated with bright brass medallions and emblems. The orchestra begins to play at 8 p.m., and the dance floor fills up as the evening moves on. Service and ambience are very much in the posh French style, as is the cuisine. Coq au vin grand'mère (250 pesos, $5), and stuffed squab Prince Rainier (the stuffing is of pâté and veal; 300 pesos, $6), are some of the standard items. In summer, begin your meal with the unfamiliar but delicious avocado and yogurt soup, served cold (130 pesos, $2.60). To close out an elegant repast you can choose from baked Alaska, crêpes suzette, chocolate mousse, or the incredible dessert soufflé Grand Marnier (order this one at the start of the meal to give the chef enough time). Note that every person pays a 50-peso ($1) cover charge at Ambassadeurs.

Although Ambassadeurs is open for lunch as well (1 p.m. to 2 a.m. are the hours), if you come then you'll be dining with expense-account clients talking business deals; save this place rather for the classic "dinner and dancing." Proper dress required, of course.

Delmonico's, at 87 Londres (tel. 514-7003), has been a famous place to dine in Mexico City for decades, and success has led the management to open another dining place in the Zócalo's Gran Hotel Ciudad de México. But the original Delmonico's is still the center of attraction, especially if you hunger for a fine, big American-style steak, or some other dish brought dramatically flaming to your table. Steaks and other meats from the grill are priced from 300 to 480 pesos ($6 to $9.60); an interesting alternative is the grilled turkey steak with ginger apple sauce (310 pesos, $6.20). For flames and flavor, nothing can beat the jumbo shrimp, grilled and brought to you on a flaming sword (450 pesos, $9). All this takes place in a softly lit room filled with live music for much of the evening, Muzak for the rest. Service is friendly rather than formal, and the mood is a very sociable one. Delmonico's is open for lunch and dinner from 1 p.m. to 1 a.m. daily; prices given above are for the more expensive (and larger) dinner portions. Although jacket-and-tie formality is not strictly required, it is appreciated.

The Best Mexican Restaurants

Of course you're out to try the local cuisine as much as possible while you're here. After a few meals in the restaurants listed below, you'll be copying down recipes in the back of this book for duplication at home. Good Mexican restaurants come in all price ranges, but those listed below fall roughly into the moderate category, with full lunches for 200 to 400 pesos ($4 to $8), full dinners for 400 to 800 pesos ($8 to $16). Remember that a 10% tax will be added to your bill.

Fonda El Refugio, Liverpool 166 (tel. 528-5823), near the corner of Liverpool and Amberes, is a very special place to dine *á la Mexicana.* Although small, it's unusually congenial with natural blond wood floors, a large fireplace decorated with gleaming copper pots and pans, and rows and rows of culinary awards and citations behind the desk. It manages the almost impossible task of being elegant and informal at the same time. Service is careful, efficient, and extremely polite, and the menu is one which runs the gamut of Mexican cuisine. You can run part-way by having a sopa de verduras (vegetable soup), then perhaps arroz con plátanos (rice with fried bananas), or tamales de elote con pollo; for a main course, you can try the chalupas poblanas (tortillas topped with chicken, onions, cheese, lettuce, and green chili sauce), or perhaps enchiladas con mole poblano (topped with the rich, thick, spicy chocolate sauce of Puebla). Desserts are the authentic traditional ones, like sweet marzipan figurines and camotes (delicate cylinders of a flavorful sweet potato paste). Wine, liquor, and beer are served, and if you go all-out and order whatever you like, plus a half bottle of wine, the check should come to something like 500 to 700 pesos ($10 to $14) per person. You can dine for not much more than half that, though, if you like. The Fonda El Refugio is very popular, especially on a Saturday night, so get there early—remember, it's small.

The **Café de Tacuba,** at Tacuba 28 (tel. 512-8482), very near the Metro station Tacuba, looks as though it's been here on this street in Mexico City since the city began—or at least for 100 years or so. The wainscoting in the two long dining rooms is of orange, white, and blue faïence, the lamps are of brass, dark and brooding oil paintings share wall space with a large mural of several nuns working in a kitchen (maybe it was here from the time of Cortes, at least?). The waitresses wear white uniforms with matching caps, and they're on duty every day from 8 a.m. to midnight. Soups here cost 50 to 65 pesos ($1 to $1.30), with the top price going to cream of asparagus with biscuits; grilled chicken costs about 140 to 200 pesos ($2.80 to $4), most meat dishes are 80 to 100 pesos ($1.60 to $2) more than chicken, but such things as enchiladas and chilaquiles con crema are cheaper. Rather than the customary *comida corrida,* the Café de Tacuba offers a selection of daily lunch plates, served with soup, costing 300 to 380 pesos ($6 to $7.60). The best is the last, however, as a tempting selection of what certainly look to be homemade cakes and pastries wait in a glass case near the front of the restaurant. Wine, beer, and liquor are served. You won't believe it either, but the Café de Tacuba was founded in 1912.

A Mexican Restaurant in a Class by Itself

Mazatlan, Cuernavaca, Acapulco, and Mexico City: the famous Mexican restaurateur Carlos Anderson operates one of his zany and guaranteed enjoyable eateries in the capital of the republic. Called **Anderson's Bar & Grill,** it's at Reforma 400 (tel. 511-5187), a short stroll from the center of the Zona Rosa, and it sports the familiar Anderson trademarks: a plaque by the front door boasts that it has been there "Since 1315," the interior is a jumble of antique junk-and-treasures, and it's open to "Members and Non-members Only." The doorman in a red bowler and coveralls will arrange for the parking of your car, while you enjoy one of the several small dining rooms on various levels (one has a ceiling covered in every conceivable sort of hat). For all its foolery, there are white tablecloths and efficient, friendly waiters, plus food that is good, if on the high side of the price range: seafood is the specialty, with most entrees costing about 300 pesos ($6), although lobster Thermidor is a cool 430 pesos ($8.60). A good bet is the concha de mariscos, a conch shell filled with various nautical delicacies for 315 pesos ($6.30). There are lots of meats featured as well, and also a full set-price meal for only 455 pesos ($9.10). The "Calories" (Andersonese for dessert) include flan, choco-late mousse, and a specialty called "Pemex-Sol," named for a lead-ing brand of Mexican motor oil (coffee with brandy and Kahlúa). Wild, but fun, and good. There's music from a combo after 9:30. Open Sunday, too.

The area to the north and west of the Zócalo is fairly rundown and dilapidated, and you would not normally have much reason to wander here. There is, however, one restaurant in this area (on a dirty, dreary street) which is a must for anyone wanting the real taste of Mexico. It is **Las Cazuelas** (tel. 522-0689), Columbia

69, just down from Carmen, five blocks north and one block east of the National Palace on the Zócalo, housed in a beautiful 18th-century tiled mansion. The dreariness of the street disappears as you enter Las Cazuelas, for you are surrounded by beautiful wall tiles, hand-painted chairs, and a lively group of mariachis. The kitchen, which is immediately visible when you enter, is lined with large earthen pots and casseroles, and thus the name *las cazuelas*. This place is always swinging with live mariachi music (especially on a Sunday when the whole family is out for a good time) and it's no wonder, considering the prices they charge: 170 to 265 ($3.40 to $5.30) for most items, which are distinctly Mexican, like costilla de res (grilled beef ribs), cabrito al horno (roast kid), chicharrón (pork crackling) with guacamole. There is no English menu here and the waiters do not speak English, so you'll have to know your Spanish menu. A full meal, with drinks, for two people will be between 500 and 700 pesos ($10 and $14). Highly recommended! Open daily noon to midnight, but the best time to come is late afternoon between 2 and 6 p.m.

With a name like **Bellinghausen** (tel. 528-6814), how could a restaurant be anything but German? Easily, at least in Mexico City, for Bellinghausen, at Londres 95 in the Zona Rosa, actually serves internationally recognized fare with a Mexican touch, although it was not always thus. Back in 1914 when the restaurant was founded, black bread and blutwurst were the rule. While the restaurant still retains much of its earlier decor—café curtains on brass bars, coat hooks all along the walls, dark wood wainscot, dark tables and chairs, and white tablecloths—the menu is in Spanish. Sopa de pescado (95 pesos, $1.90) is good for a starter. Robalito meunière (small bass sauteed in butter; 250 pesos, $5) could be either your main course or just the fish course, if you're ravenously hungry, followed by Tournedos con champiñones (with mushrooms) or cabrito al horno (roast kid), for 365 pesos ($7.30). A full meal at Bellinghausen, with a bottle of beer, will cost in the range of 650 to 780 pesos ($13 to $15.60). Don't expect to find many tourists here; the clients are mostly local people who come for the food, not a flashy "native" decor. The restaurant is open every day from 1 p.m. to 1 a.m.

Close by is another popular place with a very reasonable menu; it's **La Carretta Rosa,** Hamburgo 96 (tel. 514-3444),—you'll recognize it by the painting of the wagon over the pink door and two large wagon wheels which flank the tiled entrance. This is a down-home place patronized by Mexicans homesick for real country cooking: menudo (tripe soup), pozole (meat and hominy stew), chicharrón (pork crackling), and tacos of grilled or roasted meat. Specialty plates abound, mostly featuring northern cuisine. You can spend as little as 100 pesos ($2) or as much as 300 pesos ($6), but the average bill is 150 to 225 pesos ($3 to $4.50). Jukebox, fluorescent lights, hefty señoras—you might as well be in some small Sonoran ranching town.

Some of the cheapest and best Mexican food in the city is yours at **El Rincon Mexicano,** Uruguay 27 between Avenida Lázaro Cárdenas and Bolívar. Plain, but clean and bright with a nice tiled grill, El Rincon offers a menu on which few items are priced above 55 pesos ($1.04). The daily *comida corrida* is somewhat spartan, but an indisputable bargain for only 70 or 95 pesos ($1.40 to $1.90): chicken consommé or cream of asparagus soup, rice or spaghetti, grilled bananas or chicharrón and a choice of nine main courses. Something is sure to be right on, from Virginia ham to chicken casserole, from pork chops with chilis to three different types of enchiladas. Dessert and coffee are included in the ridiculously low price.

American Restaurants

Mexicans are so used to American food, it almost blends into the national cuisine—much as the taco is no longer a "foreign" dish to Americans. Consequently, American food in Mexico City tends to be good, reasonably priced, and reasonably authentic. Cleanliness and efficiency, highly valued north of the Río Grande, are also to be found in these American-style restaurants. When your stomach demands something familiar for a change, or you just get that craving for an old-home favorite, choose from among these recommendable places.

Right on Reforma, northeast of the Insurgentes intersection, is **Shirley's** (no phone), on the east side of the street at Reforma 108 (open 7:30 a.m. to 11:30 p.m. every day, Saturday till 1 a.m.). Shirley's is the epitome of efficiency, from the navy-blazered maître d' to the light-blue-uniformed waiters and waitresses; everything runs smoothly, and the atmosphere is one of order and friendliness—a good bet for anyone who's homesick. In fact, from first (a glass of water brought automatically) to last (the check says "Please Pay the Cashier") Shirley's shows its American heritage. You can start the day with the standard breakfast of juice, coffee, toast, and two eggs for 100 pesos ($2), or the house special, English muffins with cheese and ham for about the same; for lunch try a hamburger (88 pesos, $1.76), or a Ruben sandwich (125 pesos, $2.50—french fries included). Air-conditioned—a very pleasant place!

Shirley's has a branch in the Pink Zone at Londres 102, open 7:30 a.m. to 11:30 p.m. daily, Friday and Saturday nights till 1 a.m. Vaguely western in decor following that at the main restaurant, diners sit in red booths or captain's chairs as they pore over the long menu of appetizers, soups, salads, sandwiches, Mexican specialties, meats, fish, side orders, and desserts. Although it appears very American, Shirley's is patronized most heavily by Mexicans who know good food and service, and who want it at a reasonable price. Note that here in the Pink Zone you can order wine with your dinner.

Pam-Pam, in the arcade beneath the Hotel Del Prado at Juárez 70 (tel. 521-0524), has puzzled guests for years with the cryptic notice that it is "Affiliated with the Café de la Paix, Paris, France." (One wonders whether the menu at the Café de la Paix says "Affiliated with Pam-Pam, Mexico City.") Such speculation aside, Pam-Pam is the Mexico City businessman's version of an American luncheonette, with attractive red booths plus a handy lunch counter with stools, but with little extra touches of elegance—the lamps verge on being chandeliers. The menu comes to you in Spanish, French, and English, and offers all three meals, every day. For breakfast, 115 pesos ($2.30) will buy you two eggs, bacon or sausage, juice, and coffee; hotcakes, juice, and coffee are somewhat less. At lunchtime order the *comida corrida* for 145, 163, or 185 pesos ($2.90, $3.26, or $3.70). Attractive, efficient, reasonably priced, with food that's easy on the foreign stomach, Pam-Pam was a frequent resort on my first trip to Mexico City many years ago, when my digestive system demanded an end to enchiladas with hot sauce.

From the Bellas Artes, walk to Avenida Madero and the **Sanborn House of Tiles** ("Casa de Azulejos"; tel. 521-9100). This gorgeous antique building was once the palace of the Counts of the Valley of Orizala, but now houses a branch of the Sanborn's restaurant and variety store chain. Dining tables are set in an elaborate courtyard complete with carved stone pillars, tiles, and peacock frescoes. It's a lovely place for a rest and a cup of coffee with some apple pie à la mode. Coffee (a little pot) is 24 pesos (48¢); eggs with bacon, 110 pesos ($2.20); pork chops cost 188 pesos ($3.76); shrimp is more. If you dine, order the daily special, which, for 125, 145, or 210 pesos ($2.50, $2.90, or $4.20), gives you the best value.

Although other branches of the Sanborn's chain are not as palatial and historically significant as the House of Tiles, they are convenient, comfortable, and familiar. Besides being restaurant/lunch counters, Sanborn's branches sell newspapers and magazines, cosmetics and toiletries, film and gifts. There's a Sanborn's at Niza and Hamburgo, in the Zona Rosa; one at Reforma 45; and another on Reforma at the corner of Tiber, near the "Angel" Monument.

Of the Howard Johnson-type restaurants in Mexico City, none is ubiquitous like **Denny's,** which has 11 branches in the capital. Modern and scrupulously clean, air-conditioned, and be-Muzaked, Denny's specializes in no-fuss fast service of predictable food in predictable surroundings. While many tourists shun such places as "un-Mexican," the Mexicans themselves flock to Denny's throughout the day to down such things as club sandwiches and eight varieties of hamburgers (108 to 129 pesos, $2.16 to $2.58), and even Mexican combination plates for 200 pesos ($4). But to local people, Denny's is not a cheap fast-food place; rather, this is dining out, and indeed for what you get the prices are a bit high. When you're hot and tired and your stomach chooses not to accept unfamiliar food, Denny's is the place to go for familiar surroundings and familiar eats. The most convenient locations are those at Paseo de la Reforma 509, at Londres and Amberes in the Zona Rosa, at Avenida Juárez and corner of Humboldt, at Plaza Necaxa (in the Hotel Bristol), and at Mariano Escobedo 402.

Almost as evident as Denny's are the various branches of **VIP's** (pronounced "beeps" in Spanish), a similarly modern chain of American-style restaurants with comparable conveniences, food, and prices. Check out the menu posted in the window and you'll find soups priced at 44 to 63 pesos (88¢ to $1.26), hamburgers for 115 to 128 pesos ($2.30 to $2.56), and a sirloin steak sandwich with garlic bread, tomato, and french fries for 160 pesos ($3.20). For dessert, the peach Melba is a popular choice. Note that breakfasts at VIP's tend to be surprisingly expensive.

Around-the-World Dining

One could easily eat for a week in Mexico City without repeating national cuisines, and for many weeks without repeating restaurants. Once you've had a few *comidas corridas,* and located the best fast-service hamburger, you're ready to explore the capital's international lineup. Prices, again, are mostly in the range of 200 to 400 pesos ($4 to $8) for lunch, 400 to 800 pesos ($8 to $16) for dinner. Then there's that 10% tax.

CHINESE: There is a small Chinese section in Mexico City located on Dolores between Independencia and Articulo 123. The best of the restaurants here is **Shanghai,** a few doors up from Articulo at Dolores 30. Numerous salons open off the entrance and during the lunch hour they are almost always busy. The food here is good but the prices are high for what you get—but then if you're in the mood for Chinese food, nothing else will usually do. They offer a series of combination plates for one to four persons ranging from 235 to 540 pesos ($4.70 to $10.80) per person. The last time I ate there I got a 280-peso ($5.60) combination plate which included a quite good noodle soup, spare ribs (costilla al horno), fried shrimp (only two, unfortunately), fried rice, beef chow mein, and of course a full pot of good Chinese tea. The à la carte items are about 160 pesos ($3.20) for egg foo yung with chicken, 190 to 235 pesos ($3.80 to $4.70) for the chop sueys. Open from noon to midnight.

A clue to the authenticity of the cuisine at **Luau,** Niza 38 in the Zona Rosa (tel. 525-7474), is the large number of Chinese and Polynesian diners seen here most of the time. It is doubtful, after all, that they would come for the decor, which might be called Cantonese Disneyland: goldfish pond, rock garden, and red lamps, red tablecloths, red carpets, red this and red that. As always, a first-time visitor's best bet at the Luau is a combination plate, prices for which start at about 215 pesos ($4.30) and go to 450 pesos ($9). For the lowest price you'll receive respectable portions of soup, fried shrimp, fried rice, barbecued pork, chow mein, a fortune cookie, and tea. Another 60 pesos ($1.20) increases the quality of the bounty: wonton soup rather than broth, eggroll rather than fried rice, and so on. Luau is a longtime favorite in the capital, open daily from noon to midnight.

DANISH: **Cafe Konditori,** Genova 61, near Londres (tel. 511-1589), is a Danish coffeeshop that also serves meals and breakfast (open 7 a.m. to midnight daily). There are outdoor tables here, and the front room is glassed in and looks out on the street. They have a good onion soup for 72 pesos ($1.44). Sandwiches range from 80 to 105 pesos ($1.60 to $2.10). Their pastries are excellent —and expensive, going for about 33 to 52 pesos (66¢ to $1.04). Cappuccino is 24 pesos (48¢). This is quite an "in" spot so it will probably be busy any time you go. Breakfasts, by the way, cost 99, 135, and 175 pesos ($1.98, $2.70, and $3.50), the last being composed of two eggs, ham or bacon, fruit, a pot of coffee, bread and butter, and jam.

ENGLISH: If you crave a Yorkshire pudding, the place to go is the **Picadilly Pub** (tel. 514-1515), Copenhague 23, between Reforma and Hamburgo. Roast beef and Yorkshire pudding sell for 325 pesos ($6.50). Far swankier than the average English public house, it boasts such features as hunting prints, soft leather banquettes, an inner dining area called the Henry VIII Room, and a maître d' in a tuxedo. House specialities include Irish stew, and beefsteak and oyster pie—both priced at 235 pesos ($4.70) and both excellent. On the lower end of things is the Welsh rarebit, 170 pesos ($3.40). The Picadilly is open every day but Sunday from 1 p.m. to 1 a.m.

FRENCH: For dining in the French manner, you can save some money and aggravation by seeking out **La Belle Époque** (tel. 525-8435), at Río Sena 45, near the corner of Nazas, on the north side of Reforma. Clearly, the decor here follows the name and so you'll see lots of turn-of-the-century plush and gilt, old photographs and tintypes, posters and artifacts. Besides the several comfy interior dining rooms (once parlors in a converted house), La Belle Époque has a beautiful garden dining area in the rear, with a tremendous birdcage, vines and flowers, and awnings to protect diners from Mexico City's unpredictable afternoon showers. The chef is a veritable Frenchman (don't laugh, few are!) who knows what good onion soup is—it comes loaded with cheese for 120 pesos ($2.40). The daily special at lunch costs between 220 and 340 pesos ($4.40 and $6.80), and could be anything from a delectable red snapper through tournedos béarnaise to conejo (rabbit) done with a special touch. An exceptional treat here, because the chef worked for some years in North Africa, is a fine couscous (served Thursday and Sunday only). French wines can be had, but they're expensive at about 520 to 975 pesos ($10.40 to $19.50) the bottle; better to stick with the very good selection of Mexican wines for 350 pesos ($7). La Belle Époque is open 1 p.m. to midnight weekdays, till 6 p.m. on Sunday; closed Saturday. Lunchtime is busiest because of the embassy crowd, and dinnertime is more relaxed and quiet. Highly recommended.

Food and service at **Le Bistrot,** in the passage at Genova 76 (or Londres 104) in the Zona Rosa (tel. 533-3295), are less formal than is normally found in French restaurants. In fact, it goes far toward living up to its name by having a half-restaurant, half-sidewalk-café atmosphere. The style is ever so gently turn of the century, with curvy brass chandelier lamps and sconces, potted philodendrons, and folksy touches like a big glass bowl of oysters set near the door, fresh for the shucking. Come to Le Bistrot for any sort of occasion, from an informal café lunch set under the awnings, or an almost-fancy dinner of snails bourguignonnes, el pato al orange (canard à l'orange), and crêpes suzette, and you'll spend about 825 pesos ($16.50) per person. Le Bistrot is right next to several other restaurants—Toulouse-Lautrec, Alfredo's, etc.—in the passage between Londres and Hamburgo, which can also be entered from Genova.

One of the more delightful places to have lunch in Mexico City is at the **Champs-Élysées,** at the corner of Calle Amberes and Paseo de la Reforma (tel. 514-0450), in the Zona Rosa. Monday through Saturday from 1 to 5 p.m. the third-floor garden terrace is open and waiting, a delightful place brimming with greenery and shaded by gay striped awnings and umbrellas. Those who think ahead can reserve a table near the edge of the terrace for the view of Reforma, below.

The menu is straightforward (and comes in an English version) and classic French: start with pâté or an avocado with creole sauce for about 260 pesos ($5.20), or burgundy snails or smoked salmon for about twice that price. Red snapper or fresh salmon are usually available as a fish course, and as a main course the daring might order steak tartare at 390 pesos ($7.80), the timid but discerning might choose the tournedos in béarnaise sauce for the same price. Desserts are the delicious tried-and-true classics: chocolate mousse, strawberries chantilly, or a cold soufflé with Grand Marnier. With wine, a dinner at the Champs-Élysées might come to 1100 pesos ($22); lunch only half that much.

If you come in the evening, the terrace will be closed but you can dine in the comfortable indoor dining rooms.

ITALIAN: Lowly pasta takes on noble proportions at **Alfredo** (tel. 511-3864), in the passage at Genova 76 (or Londres 110) in the Zona Rosa. As the restaurant has both indoor and awning-shaded terrace dining areas, the spaghetti is cooked in a chafing dish at an outside table during the warm months, and the chef enjoys preparing the glistening strands with a flourish. During the cold, rainy days of winter or on especially cool summer nights, you may prefer to dine indoors where even the ceiling is paneled in dark wood and display cases set in the walls are stocked with stuffed animals and birds. (This sounds like a taxidermic nightmare, but it's not really.) The noble pasta plates cost about 120 pesos ($2.40); main courses of fish and meat are mostly in the 155- to 210-peso range ($3.10 to $4.20). Alfredo is open from 1 p.m. to 1 a.m. daily; if you come after 9 p.m. for dinner, you can enjoy the live music.

La Gondola, Genova 21 (tel. 511-6908), has a posh atmosphere of stained-glass windows, beamed ceiling, thick carpets, and a maître d' in tuxedo who cooks the spaghetti in a chafing dish at your table. It's a popular place for lunch with well-heeled businessmen and Mexico City's elegant women who shop in the area, yet the prices aren't staggering. Most Italian meat entrees —chicken tetrazzini, breaded veal cutlet—run 210 to 235 ($4.20 to $4.70). For a light lunch I can recommend their hearty minestrone soup at 52 pesos ($1.04) and a Caesar salad at 90 pesos, ($1.80). Open 1 p.m. to midnight daily.

One of the best long-standing restaurants is **Sorrento** (tel. 512-6118), in the arcade of the Banco de Industria y Comercio building which runs between Azueta and Balderas, just south of Juárez near the southwest corner of the Alameda. There's a large sign on Azueta so you shouldn't have any trouble finding it. This is a businessmen's eating house, complete with comfortable red leather chairs and white-jacketed waiters. The place is always busy but the service remains excellent nonetheless. They offer a very good *comida* (all those businessmen, remember) for 175 pesos ($3.50), with a selection of appetizer, soup (the cream of asparagus is especially good), an entree which comes with vegetable and pasta, dessert, and coffee. They also have à la carte items with some Italian specials like lasagne (very tasty) and cannelloni for 90 to 130 pesos ($1.80 to $2.60).

For Pizza

Pizza Real, Genova 28 (511-8834), at the corner of Estrasburgo, boasts that it serves 50 different varieties of pizza, priced at 24, 58, or 78 pesos (48¢, $1.16, or $1.56) the piece, 130 to 416 pesos ($2.60 to $8.32) for a "Princesa," the medium-size pie, and 170 to 545 pesos ($3.40 to $10.90) for the giant *real* ("king-size") pie, which serves eight people. They even serve a selection of five *comidas corridas* featuring soup, fruit salad, pizza, dessert, and coffee, or in the more expensive *comidas,* an Italian entree such as ravioli. Although it is billed as a pizza joint, Pizza Real is half pizza parlor, half Italian restaurant, with wide black-and-white stripes on the brick walls, yellow tablecloths, and a pizza-cutting counter by the front door. It's open from 8 a.m. to 11:30 p.m. Monday through Saturday, 1 to 11:30 p.m. on Sunday.

JAPANESE: Of the several Japanese restaurants in Mexico City, the most centrally located is the **Restaurant Tokyo** (tel. 525-3775), Hamburgo 134, at the corner of Amberes in the heart of the Zona Rosa, on the second floor. Mounting the stairs brings you to a room hung with black banners bearing the name "Tokyo" and a rosette in white, and otherwise done up in plain and simple Japanese style. Soft lighting and quiet, traditional Japanese Muzak set a relaxed mood; this is no formal place, so moderately presentable dress will do fine. The hordes of Japanese businessmen often shed their jackets here.

Plenty of Japanese delicacies to choose from, such as sukiyaki cooked at your table, or shabu shabu (fresh vegetables and beef in broth, cooked at your table; 260 pesos, $5.20). The tempura is 195 pesos ($3.90), and delicious sashimi (strips of raw fish) is the same. For those not closely familiar with Japanese cuisine, the combination plates offer the best plan: they come in various sizes and degrees of bounty, and are priced from 210 to 390 pesos ($4.20 to $7.80). The Tokyo is open every day from 12:30 p.m. to midnight; on Sunday from 2 to 10 p.m.

Daruma (tel. 546-3467), a Japanese restaurant not far from the intersection of Insurgentes and Reforma at Río Tamesis 6 (where Tamesis meets Finlay and Villalongin), is a bit hard to find but worth the effort. Informal as can be, the boys cook behind the sashimi bar while mom totals up the bills and makes change. The sashimi bar and small tables are of heavy natural wood, however, and like the rest of the simple furnishings impart a good deal of dignity to the proceedings. The food is good, and even if you're not familiar with Japanese cuisine, here you can safely order what your neighbor's having and come out all right. The specialty of the house is tori-katsu, boned chicken breast stuffed with vegetables and noodles. Sashimi (raw fish) and curry dishes with chicken and shrimp fill out the menu. Prices are moderate: about 112 to 210 pesos ($2.24 to $4.20) per plate, about 260 pesos ($5.20) for a full meal—you'll enjoy your meal here. You can dine at Daruma from 1 p.m. to midnight every day, 1 to 10 p.m. on Sunday; closed Saturday.

Although the aforementioned places can't be faulted on food, service, or prices, sometimes only a kimono-clad waitress will bring out the real spirit of Japan. For kimonos and generally lush surroundings, look for the **Restaurant Fuji** (tel. 514-6814), Panuco 128 at the corner of Tiber. Despite the costumed waitresses and the posh atmosphere, prices are fairly reasonable, and a full seven-course meal is offered for 370 pesos ($7.40). The tables and the counter remind one of the Daruma, but you're likely to find a larger number of visiting Japanese businessmen here than there.

JEWISH: Who doesn't dream now and then of having a good New York deli close at hand when in a foreign country? Mexico City has a few restaurants which hold up respectably against New York's Lower East Side, but none of those mentioned below is, as of this writing, strictly kosher.

At the corner of Hamburgo and Genova there's **Kineret** (tel. 525-6927), where you can scarcely find room to sit down, especially at the outdoor tables. It's a delicatessen with an extensive menu including such items as borscht, chopped liver pâté, herring, and blintzes. After 1 p.m. they offer dinner platters which range from 100 to 350 pesos ($2 to $7). The liver-and-onions dinner includes a choice of appetizer (the pâté is very nice), soup, dessert, and coffee. There is also a cocktail lounge called the Rana Bar, which has "happy hour" at 5:30 to 7:30 p.m. (two drinks for the price of one).

SPANISH: The **Meson del Perro Andaluz** (tel. 533-5306), Copenhague 28, very near the Hotel Aristos, has two levels inside, a few outdoor tables (always crowded in the evenings), and a very loyal clientele. Although prices in the evening are fairly high, with such delicious things as duck in olive sauce *(pato á la aceituna)* and similar items going for 285 to 365 pesos ($5.70 to $7.30), the luncheon specials 180 to 290 pesos ($3.60 to $5.80) make it especially attractive for a midday meal. Try the tuna and avocado salad or a bowl of the hearty minestrone soup. Note that entrees come ungarnished (without vegetables or salad). They have wine, both Mexican and imported, but you'll pay a high 365 pesos ($7.30) minimum for a bottle. The Meson del Perro Andaluz is open from 1 p.m. to 1 a.m. daily; arrive early in the evening if you want a seat at one of the café tables out front.

Although the menu at **El Parador de José Luís,** Niza 17 (tel. 533-1840), used to be very, very Spanish, concessions have been made to internationalism. Today, along with the Castilian garlic soup and several other traditional dishes, one can order duck à l'orange, a mixed grill, or crepes au gruyère. To finish off, there are plenty of things waiting to rob you of your last peso; but who can resist bananas flambéed in rum, or crêpes suzette? Expect to pay about 1000 pesos ($20) for a full dinner. It is possible to enjoy the comfort and elegance of El Parador at a very moderate, fixed price by ordering the *menu turistico,* or set-price dinner, which is usually something like ceviche, soup, or ham as a first course; then your choice of a main course of chicken, beef, or pork; pastry for dessert; and tea or coffee. The price is 450 pesos ($9).

You can spot El Parador easily on Calle Niza, just off Reforma, as it's in a colonial-style stone building with ornate decoration around the windows and doors. Inside, there's heavy use of heavy wood, antiques and sort-of-antiques hung on walls and posts, and a low ceiling to give a cozy feeling to the dining rooms.

SWISS: At least half my friends in Mexico swear that **Chalet Suizo,** Niza 37, between Hamburgo and Londres (tel. 511-7529), is the most dependable restaurant around. The decor is Swiss, of course, with checked tablecloths, enormous wooden horns, and Alpine landscapes; service is very good. The menu features hearty French onion soup for 90 pesos ($1.82), and a wide range of interesting entrees, some of which are changed daily, for 135 to 275 pesos ($2.70 to $5.50); among these are sausages with sauerkraut, smoked pork chops, baby veal tongue, sauerbraten, and excellent fondue. Wine is served, a half bottle of local wine costing 200 pesos ($4). Open from about 12:30 p.m. to midnight daily. Menu in English.

The specialty at **La Crepa Suiza,** Florencia 33 between Hamburgo and Londres (tel. 511-3734), is crêpes of course, but that's not all. Diners crowd the few tables set out in the courtyard off Florencia, and the cozy indoor dining room, for a plentiful luncheon buffet costing 250 pesos ($5), served from 1 to 5 p.m. After that, you must order à la carte: dinner crêpes with various delicious stuffings cost 90 to 125 pesos ($1.80 to $2.50), dessert crêpes are half that price. For more filling fare, you can't miss with the fondue bourguinonne: succulent morsels of beef which you cook yourself in a pot of hot oil, and then dip into any of six different sauces. With garlic bread, the fondue is 520 pesos ($10.40) for two people. La Crepa Suiza is open for breakfast daily, as well.

VIENNESE: Another restaurant in the tried-and-true category is the **Restaurant Viena,** Amberes 4, just off Reforma (tel. 511-3486). Amberes is a fashionable street with lots of interior-decorator and art shops, and for all this class the Viena is an unassuming little place with café tables and wood paneling. Recently the Viena has come under new management, and the menu now includes a few hard-to-find Jewish items such as matzoh-ball soup. But Viennese specialties such as stuffed cabbage and wienerschnitzel, at 200 pesos ($4) each, are still the mainstays. Menu in English. The Viena is open from 12:30 to 11 p.m. daily, 1 to 11 p.m. on Sunday.

Specialty Restaurants

Besides all of the above, Mexico City has a number of restaurants especially good for certain types of food, or certain times of day. Here, then, are tips on how to find the best octopus, the tastiest meatless meals, the most filling noontime *comidas corridas,* and the most interesting sidewalk cafés.

SEAFOOD: If you can't get down to Acapulco but you still want to wet your whistle with some of the sumptuous fish found in the Pacific, head for the **Restaurant Nuevo Acapulco** (tel. 521-5950), Lopez 9, a half block south of Juárez. They have a handsome display of fresh fish on the counter, a crocodile hanging on the wall in front of you, and a turtle on your right. Although neither of the latter two is served, there is a wide range of soups in the 90-peso ($1.80) range 125 pesos—$2.50—for oyster stew with 24 oysters), and fish entrees are 170 to 225 pesos ($3.40 to $4.50). The highest price on the menu is for lobster. Their camarones (shrimp) are fresh and flavorful, and they make an excellent camarones-and-cheese casserole. Although the food here is excellent, the prices have more than doubled over the past few years, and all sorts of seafood have become luxury items. The restaurant has three rooms which are kept busy and full (mostly with businessmen and others who can pay a bit more). If you're dying for good fish, by all means go to the Acapulco.

VEGETARIAN RESTAURANTS: I can't say enough good things about the food at the **Restaurante Vegeteriano y Dietético,** Madero 56, not far from the Zócalo (tel. 521-6880 or 585-4191). There's no sign on the sidewalk, so look for a stairway marked Panella, or the menu posted outside on the entrance; walk one flight up, and you'll enter the restaurant. Decor is nothing special but the food is fantastic, and they have a piano player who plunks out oldies-but-goodies while you feast on the 130-peso ($2.60) *comida* (or one with gigantic portions for 145 pesos, $2.90). As the name implies, they serve no meat, but you can easily have your fill starting with a huge salad (watercress, tomato, radishes, grated carrot, and beets), followed by superb cream of tomato soup, a choice of two entrees (berenjena empanizada, or breaded eggplant; ensalada trigo, or bulghur salad), a delicious cake made of whole wheat and honey, served with coffee or tea. This place is good—you must try it yourself to appreciate it. Menu in Spanish only; open every day except Sunday from noon to 6 p.m. There's another Vegeteriano at Filomeno Mata 17, between 5 de Mayo and Madero, five blocks west of the Zócalo.

Las Fuentes (tel. 525-0629), Panuco 127 at Tiber, two blocks north of the "Angel" Monument, is another branch of the Restaurant Vegetariano y Dietético. This is the most modern and luxurious of the three, filling the ground floor of a hotel building. More expensive than the other two, it's still well worth the money you pay for what you get. The daily set-price lunch costs 285 pesos ($5.70), but huge portions are the rule, and for that price you may enjoy lentil soup, carrot- and potato-filled tacos with apple salad, a side order of peas or beans, then coffee or tea and whole-wheat-and-honey cookies. Las Fuentes is open daily from 8:30 a.m. to 11:30 p.m., till 10:30 p.m. on Sunday. Highly recommended.

A DINING ROOM WITH A VIEW: One must always beware of rooftop restaurants, as the management often takes the view that diners will absorb the food as uncritically as they absorb the panorama around them. But at the **Muralto,** atop Mexico's Latin American Tower (Torre Latinoamericana) at the corner of Avenida Lázaro Cárdenas and Avenida Madero (tel. 521-7751 or 521-7752), the food is almost as good as the view. Take the elevator from the lobby, then switch elevators (you'll see) and get out at the Muralto stop on the 41st floor. At lunchtime, the variegated sprawl of city is a constant wonder, stretching for 20 miles in every direction. With luck, the clouds will drift away from the peaks of the twin volcanoes, Popocatepetl and Ixtacchihuatl, to the southeast. Unhappily, they don't drift away often and they don't drift away for long.

At night, however, you're liable to catch your breath as you exit from the elevator, turn the corner, and are confronted with the city lights—an incomparable sight. Have a drink in the bar, and take some time to choose from the menu. A moderately priced meal might consist of fruit cocktail or onion soup, filete de huachinango (red snapper) or puntas de filete (tenderloin tips), peach Melba, and coffee. With tax and tip, the bill for one person—excluding liquor—will be about 500 pesos ($10). You can spend a good deal more, or somewhat less, as you wish. Add about 100 pesos ($2) for each drink, 475 pesos ($9.50) for a bottle of Mexican wine to reach your grand total. Entertainment nightly; open from 1 p.m. to 1 a.m. every day of the week.

THE BEST COMIDAS CORRIDAS: Along the south side of the Alameda, on the back streets between Bucareli and Avenida Lázaro Cárdenas, are numerous restaurants, some old and well established, others new and modern. For a pleasant, relaxing *comida corrida* in the moderate price range I can recommend these special places.

Centrally located, open long hours and on Sunday, and with lots of tables, the **Restaurant Rhin** (tel. 521-3364), Juárez 36C, is a solid, dependable place to dine anytime. It's only a few steps from the Palacio de las Bellas Artes, and when you see the tiny entryway, half-filled with a lunch counter, you'll think I'm wrong—but I'm not. Go in past the lunch counter, and you'll find various rooms with tables and a semblance of decor. But the food's the thing here: two daily *comidas,* at 150 pesos ($3) and 200 pesos ($4), well worth every centavo. Service is reasonably efficient, but at lunchtime it's sure to be crowded.

One of the most teeming restaurants during *comida* time (1 to 4 p.m.) is the **Restaurant Danubio,** Uruguay 3 at Avenida Lázaro Cárdenas (no phone) which has a huge 220-peso ($4.40) lunch that is practically an institution. The restaurant itself is big and old-fashioned, its high ceiling carved and hung with wrought-iron lanterns. There's nearly always a marimba playing at the doorway during the lunch hours, but shoulder your way through the crowd and find a table. A typical *comida* consists of a shrimp or oyster cocktail, maybe Valencia soup or tomato consommé, boiled lentils, a choice of a hot or cold fish dish, a choice of three entrees, custard or fruit, and coffee or tea. The à la carte menu is extensive, but you get better service during the busy time if you stick to the *comida corrida*. They serve cocktails (65 pesos, $1.30), wine (250 pesos—$5—for a bottle of house wine), and beer (30 to 35 pesos, 60¢ to 70¢). There is also a room upstairs to accommodate the lunchtime overflow, although many in the overflow don't know it, so you may find more breathing space aloft. Open 1 p.m. to midnight daily.

Note: The house specialty at the Danubio is langostinos (baby crayfish) and well worth the money.

One of the lowest priced and most filling *comida corridas* in town is served daily at **Los Faroles,** Luís Moya 41, one block from Independencia (no phone). It's a big, busy place littered with tables and chairs, with several women-chefs toiling away at a central grill and kitchen. Tacos are the forte, and the *comida* may well include a few of these. The price for the set lunch is only 85 pesos ($1.70).

If you're staying near Sullivan Park, or find yourself near the intersection of Reforma and Insurgentes, walk west along Villalongin (which skirts the southern edge of Sullivan Park), turn left and walk through the little plaza bearing a bust of Giuseppe Verdi, and you'll come to the Calle Río Lerma. A half block southwest on Lerma, on the right-hand side, is the **Restaurant Nucleo,** Río Lerma 5 at the corner of Río Marne (no phone), a small and simple restaurant worth a walk because of its two daily *comida corridas,* one costing 70 pesos ($1.40), the other at 90 pesos ($1.80). For the lower price you might get a cream soup, rice, charcoal-grilled beef, frijoles, and dessert; for the higher price you get a wider selection of main courses and slightly larger portions. The Nucleo is very popular with young office workers, and is sometimes crowded, but seats seem to become available quickly, and sharing tables with strangers is the custom here. Nucleo is open for breakfast and supper as well, but it's closed on Sunday. By the way, two other similar eateries with similar prices are within a half block of the Restaurant Nucleo, one of these being the café-restaurant in the Hotel Maria Angelo's.

SIDEWALK CAFÉS: For all its broad sidewalks and leafy promenades, the Paseo de la Reforma has very few sidewalk cafés. Of these few, one of the best for watching the pedestrian traffic is at Reforma 92, just off the traffic circle sporting a statue of

Columbus. It's the **Café Vendôme** (tel. 535-8513), and while it can't live up to the splendor of the one in Paris, it has just enough of a Parisian flavor to make it pleasant: red-and-white striped café awnings and wooden railings enclose the tiny tables. The clientele changes depending on the time of day, with the leisurely and retired types showing up midmorning, office workers for a quick lunch around 1 or 2 p.m., businessmen for coffee after a lengthy *comida* at 4, and movie-goers in the evening (a cinema's right next door). They all come for coffee or tea (18 to 26 pesos, 36¢ to 52¢), and for light meals such as a cheese omelet, hot roast beef sandwich, or a bowl of chili con carne (80 to 98 pesos, $1.60 to $1.96). The Café Vendôme serves more expensive items as well, but it's fundamentally a light-lunch place, so save your extra pesos for a more elegant meal in a full restaurant. Open morning to late night daily.

Find your way to the passageway at Londres 104, just off Genova. Here you'll see outdoor cafés, art galleries, craft shops, and cappuccino drinkers. This is the heart of the Zona Rosa, and the home of the **Restaurant Toulouse-Lautrec,** an outdoor café-restaurant. During the day many of Mexico's young artists and writers drop in here for a cappuccino, but the weekday lunch specials (195 pesos, $3.90) are fine bargains—watermelon juice or vegetable soup; either breaded pork chops, green tomato enchiladas, or a ham omelet; frijoles refritos (refried beans); custard and coffee. À la carte items include a very fine—and huge—Mexican combination plate for only 275 pesos ($5.50). And it's a colorful place—red-checkered tablecloths over old-fashioned ice cream parlor tables with wire chairs. Open 9 a.m. to 1 a.m. They serve drinks and have live entertainment in the evenings.

AFTERNOON TEA: The Zona Rosa would have to have some fine places for afternoon tea as they serve it on the continent, and the finest we've found yet is **Auseba,** Hamburgo 159B at Florencia (tel. 511-3769), which serves pastries and candies along with its tea and coffee. The glass cases hold the most delicious-looking display of cookies, meringues, bonbons, cakes, pies, puddings, and *tortas* I've ever seen in the city. Paintings decorate one wall, fancy candy boxes another, and the little circular tables with white cloths all have modern black plastic chairs—eclectic, but comfortable. Pastries cost about 65 pesos ($1.30); coffee or tea, 26 to 40 pesos (52¢ to 80¢). You can get away with spending only

65 pesos ($1.30—for coffee and croissants) or you can spend 130 pesos ($2.60—for a rich pastry and Viennese coffee). Auseba is open daily for breakfast, and stays open until about 10:30 p.m. On Sunday, the hours are 11 a.m. to 10:30 p.m.

Very near Auseba, right on the corner of Florencia and Hamburgo, is the **Duca d'Este,** another *salon de thé* with a rich decor and prices to match.

Not far from the intersection of Reforma and Insurgentes, off Sullivan Park, is **Giorgio's Café y Arte,** Villalongin 28 at Río Marne. Totally modern in design, Giorgio's is very traditional when it comes to pastries and coffee. The choice of cakes and cookies is diet-destructive and delightful, and a portion with coffee will cost about 60 to 98 pesos ($1.20 to $1.96). Breakfast is on from 8 to 11:30 a.m. every day, and light lunches are a possibility the rest of the day. The windows which surround Giorgio's make it as close to a sidewalk café as is possible without actually being one. The crowd here is usually young and art-happy, especially on Sunday mornings when the free paintings exhibitions are set up in neighboring Sullivan Park.

CHURROS AND HOT CHOCOLATE: Those interested only in a snack at lunchtime should head for **El Moro,** Avenida Lázaro Cárdenas 42, at Uruguay. A little man in the window turns out fresh doughnut-type treats called churros or estillos, which he then smothers in sugar and serves piping hot. The churros are offered in combination with hot chocolate (the best and richest chocolate I've ever tasted): 45 to 48 pesos (90¢ to 96¢) for the delectable hot chocolate and a plate of four churros, or 30 pesos (60¢) for the plate of churros plus coffee and milk. Try it—an authentic *churrería* is a bit of true Mexico City daily life.

A DELICATESSEN: The Mexican equivalent of a deli is a shop that sells *productos ultramarinos* (imported goods). Although it's not a deli as we know it, **La Villa de Madrid,** Uruguay 36 at the corner of Bolívar (tel. 512-3782), still has a tempting assortment of hard-to-find goodies in its sidewalk windows, with more inside. (Don't confuse the deli entrance with the nearby grubby cantina of the same name). Imported liquor—everything from Schlitz to Dom Perignon—cookies, crackers, nuts, cheese, and cold meats are sold daily, 9 a.m. to 9 p.m.; closed Sunday.

To fill out your picnic basket, cross Bolívar and right there is the **Rosticería Italiana,** where a freshly roasted chicken will set you back only 300 pesos ($6).

STARVATION BUDGET EATS: All over Mexico are phenomenally cheap working-class eateries that could almost be classified as soup kitchens. They're called *taquerías* or *fogatas,* and are much patronized by families who find it cheaper to eat here than to cook at home. Sometimes they're dives, so it's best to look them over carefully and test them gingerly. Also note that no English will be spoken, so know your Spanish menu.

Cheap eats in Mexico usually means tacos, and at **El Caminero Tacos al Carbon** you'll find three cooks very busily chopping and filling to make a dozen different types. A plate of three tacos costs 85 pesos ($1.70); a beer, only 34 pesos (68¢). The counters are usually crowded with hungry taco-munchers who come for the good food, low prices, and clean, attractive atmosphere. El Caminero is north of Reforma, at Calle Río Lerma 138, near the intersection with Río Po.

Right in the Pink Zone—and at many other locations around the city—you'll come across **Tacos Beatriz,** a chain of eateries serving up the national dish at rock-bottom prices, even in the high-rent districts. The Zona Rosa outlet is at Londres 148, between Florencia and Amberes. The tacos are only 21 pesos (42¢) each. Closed Sunday.

For a varied assortment of taquerías (taco shops), head for Calle de Uruguay between Bolívar and Avenida Lázaro Cárdenas. You may find it hard to believe that one can buy a full meal for about a dollar, but here you can. The shop at Uruguay 27 seems to be about the best.

The **Lonchería "Los 2 Pericos,"** located at Donceles 2, just two blocks north of the Bellas Artes and near the corner of Avenida Lázaro Cárdenas, is a restaurant with two parts. The fruitería sells every imaginable sort of fruit (22 varieties). Licuados made from the fruit cost 13 to 26 pesos (26¢ to 52¢), depending on the size; the *vaso* (glass) is small; *cupo* (goblet) is the large size. Try the guanabana, with a taste somewhere between that of a pear and a lichee-fruit. The other part of the place serves tacos and tostados made of grilled or roasted meat, onions, and other nice things. There's a huge wooden bowl of pickled carrots, peppers, and chilis, and all in all it's a mouthwatering sight. But watch what you order, for some of their tacos are not for the squeamish: *cabeza* (head), *ubre* (udder), tripe, *lengua* (tongue), and various other organs are all offered. There are more conventional stuffings as well, including *Milanesa* (veal), *cecina* (dried beef), and *salchicha* (sausage). Prices vary according to the filling, but are generally 13 to 36 pesos (26¢ to 72¢). It's a bargain, and the beautiful wall tiles give you more than your pesos' worth of taco enjoyment: the place stays open all day.

Let's assume you're near the Zócalo, tired of sightseeing, hungry for lunch, low on cash. Search out the **Comedor Familiar "Minerva,"** at Carranza 105 just east of Pino Suarez: walk through the arcade of leather shops, turn right, go through a double door, climb a flight of stairs (watch your head!), walk past the busy kitchen, and there you are. In a few minutes you'll get your chance at a seat, and at the filling 65-peso ($1.30), six-course *comida corrida*. Don't get to the Comedor Familiar before 1 p.m., however, as the *comida* isn't served before that time.

Although culinary delights are one of Mexico City's strong points, there's plenty more to see and do here. Read on for full details.

National Cathedral

Chapter V

MEXICO CITY SIGHTS

YOU'VE SEEN something of the city as you found your way to a hotel and located some of the better places to dine, but now it's time for a systematic introduction to the wonders and delights of this, one of the greatest cities in the world. You might want to review the layout of the city as described in Chapter II of this book before starting out on the following sightseeing tour, arranged as a walk through the most interesting sections with stops at the major sights. You won't be able to finish seeing all the things below in a day, or even two or three. You'll need at least a week to get a good introduction to the city's major attractions, a month to get to know them well.

Start your walking tour at the center of Mexico City's history, the colonial Zócalo. Take the Metro to the Zócalo station, or an Expresso Reforma bus ("Zócalo") along Reforma or Juárez.

The City Center

THE ZÓCALO: Every Spanish colonial city in North America was laid out according to a textbook plan, with a plaza at the center surrounded by a church, government buildings, and military headquarters. As capital of New Spain, Mexico City's Zócalo is one of the grandest, and is graced on all sides by darkened 17th-century buildings.

There's a wonderful view of the Zócalo from the seventh-floor restaurant, partly open air, of the Hotel Majestic, which is on the corner of the Zócalo and Madero. You can start your trip with breakfast here, or pay a late visit to the bar which adjoins the restaurant. From this vantage point, the people strolling casually in the vast expanse of square below look as though they have been choreographed by some omnipotent chess player, as indeed they may have been.

The odd Indian word *zócalo* actually means "pedestal," or

"plinth." A grand monument to Mexico's independence was planned, and the pedestal built, but the project was never completed. The pedestal became a landmark for visiting out-of-towners, and pretty soon everyone was calling the square after the pedestal, even though the pedestal was later removed. Its official name is Plaza de la Constitución. In imitation, the main square in any other Mexican town is often called "el zócalo," whether it ever bore a pedestal or not!

The Zócalo is being closed to vehicular traffic as Mexico City's pedestrian plans reach fulfillment. Soon, most of the streets around the square will be for people only, not cars, and you'll be able to stroll at leisure through what used to be the very center—the *tianguis* (market) and *teocalli* (sacred center)—of ancient Tenochtitlán. The paving in the square is being given a stone mosaic which shows a portion of the Mendocino Codex, an Aztec "picture-text" of the founding of Tenochtitlán.

The National Cathedral

Take a look inside the cathedral, begun in 1573 and finished in 1667. If you wander quietly around past the innumerable small chapels, you'll almost certainly come across a guide who is busily demonstrating some of the cathedral's more outstanding features: the tomb of Agustín Iturbide perhaps, placed here in 1838, or the fact that the holy water fonts ring like metal when tapped with a coin. Like all good big churches it has catacombs underneath; unlike some churches it is immense, brilliant almost to blinding, overpowering.

Next to the cathedral, and communicating with it, is the chapel known as **El Sagrario,** another tour de force of Spanish baroque built in the mid-1700s.

In your look around the cathedral and the Sagrario, be sure to note the sinkage of the great building into the soft lake bottom beneath. The base of the facade is far from being level and straight, and when one considers the weight of the immense towers, the sinkage is no surprise.

Around to the east side of the cathedral is a quaint reminder of medieval trade life. Here is where carpenters, plasterers, plumbers, painters, and electricians gather who have no shops of their own—modern journeymen. Each has his tool box and may display the tools of his trade along with pictures of his work, paint color charts, and various other attractions.

Big things are about to happen to the area off the cathedral's northeast corner. Several years ago the ruins of an immense Aztec temple were discovered near the corner of Calle República de Guatemala and Avenida República de Argentina. Excavations are well under way, and plans call for an open-air museum and theater. The surrounding district, one of the oldest in the city, has suffered long neglect, but a project inaugurated in 1980 should restore much of its colonial charm. Designated a Historical Zone, the district is eligible for urban-renewal funds. The first product of the plan is the beautifully restored mansion at the corner of Donceles and República de Chile. Built as the home of Don Manuel de Heras y Soto in the 18th century, it is now the **Mexico City Historical Center.** Take a look in through the gates. Don Manuel, by the way, was one of the notables who signed Mexico's Act of National Independence.

The National Palace

On the east side of the Zócalo stands the impressive National Palace, begun in 1692, the last addition completed late in the 19th century. A complex of countless rooms, reached by wide stone stairways and adorned with carved brass balconies opening onto a series of courtyards, the National Palace is where the president works from 8 a.m. to 2:30 p.m. (regular hours for government employees in Mexico). Enter by the central door any day from 8 to 6. The guards will let you by if you ask.

Continue across the courtyard to the biggest attraction here, for Mexicans and tourists alike, the enormous murals painted over a 25-year period by Diego Rivera. All the murals are quite easy to understand. There is, for instance, *The Legend of Quetzalcoatl,* depicting the famous legend of the flying serpent bringing a white man with a blond beard to the country; when Cortes arrived, many of the Aztecs remembered this legend, and believed the newcomer to be Quetzalcoatl. Another mural tells of the *American Intervention,* during the War of 1847, when American invaders marched into Mexico City. It was on this occasion that the military cadets of Chapultepec Castle (then a military school) fought bravely to the last man; the final six wrapped themselves in Mexican flags and leaped from the windows to avoid surrendering. (You'll see a monument to the boy heroes later, in Chapultepec Park.) The pride and joy of palace murals is one called the *Great City of Tenochtitlán,* a pictorial study of the original settlement in the Valley of Mexico. The city takes up only a small part of the mural, and the remainder is filled with what appears to be four million extras left over from a Cecil B. De Mille epic. In fact, no matter what their themes, most of the murals incorporate a piece of ancient Mexican history, usually featuring Cortes and a cast of thousands.

On Saturday and Sunday night from dusk to 11:30 p.m., and throughout the month of September (Mexico's independence month), the palace and other buildings around the Zócalo are beautifully lit. The **Municipal Palace,** seat of government for the Federal District (Departamento del Distrito Federal), is the structure on the south side of the Zócalo.

THE JUÁREZ MUSEUM: A comparatively little-discovered (by tourists) museum in the Zócalo area (Metro: Zócalo) is the one dedicated to Benito Juárez, and situated in the National Palace. When facing the palace, take the farthest left of the three entrances, walk across the courtyard to the statue of Benito Juárez and then up the stairs to the left. The Juárez Museum consists of the well-preserved home of the former president of Mexico, and is usually bustling with school children studying the handwritten letters and papers that are carefully kept in glass cases around the room. In other cases are tablecloths, silverware, medals, shirts, watches, a briefcase, and symbolic keys to the city— all personal effects of the much-loved former president.

There's a beautiful library here (same hours as the museum), with lots of wood paneling, desks, history books arranged around the walls, and the wonderfully musty smell of mellow leather and aging paper that's indigenous to all respectable libraries. Anyone may study the books.

The last room at the rear is Juárez's bedroom, which gives one the eerie feeling that the former president might walk in at any moment; his dressing gown is laid out on the four-poster bed, and a chamber pot peeks from beneath the coverlet. Authenticity to the nth degree.

The museum is open from 10 a.m. to 7 p.m. Monday through Friday, to 3 p.m. on Saturday and Sunday. Admission is free after signing the registry books.

NATIONAL MUSEUM OF THE CULTURES: The pedestrian street just to the left of the National Palace, on the east side of the Zócalo, is Moneda. The museum is in the middle of the block at no. 13. It is not tremendously exciting, but does give an idea of what was going on outside Mexico while the Aztecs were building their pyramids. It displays art from North America, Japan, Peru, Greece, and Italy. They also have temporary exhibits here, as well as a bulletin board of current cultural events in the city. Open every day, except Sunday from 9:30 a.m. to 6 p.m.; small charge for admission.

MUSEUM OF THE CITY OF MEXICO: The easternmost of the three roads leading from the south end of the Zócalo is Pino Suarez. Three blocks south on this road, just before the corner of Calle El Salvador and Pino Suarez, pop through a stone doorway and you'll find yourself in the courtyard of a mansion built in 1528, and known originally as the House of the Counts of Santiago de Calimaya. Back in 1964 this classic old building, with its massive stone staircase and crumbling walls, was converted into the Museum of the City of Mexico (Metro: Pino Suarez or Zócalo—equal distance).

This museum is underrated, and should be visited by any newcomer to Mexico who wants to get the historical and prehistorical outlines of a fascinating culture. It deals solely with the Mexico Valley. The first arrival of man in the valley was in 8000 B.C. There are some fine maps and pictographic presentations of the initial settlements, outlines of the social organization as it developed, and a huge mock-up of Tenochtitlán, the city of the Aztecs. The conquest and destruction of Tenochtitlán by the Spaniards is fantastically portrayed with a mural of Capdevila that appears to have been painted in fire.

After a brief inspection of the elegant old carriage in the courtyard and the little room behind it devoted to the history of transportation in Mexico City, ascend the broad stairs and turn right. The second-floor exhibits begin with a potpourri of beautiful religious paintings, then continue the story of the city's history. Portrayals and notes on the "founding fathers," a fine picture of the Plaza of Mexico, and a series of figures clad in period costumes bring you up to the 1857 revolution. Among the tributes to Juárez and photos of the Villa/Zapata insurrection, there's a marvelously fierce and slightly cross-eyed painting of "the agrarian martyr," Emiliano Zapata, with so much artillery strapped to his chest that he could have won a good-size battle single-handed. (He probably did!)

Calmer, but no less interesting, are the photos and sketches of Mexico City in the present and the future. And on the third floor, you'll find the sun-drenched studio of Mexican impressionist

Joaquin Clausell (1866–1935). The walls are completely covered with his fragmentary works, and two easel paintings still stand.

The Museum of the City of Mexico is open from 9:30 a.m. to 7:30 p.m. Tuesday through Sunday; closed Monday; admission is free. Every Thursday evening at 7 p.m. there is a scheduled lecture at the museum.

NATIONAL PAWN SHOP (Nacional Monte de Piedad): Who ever heard of touring a pawn shop? In Mexico City it's done all the time, for the Nacional Monte de Piedad, across the street (Monte de Piedad) from the west side of the cathedral, is a huge and rather imposing building which turns out to be a department store for used items—the world's largest and most elegant Good Will/Morgan Memorial thrift store. Electric power tools, jewelry, antique furniture, heavy machine tools, sofa beds, and a bewildering array of other things from trash to treasure are all on display. Buying is not required, but taking a look is recommended.

RIVERA MURALS: From the northeast corner of the Zócalo, Calle República de Argentina heads north. If you head north too, you'll soon cross Calle Gonzalez Obregon, and on your left will be the headquarters of the Secretaría de Educación Publica. The building is open during normal working hours (9 a.m. to 2 p.m.), and the attraction is its courtyards. The walls are decorated with a great series of over 200 murals by Diego Rivera, Mexico's outstanding artist in this medium. Other artists did a panel here and there, but it's the Riveras that are superb. The building itself dates from the 1930s.

On your way back to the Zócalo, take a peek at the murals in the Escuela Nacional Preparatoria, a block south of the Secretaría, at the corner of Argentina and Donceles. Here the murals are by the three Mexican greats: Rivera, Orozco, and Siqueiros.

TIME FOR A REFRESHER: Want a refresher before you head on? We have just the place to recoup. For sunshine and a view of the Zócalo, it's the rooftop café-restaurant of the aforementioned **Hotel Majestic.** But if you don't mind being inside, make your way past the jewelry shops on the west side of the Zócalo to the southwest corner of the square and the beginning of Avenida 16 de Septiembre. A few steps west on this street (back in the direction of the Alameda, more or less) will bring you to no. 82

and the entrance of the **Gran Hotel Ciudad de México.** Full particulars are given in the hotel chapter. The lavishly old-fashioned lobby, topped with its breathtaking stained-glass canopy, is served by a bar off in one corner, and a restaurant off in another. Both are sort of expensive, but a drink in the bar, about 100 pesos ($2), is a real pleasure. Beer or a soft drink will be cheaper; you should get a bowl of peanuts, *gratuito.* Even if you don't want to stop, and even if you don't plan to stay here, you should have a look at the magnificent lobby. By the way, the reason the birds in their splendid cages aren't flitting here and there is because they're stuffed. The bird calls you hear are electronic simulations!

Refreshed by a cup of coffee or a drink in the Gran Hotel, head back into the Zócalo and then west down Avenida Madero to take in some of its colonial buildings.

ITURBIDE PALACE: Walk along Madero until you come to no. 17, a beautiful ornate stone palace with huge hand-carved wooden doors and a wildly baroque 40-foot-high carved stone archway. The mansion was built in the 1780s for a wealthy Mexican family, but was ceded in 1821 to Don Agustín de Iturbide, who later became the self-proclaimed Agustín I, Emperor of Mexico (1822–1823). His reign lasted only a matter of months, for although he was a partisan of Mexican independence, his political outlook was basically royalist and conservative, and the future of Mexico lay in the liberal social reforms advocated by the great revolutionaries Hidalgo and Morelos.

Financiera Banamex, present owner of the building, undertook restoration of the palace in 1972 and the result is beautiful, if a bit stark. Enter a courtyard with three tiers of balconies: the ground floor is a banking office; the upper floors have executive offices. Period paintings and statues grace walls and corners, and the second-floor chapel has been beautifully restored. Banamex has had a brief guide to the building printed up, and this leaflet, like your guided tour of the palace, is free of charge. Come in and have a look anytime Monday through Friday from 9 a.m. to 5 p.m. Closed holidays.

THE HOUSE OF TILES ("Casa de Azulejos"): Just before Avenida Madero meets Avenida Lázaro Cárdenas, you'll pass on your right a curious building, a wizened oldtimer decked out in gorgeous blue-and-white tiles. This building is one of Mexico City's most precious colonial gems, and was built at the very end of the 1500s for the Counts of the Valley of Orizaba. The tiles are a fine example of Puebla's craftsmen's work, and the making of faïence is still one of Puebla's outstanding crafts. Today the House of Tiles is used as a branch of the Sanborn's restaurant-newsstand-gift shop chain. You can stroll through to admire the interior (and it's air-conditioned!) or sit and have a refreshing drink or a cup of something hot. You can even have a meal here if it happens to be that time (see the description of the House of Tiles in Chapter IV).

Refreshed again, it's time to set out for the teeming intersection of Avenida Madero/Avenida Juárez and Lázaro Cárdenas. Here you'll find the mammoth **Banco de México** buildings (main building and Guardiola Annex); a block north on Lázaro Cárdenas, at the intersection of Hidalgo/Tacuba, is Mexico City's **main post office** ("Correos," but there's no sign on this grand building indicating its business!). There's a philatelic museum here. The building was finished in 1908, the work of an Italian architect—hence, the Renaissance style.

Two more buildings are important to visit at this intersection, the Palacio de las Bellas Artes and the Latin American Tower.

THE BELLAS ARTES: At the east end of the Alameda is the Palacio de las Bellas Artes, the supreme achievement of art-deco lyricism, which, aside from being the concert hall, also houses permanent and traveling art shows. You can visit the galleries free of charge Tuesday to Sunday from 11 a.m. to 7 p.m. There are galleries on both the first and second levels which exhibit temporary shows. I have seen a number of exhibits here, all of them excellent: a delightful Rumanian art show; works by a Mexican-Hungarian, Gunther Gerzso, whose use of texture and contrasting colors creates a particular intensity of depth in his paintings; Carlos Merida's Braque-like cubism, outstanding sculptures of Auguste Rodin . . . and the list goes on.

On the third level are the famous murals by Rivera, Orozco, and Siqueiros; they simply surpass your wildest imagination, so by all means go to see them. So much emotion and human struggle has been painted into the work! Don't miss Rivera's mural *Man in Control of His Universe,* which is a copy of the one commissioned for Rockefeller Center in New York in 1933 and later painted over because of its leftist views. There are four rooms off the corridor which contain some excellent paintings by Mexican artists from the late 19th century to the present.

LA TORRE LATINOAMERICANA (Latin American Tower): A
true bird's-eye view of the city is to be had from the Observation Deck of the Torre Latinoamericana, soaring above the intersection of Juárez and Lázaro Cárdenas.

Buy a ticket for the deck (open 10 a.m. to midnight every day) at the booth as you approach the elevators—admission fee is 50 pesos ($1); tokens for the telescope up top are on sale here, too. You then take an elevator to the 37th floor, cross the hall, and take another elevator to the 42nd floor. Someone will ask for your ticket as you get off.

The view is magnificent. Mountains surround the capital on all sides, but those to the north are the nearest, and Avenida Lázaro Cárdenas seems to head for them straight as an arrow. To the north just below is the marble pile of the Bellas Artes, and, west of it, the green patch of the Alameda. Due west is the Monument to the Revolution, just beyond the intersection of Juárez and Reforma. You can't see Reforma too well because it's hidden by the buildings which line it, but the green swath of Chapultepec Park and its palace on the hilltop are easy to spot. To the east is the Zócalo, dominated by the cathedral. To the south is an area densely packed with homes, factories, and tall apartment buildings.

Climb the spiral staircase—if it's open—two flights and you're on the open roof. You can climb even higher—assuming you don't suffer from acrophobia—round and round for 129 steps in a spiral tower, until you are alone in a circular framework of steel 500 feet above the ground, the wind whistling through your hair. Now you've seen it all!

In the **Muralto** bar, a floor below the observation deck, you can contemplate the panorama at your leisure over a soft drink, beer, or margarita (100 pesos, $2) without paying the admission charge. In fact, if you'd rather take a quick look than spend money for a long look, head for the Muralto (without buying that 50-peso ticket), walk around for a glance at the view, ask to see a menu, and then "decide you're not that hungry" and take the elevator back down. No one will mind.

Having had your bird's-eye view of the city, continue on your walk by heading west along Avenida Juárez. Soon on your right you'll come upon the **Alameda Central,** a beautiful park good at all times of the day for a quiet stroll to collect your thoughts. The large white marble semicircle of columns fronting on Juárez is the **Juárez Monument.** The poor Zapotec Indian boy from Oaxaca who became a lawyer, and then president of the republic, and then vanquisher of Maximilian and the Napoleonic force, sits grandly here, virtually enthroned, as angels crown him with a laurel wreath. While you're right here, take the time to cross the street and take a turn through the Hotel Del Prado's lobby.

Main reason for the last-mentioned is the Del Prado's famous mural *A Sunday Dream at the Alameda Park,* 50 feet long and 13 feet high, painted by Diego Rivera in 1947. The mural, if you can figure it out, shows all the personalities who have gone through the park since Hernan Cortes.

This section of Avenida Juárez is also a prime area for crafts shops, details of which are given in Chapter VI. While you're right here, you may want to refer to that section and drop in to some of these fascinating stores.

Take a short detour to the northwest corner of the Alameda for a look at an interesting old picture gallery.

PINACOTECA VIRREYNAL DE SAN DIEGO: As mentioned above, the Palacio de las Bellas Artes is an art gallery as well as a concert hall. The same administration responsible for the Bellas Artes's shows is in charge of the Pinacoteca Virreynal de San Diego, Dr. Mora 7, at the northwest corner of the Alameda near the Hotel de Cortes (Metro: Hidalgo). This former church is now a gallery of paintings, mostly from the 16th and 17th centuries, and mostly ecclesiastical in theme. Highlights are apparent immediately as you walk around: in the wing to the right of where the altar would have been is a room with a gorgeous blue-and-gilt ceiling with gleaming rosettes and a striking mural by Federico Cantu (1959), one of the few modern works. Upstairs in a cloister are many small paintings by Hipolito de Rioja (who worked in the second half of the 17th century), by Baltazar de Echave Ibia (1610–1640), and others. By the way, the tremendous painting on the cloister wall called *Glorificación de la Immaculada,* by Francisco Antonio Vallejo (1756–1783), can be viewed better from upstairs—the lighting is better.

The Pinacoteca is open Tuesday through Sunday from 10 a.m. to 5 p.m.; entry is free.

The street north of the Alameda, Avenida Hidalgo, heads west, crosses the Paseo de la Reforma, and becomes the Avenida

Puente de Alvarado. A few blocks west of the intersection with Reforma is the former Palace of Buenavista, at the corner of a side street named Calle Ramos Arizpe. This old mansion now houses one of the capital's better small museums, associated with the San Carlos Academy:

MUSEO DE SAN CARLOS: The San Carlos Academy is Mexico's foremost school for artists, and most of the country's great painters—Diego Rivera among them—count it as their alma mater. Connected with the academy is the San Carlos Museum, Alvarado at Arizpe. The converted mansion which now houses the museum is very fine indeed, having been built in the early 1800s by architect Manuel Tolsa for the Marqués de Buena Vista.

In the mansion's elliptical court you'll first come to displays of 19th-century Mexican statuary and busts by Manuel Vilar and his pupils, and off to one side is a pretty garden court shaded by rubber trees.

The various rooms on the first and second floors hold some of Mexico's best paintings, by both Mexican and European artists. In Sala IV, for instance, you can view *Christ in Limbo* by Mostaert (ca. 1534–1598), and also two paintings by Lucas Cranach the Elder: *Adam and Eve,* and *Federico de Sajonia.* Upstairs treats include *La Coqueta y el Jovenzuelo* by Fragonard and a portrait of Sir William Stanhope attributed to Sir Joshua Reynolds.

Admission to the Museum of San Carlos is free as of this writing, and it's open from 10 a.m. to 5 p.m. Tuesday through Sunday.

The next group of sights is several miles down the Paseo de la Reforma from the intersection of Reforma and Juárez. If you have the time, the walk is ever-fascinating and the curious sights never-ending. If you're in a hurry, you can take the Metro from the Hidalgo station (near the intersection of Hidalgo/Puente de Alvarado and Reforma) or the Revolución station (two short blocks west of the San Carlos Museum along Puente de Alvarado) to the Chapultepec station. But if you walk to the intersection of Juárez and Reforma, you can pick up an Expresso Reforma bus ("Auditorio" or "Observatorio"); that will take you down Reforma, past the golden angel on the Independence Monument, past the fountain with a statue of Diana in the center, to the beginning of Chapultepec Park, where you alight.

You do get to see at least something in the bus, while the Metro shows you only tunnels.

Chapultepec Park and Its Museums

One of the biggest city parks in the world, Chapultepec Park is more than a playground: it's a whole way of life. Every day of the week the number of holidaying Mexican families that it can accommodate must be seen to be believed. They swarm over the grass, picnic under the century-old trees, stroll around the *lago* (lake) or crowd into rowboats, buy colorful balloons, trinkets, and eats from the numerous vendors, and file through the beautiful 18th-century castle that tops the 200-foot hill. It's here that you can really begin to understand the diversity and enormity of the population of Mexico City. As David Gordon remarked, "Mexico, a country that is so full of life, is also too full of lives."

CHAPULTEPEC CASTLE: As you come down Reforma, at the foot of Chapultepec hill you'll notice six marble shafts carved as stylized torches placed in a semicircle around a small plaza. This is the Monument to the Boy Heroes (Niños Héroes)—the six cadets who jumped to their death rather than surrender to the U.S. Marines who attacked the castle during the war with Mexico in 1847. You can walk up the hill from here by following the right fork at the small castle-like gatehouse (now a house of mirrors) or take the elevator which is on the left a short way up the hill (usually a very long line on Sunday). Better to take the minibus to the top which runs daily from 9 a.m. to 4:45 p.m. Catch it at the foot of the hill where the road begins its ascent.

Although on the site of Chapultepec Castle there had been a fortress since the days of the Aztecs, the present palace was not built until the 1780s. At the time of the previously mentioned U.S. invasion, it was in use as a military college, which is how it came about that Mexican army youths, including the heroic sextet, were defending it.

The castle offers a beautiful view of Mexico which, from the balconies, appears to be covered solid with trees. It's reported that in the days of the French occupation during the 1860s, Carlotta could sit up in bed and watch her husband Maximilian proceeding down the Reforma on his way to work. Carlotta, incidentally, designed the lovely garden surrounding the palace,

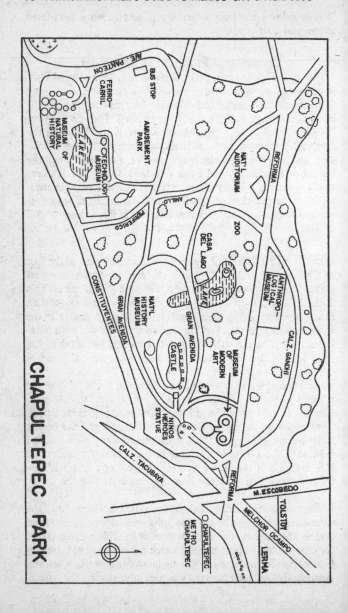

and until recent times it was still the official home of Mexico's president.

Today the palace houses the **Museum of National History,** which covers the post-Hispanic period to the present—large paintings and statues of the Spanish leaders and heroes. On the second floor are rooms displaying jewelry, colonial art objects, and the impressive malachite vases. It's an intriguing place through which to stroll, from the elaborate furnishings brought over from Europe by Maximilian and Carlotta, to the patios and fountains and the panorama of the city spread out below. Open 9 a.m. to 5:40 p.m. (last ticket sold at 5 p.m.) every day except Tuesday. Admission is 15 pesos (30¢), except Sunday when it's 10 pesos (20¢). (*Note:* Hold on to the ticket the entire time you're on the hill—you may be asked to show it.)

HISTORICAL GALLERY: On your way up the hill, about 200 yards below the castle you probably noticed the circular glass building that spirals down the hillside. This is the **Gallery of Mexican History,** and in content it's a condensed history of Mexico complete with portraits, reproductions of documents, and dramatic montages—in three dimensions—of famous scenes from Mexico's past. The more recent years are also represented, with large photographic blowups, and some of the scenes, such as the execution of Maximilian, are staged with a great sense of drama and imagination.

Admission to the museum is free, and all the way down you're torn between how attractive it is inside and how beautiful the park looks outside through the big picture windows. When you reach the exit, halfway down the hillside, a policeman tries to stop you from going through the park down the rest of the hill. Wait until his back is turned and then walk past; otherwise you'll have to climb the steps right back up the hill to come down again. The museum is open every day except Tuesday from 10 a.m. to 5 p.m.

THE MUSEUMS: The nicest thing about Chapultepec Park is its timelessness and spaciousness; it is big enough to accommodate almost anything that can be designed for it. Within this complex have been built four of the most varied, beautiful, and exciting museums ever conceived. They combine a superb sense of proportion with an equally good sense of design.

National Museum of Anthropology

By general consent, the finest museum of its kind in the world is Mexico's National Museum of Anthropology, which was built by architect Pedro Ramirez Vasquez and a team of worthy helpers in 1964. If Sr. Ramirez never did another thing, he'd still deserve the fame of centuries.

An Expresso Reforma "Auditorio" bus up Reforma will drop you right outside the museum, which is situated off the broad boulevard about half a mile past the Diana statue, opposite Chapultepec Park Zoo. Line 1 of the Metro will take you to just outside the park; walk through the park, past the Museum of Modern Art, along Reforma and you're there in 15 minutes. The museum is open Tuesday through Saturday from 9 a.m. to 7 p.m., on Sunday from 10 a.m. until 6 p.m.; closed all day Monday. Admission Sunday is 10 pesos (20¢), 15 pesos (30¢) all other days.

The museum, breathtaking in its splendor, with a massive patio half-sheltered by a tremendous stone "umbrella," will take at least two or three hours to look around even if you are a dedicated museum rusher.

There are three sections, to all intents and purposes. First of all is the entrance hall to the museum proper. Here you'll find a checkroom, and a sign which states that you *must* check coats, umbrellas, all cameras and camera bags, and any handbag that is at all large. You simply cannot take your camera into the exhibition rooms with you. The museum shop, off the entry hall, has a nice collection of souvenirs and an excellent collection of guidebooks, large and small, to cultural, culinary, and archeological attractions in Mexico.

Inside the museum proper is an open courtyard with beautifully designed spacious rooms running around three sides at two levels. The ground-floor rooms are theoretically the most significant, and they are the most popular among studious visitors, devoted as they are to history and prehistoric days all the way up to the most recently explored archeological sites. These rooms include dioramas of the way Mexico City looked when the Spaniards first arrived, and reproductions of part of a pyramid at Teotihuacan. The Aztec calendar stone "wheel" takes proud place here.

Save some of your time and energy, though, for the livelier and more readily understandable upstairs rooms. They're devoted to the way people throughout Mexico live today, complete with straw-covered huts, tape recordings of songs and dances, and lifelike models of village activities.

Since you may be spending the better part of a day in the museum, it's good to know that there is a restaurant right in the building, serving meals at moderate (although not cheap) prices.

Museum of Modern Art

The Museum of Modern Art is actually two buildings, set together in a statue-dotted section of grassy park, with two entrances: one on Reforma, the other across from—sort of behind—the Niños Héroes monument. The museum's interior is the perfect vehicle for showing works of art, simple with its handsome parquet floors, marble and stone walls, wood slatted ceiling, and circular windows (always covered by heavy drapes, presumably so the pictures don't get bleached by the sun).

The museum is open daily except Monday from 11 a.m. to 7 p.m.; admission is 15 pesos (30¢; 10 pesos with a student card). You get to it just through the entrance to Chapultepec Park at the western end of Reforma.

The museum section at the Reforma entrance has four salons, two on each level, around a central dome of incredible acoustic properties. The salons are attractive in their spaciousness, and give you the nice feeling that you're the only person in the museum. Exhibits in salons I, II, and III are temporary, and have featured both Mexican and foreign artists including greats such as Magritte, Delvaux, Antonia Guerrero, Bissier, and Nay. Last time I visited there was also a fine show of Latin American photographs.

Salon IV houses a permanent collection of contemporary art, which seems to get even better each year. Most of the works are by Latin American artists and I—very critical when it comes to modern art—find most of them palatable, and a few exceptional, such as Juan O'Gorman, Moro Hideo, and others.

In the circular rooms across the garden, near the Niños Héroes entrance to the museum, are more temporary exhibits. Note that the permanent collection of works by Mexican artists which used to be here has been moved to the Museo de Arte Carrillo Gil, in San Angel (described later in this chapter). This exceptionally fine collection encompasses works by Rivera, Kahlo, O'Gorman, Siquieros, Tamayo, Merida, Orozco, Gerszo, Romero, and others, and deserves a visit by all devotees of modern Mexican painting.

THE BOSQUE (WOODLAND): Going down the hill from the castle, turn left and follow the Gran Avenida through a landscape of trees, flowers, rock gardens, fountains, and hills. There is a beautiful man-made lake (although a bit mucky on my last visit), complete with an island, a geyser-like fountain, and boats which can be rented. On the west side of the lake is the **Casa del Lago,** originally built as a restaurant and now housing exhibits of local artists from the various art schools in and around Mexico City. There are four galleries (currently under restoration) with exhibits of the works of sundry artists in oil, lithograph, sculpture, etc. I found it very interesting to see the type of art which is currently being produced in Mexico. Most of the art is for sale. Nearby is the **Galería del Bosque,** with similar exhibits. There is no entrance fee for any of the galleries, so stroll around as you please. Hours are from 11 a.m. to 5 p.m. Wednesday through Sunday only.

ZOO: Continue down the Gran Avenida, and off to your right you'll spot the spacious zoo. A good way to see the animals without much effort is to join the line of kids waiting to ride the miniature railway. For a few pesos you can ride in comfort around the whole zoo, catching tantalizing glimpses of monkeys, hippos, herons, polar bears, zebras, and most of the other creatures. Admission to the zoo is free.

AMUSEMENT PARK: This, complete with roller coaster (named the "Montana Rusa," or Russian Mountain) and ferris wheel, is in **New Chapultepec Park**—the area at the far western end. Continue in a southwesterly direction from the zoo and you'll come to the Periferico Highway (about half a mile or a 20-minute walk); the amusement park is just on the other side. If you are coming straight from downtown, you can take bus no. 30 along Servando Teresa de Mier, Río de la Loza, and Avenida Chapultepec to Avenida Constituyentes. Alight at the Natural History Museum, and it's a 15-minute walk to the concessions (for walking directions, see under "Technological Museum," below).

Admission is 10 pesos (20¢); children under 3, free. The gates are open Wednesday and Thursday from 11 a.m. to 6:30 p.m., on Saturday and Sunday from 10:30 a.m. to 7 p.m. The two large buildings to the right of the amusement park are the Technological Museum.

Museum of Natural History

An outstanding part of New Chapultepec Park is the series of ten interconnecting domes which comprise the Museum of Natural History. From a distance the Museum looks like a set of "topes" or brightly colored inverted bowls surrounded by foliage and flowers.

You can get there by bus no. 30 (see above, "Amusement Park"). Although it takes longer and costs more, you can also take the Metro to "Chapultepec" and pick up the no. 30 bus there.

Inside the museum, you'll see stuffed and preserved animals and birds, tableaux of different environments such as desert, seashore, tropical forest, and arctic tundra with the appropriate wildlife. Other domes contain exhibits relating to geology, astronomy, biology, the origin of life, and such displays as a relief map of the world's mountains and an illuminated map of Mexico showing the origin of various minerals.

The museum, fascinating for anyone with the slightest curiosity about nature and totally absorbing for youngsters, is open from 10 a.m. to 5 p.m. daily except Monday. There is no admission fee. *Note:* The large display cases of arctic bears and moose have pushbutton lighting (on the left)—a good idea in our age of conservation.

Just outside the museum and to the left is the **Ferrocarril,** a rubber-wheeled train, on which for a few pesos you can ride around this area. From here you can take the 15-minute walk to the amusement park or the Technological Museum, or if returning to the downtown area, catch any of the no. 30 buses outside the museum.

Technological Museum

This museum is located in the western end of Chapultepec Park between the amusement park and Avenida Constituyentes. The best way to get there is to follow the directions to the Museum of Natural History given in the preceding section; from there it is only a 15-minute walk through very pleasant surroundings, as follows: take a northeasterly direction, past the ferrocarril station on your left and then the lake on your right. When you come to a fork, bear left (downhill) to the large fountain and domed building on the left. Turn left at this rather weird fountain, then right through a series of fountains with circular snake reliefs. The amusement park and Technological Museum are a short distance straight ahead.

The museum is open from 9 a.m. to 5 p.m. daily, closed on Monday. Entrance is free. The polyhedral dome outside is the **Planetarium,** which has scheduled shows at 10 a.m., noon, and 2 p.m. daily.

The museum is educational, to say the least. It is always filled with students madly taking notes on scientific developments through the ages. Inside and outside there are trains and planes, mock-up factories, experiments of Morse and Edison, and various energy exhibits. When you're thoroughly exhausted, head for the basement, wherein lies a cafeteria for food or *refrescas.*

Attractions on the Outskirts

Now that you've seen some of Mexico City's best downtown attractions, you might want to take an adventure farther afield. We'll look now at sights and activities in the southern and northern reaches of the city which you can explore in a day or less. I've grouped these sites together into "southern" and "northern" headings so that you can most efficiently plan your excursions, and avoid backtracking.

Speaking of planning, you should make your trip to San Angel on Saturday if possible, as that's the day for the famous Bazar Sabado ("Saturday Bazaar"). On Saturday, Coyoacán has a small market as well. For many other sights—the Polyforum, University City, Plaza de las Tres Culturas—the day of the week doesn't matter. As for Xochimilco, it's busiest on Sunday, which is good if you like colorful crowds and activity, but bad if you hate crowded buses and haggling over prices. Don't go south on Monday, as most museums are closed then.

HEADING SOUTH: It might be best to plan two days for southern Mexico City. On a Saturday, catch a *pesero* ("San Angel") or bus no. 17 ("Indios Verdes–Tlalpan") south along Insurgentes near the Zona Rosa. It will take you past the Polyforum Cultural Siqueiros to San Angel and its Bazar Sabado. After you've visited these places, hop the same bus south to University City, Pedregal, and the Cuicuilco Pyramid. The bus trip takes almost an hour, straight through.

In a short while the Metro should be completed to the "Universidad" station, which will give you a fast way to get back into town.

Heading south along Insurgentes, your first stop is at the mind-boggling edifice called the Polyforum.

Polyforum Cultural Siqueiros

Although this gleaming new arts center is much lauded by promoters, there's no way I can hide my lack of enthusiasm—it's a modern monstrosity with overpowering murals, low claustrophobic ceilings, and poor acoustics that echo the slightest sound. However, it does contain the world's largest mural (90,655 square feet) by a very well-known muralist, David Alfaro Siqueiros.

The Polyforum is open from 10 a.m. to 9 p.m. every day and costs 40 pesos (80¢) if you want to see the overambitious sculptured murals, *The March of Humanity on Earth* and *Toward the Cosmos,* by Siqueiros. They also stage a sound-and-light show here every evening at 6 in English, for 150 pesos ($3) a head.

Most of the Polyforum is devoted to art: on the floor that you enter is a small exhibition of visiting artists; on the two floors below are handicrafts from Mexico which you can purchase, although the prices are a bit high: the first level down has some art objects in glass display cases, while the floor below is basically the basement and things are just here and there in a wide open space.

After boggling your mind at the Polyforum, get back to Insurgentes and escape south in another *pesero* or bus, to San Angel.

In San Angel

In the suburb of San Angel there are several famous colonial houses and the convent of the Carmelites. If you go on Saturday, you can combine your museum tour with a visit to San Angel's Sabado (Saturday) Bazaar—see Chapter VI for details.

A *pesero* will terminate at the intersection of Insurgentes and Avenida La Paz; as for the bus, ask to get off at La Paz. There's a pretty park here, to the east, and on the west side of Insurgentes is a Sanborn's store and restaurant, good for a quick, moderately priced lunch. (My favorite is the fruit-and-sherbet salad plate, with a soft drink, for 150 pesos—$3—all in.)

Walk west, up the hill on La Paz, and in a block you'll come to Avenida de la Revolución. To the left (south) is the dark colonial stone bulk of the Museo Colonial del Carmen. To the right, a few blocks north, is the Museo de Arte Carrillo Gil. And straight ahead, across Avenida de la Revolución, is the shady Plaza del Carmen.

The **Museo Colonial del Carmen** is a former Carmelite convent, now filled with religious paintings, other ancient artifacts, and a batch of mummified nuns in glass cases in the cellar! The museum, a maze of interlocking halls, corridors, stairways, chapels, and pretty flower-filled patios, is very pleasant to look around and is open from 10 a.m. to 5 p.m. every day except Monday for a few pesos admission.

San Angel's outstanding contribution to Mexican painting is the **Museo de Arte Alvar y Carmen T. Carrillo Gil**, sometimes called the Museo de la Esquina ("Museum on the Corner") as it is at a major intersection on the Avenida de la Revolución, at no. 1608. This modern gallery's collection of exhibit rooms include those dedicated to the works of José Clemente Orozco (1883-1942), Diego Rivera (1886-1957), David Alfaro Siqueiros (1896-1974), and rooms with works by a variety of Mexican painters. Lectures and concerts are also held here—programs can be picked up at the door.

You can see the collections at the Museo de Arte Carillo Gil from 11 a.m. to 7 p.m. every day but Monday; admission is 10 pesos (20¢).

Having filled yourself with Mexican culture, both colonial and modern, head up the hill through the Plaza del Carmen on Calle Dr. Calvez. Soon you'll come to the beautiful **Plaza San Jacinto**, filled with artists and their paintings on Saturday. Many of the old buildings surrounding the Plaza San Jacinto have fine courtyards where crafts are sold. The **Centro Cultural Isidro Fábela**, at no. 15, deserves special mention.

Many famous personalities of show business, government, and social life maintain homes in San Angel, but the most famous house now belongs to the nation, to which it was recently donated by Isidro Fábela, an international jurist, statesman, and art collector. His house, the **Casa del Risco** ("House of Broken Porcelain"), was built during the 17th century and furnished in magnificent colonial style with ornate doors, fireplaces, coats-of-arms, statues, portraits, chairs, chests, and, as the pièce de résistance, a fantastically decorated fountain which sits against one wall of the open patio. You'll have to see this fountain to believe it, for the decorative tiling consists of broken and unbroken pieces of porcelain that once comprised half a dozen banquet-sized sets of porcelain. The Casa del Risco is open 10 a.m. to 6 p.m. every day except Monday; entrance free.

Two doors away from the Casa del Risco is the famous **Bazar Sabado**, in another colonial building. Be sure to take a turn through the building, whether or not you intend to buy. The crafts, the crowds, and the building itself are all wonderfully colorful.

Leaving the bazaar, spend some time in the plaza examining paintings. Some are excellent, others are quite good, and still others are, well, rather unfortunate. Prices are open to haggling.

Up the hill a few more steps from the Plaza San Jacinto is another, smaller plaza crowded with sellers of crafts, art objects, souvenirs, and tourist junk. The square is shady and interesting, festooned with printed and woven wall hangings.

After your shopping, are you up for a stroll? Continue uphill past the aforementioned little plaza on Calle Juárez. Soon you'll see a big old house—now a school—on your right at an intersection. Turn left, then left again, and you'll find your way to the gorgeous little **Plaza de los Archangelos.** Filled with bougainvillea (and often with adolescents in love), the plaza is a peaceful, flower-filled refuge away from the market bustle. The houses all around have high walls, exotic gardens, enormous gateways, and breathtaking pricetags. When you're ready, retrace your steps; if you take that other road out down the hill you'll walk farther, and in traffic, to get back to the plaza.

Ready for lunch? The Sanborn's on Insurgentes (mentioned above) is a good, inexpensive bet. You can also have the buffet in the courtyard of the Bazar Sabado (about 500 pesos—$10—all in). Or you can dine in a marvelous colonial setting at the **San Angel Inn** (tel. 548-6746), at the corner of Palmas and Altavista. To get to the inn, walk up Calle Juárez out of the Plaza San Jacinto, past the little plaza, and turn right on Calle Reyna (or Reina). At the end of Calle Reyna, turn left onto Avenida Altavista. The inn is four blocks up—you can see it in the distance where the road curves.

The inn's courtyard is, well, like heaven I guess—lush, green, peaceful, tasteful, a quiet refuge absolutely essential for anyone touring Mexico City. You can order a drink to be brought to one of the small, low tables here, or you can dine. The luncheon *menú turístico,* with tax, tip, and beverage all in, will run you 750 pesos ($15) or so.

All done in San Angel? Catch a no. 56 bus ("Alcantarilla–Col. Agrarista") at the San Angel Inn, or along Altavista, to get to Coyoacán or the Anahuacalli (see below). For University City, get back to Insurgentes and catch anything, *pesero* or bus, with "Ciudad Universitaria," or simply "C.U." in the window.

University City

This is the site of the world's most flamboyant college campus and, indeed, of one of the world's most flamboyant architectural groupings. Appropriately enough, it is located about 11 miles south along Insurgentes.

University City (it houses Mexico's National Autonomous University) was planned to be the last and grandest achievement of the regime of former president Miguel Aleman. The original university is said to date back to 1551, which would make it the oldest university in the Western Hemisphere.

It's an astonishing place and well worth going out to see for its gigantic and brilliantly colored mosaics and murals. The most outstanding of these, by Juan O'Gorman, covers all four sides and ten complete stories of the library building. Fittingly, the mosaic wall depicts the history of Mexican culture and covers a space in which 2½ million books can be stored. The two lower stories are glass-enclosed and are used as the library's reading rooms.

The administration building, closest to the road, is mostly travertine onyx but also has an immense outer mural. This was executed by David Alfaro Siqueiros and depicts Mexican students returning the fruits of their labors to the nation. Diego Rivera's famous contribution is a sculpture-painting which adorns the world's largest stadium (capacity: 102,000) across the highway. The stadium was used for a number of events in the 1968 Olympics.

Nobody will object if you wander at random around the campus, which accommodates 300,000 enrollment. There is a cafeteria on the ground floor of the humanities building and this, especially in summer, is well patronized by American students attending classes. All the university cafeterias are open to the public, and charge very reasonable prices.

The university will soon boast its own Metro station, at the end of the Indios Verdes line. If it's not open when you go, plan to catch a no. 17, 19, or 19A bus north, back to Reforma. Are you interested in seeing a pyramid? Then catch a no. 17 bus heading south on Insurgentes, and just after it crosses the Anillo Periférico Sur, hop off. You're only a 15-minute walk from the **Museo y Ruinas de Cuicuilco.**

The pyramid, open to visitors at all hours, represents some of the earliest civilization in the Valley of Mexico. Built in the preclassical period, around 1800 B.C., it was completely covered by a volcanic eruption (in A.D. 300), surviving only because it was protected by a strong outer wall.

The Pedregal

Just west of University City is Mexico's most luxurious housing development, the **Jardines del Pedregal de San Angel.** The word *pedregal* means lava, and that's precisely what this enormous area, stretching well beyond the university, consists of. In the Jardines del Pedregal, the only restriction placed upon homeowners is that they have enough money to buy at least 2000 square meters of land and hire an architect to design their home. The result is that all the houses are exceptionally lavish, with swimming pools scooped out of the rock, split-levels with indoor gardens, solid-glass walls, and, in one case, an all-glass sunroom on a narrow stilt above the house—like an airport's observation tower.

The pedregal, or lava, all came from the now-extinct volcano Xitle, whose eruption covered the abovementioned Cuicuilco Pyramid. Only in recent times has the pedregal been regarded as anything but a nuisance; at one time, many of its caves hid bandits. Today, all kinds of odd plants and shrubs grow from its nooks and crevices, and if you are interested in botany, you'll want to take a good look around. The main street is the north-south Avenida Paseo del Pedregal.

Two in Coyoacán

There are two interesting museums in the suburb of Coyoacán, south of the city near San Angel. If you have an extra morning I would strongly recommend a visit to the House and Museum of Trotsky and the Museo Frida Kahlo, the latter the former home of muralist Diego Rivera and his painter wife, whose name the house bears.

Coyoacán is a pretty, and wealthy, suburb with many old houses and cobbled streets. At the center are two large, graceful plazas, the Plaza Hidalgo and Jardín Centenario, and the Church of San Juan Bautista (1583). Once the capital of the Tepanec kingdom, Coyoacán was later conquered by the Aztecs, then by Cortes. The great *conquistador* had a palace here for a while.

The Metro will soon reach to the Bancomer station, within walking distance of Coyoacán's museums. As of this writing, however, you'll have to depend on buses nos. 23 and 23A ("Iztacala–Coyoacán") to get you from the center to this suburb. Catch the no. 23 going south on Bucareli, or the no. 23A on Miguel Schultz, Antonio Caso, Río Rhin, or Niza.

Coming from San Angel, catch a no. 56 bus ("Alcantarilla–Col. Agrarista") heading east along the Camino al Desierto de los Leones or Avenida Altavista, near the San Angel Inn. When the bus gets to the corner of Avenida México and Xicoténcatl in Coyoacán, descend. Or, simpler, take a cab for the 15-minute ride.

Museo Frida Kahlo

The museum is about six blocks north of the plazas. There is a sign pointing east off Calle Centenario to the museum; follow this one block east to Allende. The house is on the corner of Allende and Londres—you can't miss it, for it is painted a brilliant blue with red trim.

Frida was born here on July 7, 1910, and occupied the house with Rivera from 1929 to 1954. The house is basically as she left it, and as you wander through the rooms you will get an overwhelming feeling for the life that they led. Their mementoes are in every room, from the kitchen, where the names Diego and Frida are written on the walls, to the studio upstairs, where a wheelchair sits next to the easel with a partially completed painting surrounded by paint brushes, palettes, books, photographs, and other paraphernalia of the couple's art-centered lives.

The bookshelves are filled with books in many languages, nestled against a few of Rivera's files bearing such inscriptions as "Protest Rockefeller Vandalism," "Amigos Diego Personales," and "Varios Interesantes y Curiosos." Frida's paintings hang in every room, some of them dominated by the exposed human organs and dripping blood that apparently obsessed her in the final surgery-filled years of her life.

Frida was a collector of pre-Columbian art, so many of the rooms contain jewelry and terracotta figurines from Teotihuacán and Tlatelolco. She even went to the extreme of having a mockup of a temple built in the garden where she could exhibit her numerous pots and statues. On the back side of the temple are several skulls from Chichen-Itza.

You will no doubt be spurred on to learn more about the lives of this remarkable couple. I can recommend the book written by Bertram D. Wolfe entitled *Diego Rivera: His Life and Times*.

House and Museum of Leon Trotsky

This most interesting place is located two blocks north and

2½ blocks east of the Frida Kahlo house (a ten-minute walk), at Viena 45, between Gómez Farías and Morelos. You will recognize the house by the brick watchtowers on top of the high stone walls. There is a thick steel door which will be open from 10 a.m. to 2 p.m. and 3 to 5:30 p.m., Tuesday through Friday; 10:30 a.m. to 4 p.m. on weekends; closed Monday.

During Lenin's last days, when he was confined to bed, Stalin and Trotsky fought a silent battle for control of the Communist party in the Soviet Union. Stalin won, and Trotksy fled in terror for his life. He settled here on the outskirts of Mexico City (this area was mostly fields then) to continue his work and writing on political topics and Communist ideology. His ideas clashed with those of Stalin in many respects, and Stalin, wanting no opposition or dissension in world Communist ranks, set out to have Trotsky assassinated. A first attempt failed but it served to give warning to Trotsky and his household, and from then on the house became a veritable fortress, with riflemen's watchtowers on the corners of the walls, steel doors (Trotsky's bedroom was entered only through thick steel doors), and around-the-clock guards, several of whom were Americans who sympathized with Trotsky's philosophies. Finally a man thought to have been paid, cajoled, or blackmailed by Stalin directly or indirectly was able to get himself admitted to the house by posing as a friend of Trotsky and of his political views. On March 20, 1940, he put a mountaineer's axe into the philosopher's head. He was, of course, caught by the guards; Trotsky died of his wounds shortly after.

If you saw the film *The Death of Trotsky* with Richard Burton, you already have a good idea of what the house looks like, for although the movie was not made here, the set which was used was a very good replica of the house and gardens. You can visit Natalia's (Trotsky's wife's) study, the communal dining room, Trotsky's study (with worksheets, newspaper clippings, books, and cylindrical wax dictaphone records still spread around), and his fortress-like bedroom. Some of the walls still have the bullet holes left during the first attempt on his life. Trotsky's tomb, designed by Juan O'Gorman, is in the garden of the house.

Once you've seen Coyoacán, find your way to Calle Centenario or Avenida México-Coyoacán, and catch the no. 23 or 23A bus north to get back to the center. If you're heading west to San Angel, catch a no. 56 on Calle Cuauhtémoc; going east to the Anahuacalli, catch a no. 56 on Calle Xicoténcatl, then transfer to a no. 25 ("Zacatenco–Tlalpan") or no. 59 ("El Rosario–Xochimilco") going south on the avenue called División del Norte.

Diego Rivera Museum (The Anahuacalli)

Probably the most unusual museum in the city is that designed by Diego Rivera before his death in 1957 and devoted to his works as well as an extensive collection of pre-Columbian art. Called the Anahuacalli Museum and constructed of pedregal (lava rock, with which the area abounds), it is similar in style to Mayan and Aztec architecture. The name Anahuac was the old name for the ancient Valley of Mexico.

The museum, admission free, is open daily from 10 a.m. to 6 p.m. (closed Monday), and is situated on the southern outskirts of the city in the suburb of **San Pablo Tepetlapan,** at Calle Tecuila 150, off Calle del Museo. Take the Metro (Line 2) to the Taxqueña terminal. From the terminal, catch a SARO bus no. 136 ("Taxqueña–Peña Pobre") west, and it'll take you right past the museum.

Another way to get there is bus no. 25 ("Zacatenco–Tlalpan") south along Balderas, or no. 59 ("El Rosario–Xochimilco") south along Avenida Vasconcelos, Nuevo Leon, and Avenida División del Norte. Hop off at the Calle del Museo stop.

The museum is a ten-minute walk west along Calle del Museo from Avenida División del Norte. Signs point the way. If you see the no. 136 bus coming, you might as well hop aboard.

In front of the museum is a reproduction of a Toltec ball court, and the entrance to the museum itself is via a coffin-shaped door. Light filters in through translucent onyx slabs and is supplemented by lights inside niches and wall cases containing the exhibits. Rivera was a great collector of pre-Columbian artifacts and the museum includes literally hundreds of them, stashed on the shelves, tucked away in corners, and peeking from behind glass cases.

Upstairs, a replica of Rivera's studio has been constructed, and there you'll find the original sketches for some of his murals and two in-progress canvases. His first sketch (of a train) was done at the age of three, and there's a photo of it, plus a color photograph of him at work later in life in a pair of baggy pants and a blue denim jacket. Rivera (1886-1957) studied in Europe for 15 years, and spent much of his life as a devoted Marxist. Yet he came through political scrapes and personal tragedies with no apparent diminution of creative energy, and a plaque in the museum proclaims him "a man of genius who is among the greatest painters of all time."

Xochimilco

As you might guess from its name, Xochimilco (pronounced "so-chee-MEEL-co") is a survival from the civilization of the Aztecs. They built gardens on rafts (called *chinampas*), then set them afloat on a series of canals. Now, of course, the gardens are gone, but flower-bedecked boats still run to and fro.

Sad to say, Xochimilco is not in the best of shape today. Aside from the fact that it's become badly commercialized (from the moment you arrive, you'll be pestered by people trying to sell you something or persuade you to take one boat over another), the canals themselves are a bit polluted. On Sunday, the place is jammed with foreign tourists and Mexican families with babies and picnic hampers; on weekdays, it's nearly deserted.

To reach Xochimilco, take the Metro to Taxqueña and then a bus. The buses (31, 33, 35, 37, 39, 59) run all the way across the city from north to south to end up at Xochimilco, but they take longer than the Metro. Of the buses coming from the center, the most convenient are nos. 31 and 33 ("La Villa–Xochimilco"), which you catch going south on Correo Mayor and Pino Suarez near the Zócalo; or no. 59, which you catch near Chapultepec on Avenida Vasconcelos, Avenida Nuevo Leon, and Avenida División del Norte.

When you get to the town of Xochimilco, you'll find a busy market in operation, specializing in garish, brightly decorated pottery. Turn along Madero and follow the signs that say **Los Embarcaderos.** If you can resist the blandishment of the inevitable salesmen and shills, you will eventually arrive at the riverbank.

The boats are priced according to their size and the number of people they can hold, plus your skill as a bargainer. The going rate for a medium-size boat which can hold five or six persons is about 350 pesos ($7) per hour. If you have a group of four or five people, a picnic lunch, and a few six-packs of beer or soft drinks, the ride can be a pleasure. For single people or even couples, the minimum rental fee is a bit much, and Xochimilco is definitely the sort of place which is best enjoyed in a small group.

HEADING NORTH: Within the northern city limits are two more interesting locations, and another is just a short ride outside. You can take the Metro to the Plaza de las Tres Culturas (Tlatelolco station), and then continue up the same line to the Basilica de Guadalupe (Basilica station). Finally, the terminus at Indios Verdes is the place to catch a bus for the short ride to Tepotzotlán.

Plaza de las Tres Culturas

A few miles north of the Alameda, in **Tlatelolco**, stands this monument to the long and varied history of Mexico: all three cultures—Aztec, Spanish, and contemporary—are architecturally represented here.

During the Aztec Empire, Tlatelolco was on the northern edge of Lake Texcoco and for a long time it maintained its autonomy, independent of the Aztecs. In May of 1521, it was to Tlatelolco that Cuauhtemoc and his army withdrew when Cortes marched for the second time on the great city of Tenochtitlán. Cuauhtemoc would not surrender and after a three-month siege, with thousands of his army dead from starvation or wounds, he was finally captured. Reduced to a wretched state of captivity, he grabbed Cortes's dagger and fell upon it. The Plaza de las Tres Culturas is where this heroic siege took place, and a plaque commemorates it.

Afterward, Tlatelolco was officially abandoned, and it remained so until 1960 when the government began a redevelopment program to clean up the slum area which had grown during the years of neglect. Tlatelolco today is a suburb of housing projects, and not a very attractive one at that, but these tall building complexes represent the "contemporary" aspect.

The beautiful Spanish church which stands in the plaza, albeit at a slight angle as a result of sinking into the lake bed, is the famous **Cathedral of Santiago Tlatelolco.** Built in the 16th century entirely of volcanic stone, it echoes Aztec construction, which was made from the same stone. Inside, most of the frescoes have been badly damaged over the years; the interior has been tastefully restored, preserving little patches of fresco in stark white plaster walls, with a few deep-blue stained-glass windows and an unadorned stone altar.

To get to the plaza, take the Metro (Line 3) to Tlatelolco, leave the terminal by the exit to Manuel Gonzalez, and turn right on this street. Walk two blocks to Avenida Lázaro Cárdenas, and turn right again. The plaza is about half a block south, on the left, just past the Clinico Hospital. The walk takes less than 15 minutes.

Basilica of Our Lady of Guadalupe

The Basilica of Our Lady of Guadalupe is on the site of the spot where a poor Indian named Juan Diego is reputed to have seen a vision, on December 9, 1531, of a beautiful lady in a blue mantle. The local bishop was reticent to confirm that Juan had indeed seen the Virgin Mary, and so he asked the peasant for some evidence. Juan saw the vision a second time, and it became miraculously emblazoned on the poor peasant's cloak. The bishop immediately ordered the building of a church on the spot, and upon its completion the image was hung in the place of honor, framed in gold. Since that time millions upon millions of the devout and the curious have come to this spot to view the miraculous image which experts, it is said, are at a loss to explain. The blue-mantled Virgin of Guadalupe is the patron saint of Mexico.

So heavy was the flow of visitors—many of whom approached for hundreds of yards on their knees—that the old church became insufficient to handle it, and an audacious new basilica is being built, designed by the same architect who did the breathtaking National Museum of Anthropology. It won't be completed for many years, in the tradition of great religious edifices the world around, but it's in service already and you can visit and admire this all-new monument to the humble peasant's miraculous experience. The problem of handling the flow of traffic past the portrait of the Virgin has been solved by modern means: a moving walkway provides a brief look at the image, and keeps small groups from monopolizing the ground immediately in front of it.

At the top of the hill, behind the basilica, is a cemetery and also several gift shops specializing in rather tasteless trinkets encased in seashells and other irrelevancies. The steps up this hill are lined with flowers, shrubs, and waterfalls, and the climb, although tiring, is worthwhile for the view from the top.

Should you be lucky enough to visit Mexico City on December 12, you can witness the grand festival in honor of the Virgin of Guadalupe. The square in front of the basilica fills up with the pious and the party-minded as prayers, dances, and a carnival atmosphere attract thousands of the devout.

Easiest way to reach the basilica is to take the Metro (Line 3) to the Basilica station.

If you are driving, a trip to the basilica can be fitted conveniently into a day's outing to the pyramids, farther north. Drive northward up Insurgentes, past the Buena Vista Railroad Station on your right and the pyramid-shaped Monumento a la Raza, and then, about six miles from Juárez, turn off to the right beside the Lindavista Cine sign (in the suburb of Lindavista) and head down Avenue Montevideo about half a mile to Guadalupe Plaza.

Tepotzotlán

Interested in baroque architecture? Want a close-up view of small-town Mexican daily life? Set aside a morning or afternoon for an excursion to the colonial town of Tepotzotlán, 24 miles north of Mexico City. Tepotzotlán's church (1682) is among the finest examples of Churrigueresque (Mexican baroque) architecture, and the museum attached to it has a rich collection of paintings (including a Tintoretto), church ceremonial objects, vestments, pottery, and carving. Plan your visit for any day, Wednesday through Sunday (the church is closed on Monday, and the museum is closed on Tuesday).

You can make the trip in a morning or an afternoon by taking the Metro to the Indios Verdes terminus station, and then catching a bus to Tepotzotlán. If you drive, go west on Paseo de la Reforma, and shortly after you pass the Auditorio Municipal (on your left) in Chapultepec Park, turn right (north) onto the Anillo Periférico. This soon becomes the Avenida Manuel Avila Camacho, which in turn becomes Hwy. 57D, the toll road to Querétaro. About 35 km (22½ miles) out of the city, look for the turn to Tepotzotlán, which is about 2 km west of the highway.

Whether you come by bus or car, you'll soon end up in the town's main square, where you'll spot the church's extravagantly elaborate facade at once. This is considered one of the three finest examples of Churrigueresque decoration, the other two being the Santa Prisca in Taxco, and La Valenciana in Guanajuato.

The grand extravagance of the facade is echoed inside the church, which is richly decorated with carved altarpieces and paintings. When your senses start to reel from the power and weight of it all, stroll outside, turn right, and enjoy the shady park standing in front of the museum.

The National Viceroy's Museum was once the Novitiate of the

Company of Jesus (1585). Besides the dozens of rooms with displays of colonial treasures, be sure to inspect the Domestic Chapel, dating from about the same time as the neighboring church.

After you've seen Tepotzotlán's colonial monuments, you might want to have a look at the market, or simply wander the cobbled streets for a while. The bus back to Mexico City passes right through the main square. Those with cars might want to continue on (north) along Hwy. 57D, the Querétaro toll road, to the ruined Toltec city of Tula (see Chapter VIII).

The Bullfights and Horse Races

THE BULLFIGHTS: The capital's **Plaza México** is the biggest bullring in the world. It seats 64,000 people and on Sunday during the professional season (usually December through April, but no fixed dates) most of them are taken. On other Sundays through the year, the arena is given over to the beginners or *novilleros;* most of them are as bad as the beginners in any other sport. Six fights make up a *corrida,* which begins precisely at 4 p.m. and is one of the few things in Mexico that's always on time.

There are several ways to reach the Plaza México, which is situated two or three miles south along Insurgentes. Any big hotel or tour agency will be happy to book you onto a tour with limousine, guide, and reserved seat; this can cost anything from 750 pesos ($15) and up. Alternatively, you can take a *pesero;* the meager number of *peseros* that normally roam Insurgentes is supplemented by Sunday afternoon taxis headed for the plaza, and they'll often pick up extra passengers going their way. Or you can catch the buses marked "Plaza México" which travel down Insurgentes on Sunday afternoon. Finally, you can catch a no. 17 bus ("Indios Verdes–Tlalpan") along Insurgentes.

Roughly 25 minutes after you start out, the bus will pass the bullring on the right. At the point at which you should alight, the ring is hidden by buildings, so you'll have to watch for a gray, modern apartment building to your right, its exterior more windows than walls. (This is Insurgentes 949, and its owners are so proud of it that, as in many cases of modern buildings in Mexico, they have listed the architect's name, Francisco Artigas, above the entrance.)

Most of the people on the bus will alight here, so you'll know you're at the bullring, which is just around the corner ahead. On the way you'll see dozens of men and women squatting on blankets selling nuts, hats, and all kinds of whatnots. Look for a woman or *muchacha* selling chewing gum and waving small "programs." If you buy the chewing gum, she'll give you (free) the one-page sheet which lists the names of the day's *toreros.*

Unless you want to pay more, take your place in the line at one of the windows marked "*Sol General.*" It will be in the sun and it will be high up. But the sun isn't too strong (it sets soon, anyway), and you won't see many other tourists that way. Try to avoid the seats numbered 1 to 100; for some reason, the roughnecks prefer to gather in this section. Seats in *la sombra* (shade) are more expensive, of course.

Usually, there are six separate bulls to be killed (two by each matador) in a *corrida*, but I'd suggest that you leave just before the last bull gets his—to avoid the crowds. Outside, around two sides of the bullring, is a scene of frantic activity. Hundreds of tiny stalls have masses of food frying, cold beer stacked high, and radios blaring with a commentary on the action inside the ring.

A DAY AT THE RACES: Mexico City's racetrack, the **Hipodromo de las Americas,** is as extraordinarily beautiful as many of its other tourist-popular spots. Approached by way of a tree-lined boulevard and containing a small lake on which an occasional swan or heron basks, it has stands built on the hillside for a good view of the track.

The track operates on Tuesday (in winter only), Thursday, Saturday and Sunday for 11 months of the year; it is closed only for part of September and October. Take a *pesero* marked "Hipodromo" along Reforma, which takes you through Chapultepec to the Anillo Periférico (which parallels Avenida Manuel Avila Camacho). The track is just off this main artery, near the intersection with Calzada Legaria.

Once at the track, you may enter through a special (free) tourist gate (you pay only the tax). The normal price of admission is through purchase of a program. If you don't get a program, you won't have much idea what's going on, so better buy one at the gate. Two or more people may enter on one program, but each must pay the program's tax. Inside, head for the stands and grab a seat. If you're willing to spend the extra loot, you can climb one level higher and sit at a table where the view is excellent and a minimum amount must be consumed in either food or drink. Racing begins at 2:15 p.m.

Betting: You can bet either to win *(primera)*, to place *(segun-*

da) , or to show *(tercera)*. All windows have signs in both English and Spanish. On certain races, marked on the program with bold letters—**"SELECIÓN 1-2"**—you can win a substantial sum by picking the horses that will come in first and second and placing a bet on your selections. In some races, there is an alternative way of betting called the *quiniela*. This operates on a similar principle, except that your choices for first and second can come in second and first.

To get back into town, take any bus marked "Zócalo."

———————

Few people come to Mexico City these days without expecting to spend some time (and money) in the shops and markets. The following chapter is devoted to browsing and buying in the capital's markets.

Bullfight

Chapter VI

MEXICO CITY'S MARKETS AND SHOPS

WHEN YOU FIRST lay eyes on a good selection of Mexican crafts, you won't believe the colors. Besides the ingenious, fanciful, and painstaking creations themselves, it's the brilliant mottled colors that make Mexican handicrafts so enjoyable to shop for and to take home as souvenirs or as gifts.

No longer is it true that the best craft bargains are to be had in the regions where the crafts are made. Now, with regional and national craft cooperatives, many craft items may be bought in the capital for about the same prices, or only slightly more, as in the region of origin. And national cooperatives and crafts unions have organized transport and marketing so that large assortments of craft items can be found at several locations in Mexico City.

Places to shop in Mexico City can be separated conveniently into three types: the large general markets, usually housed in sprawling buildings with rows and rows of tiny shops; the small, specialized, and highly selective arts and crafts shops, best for top-quality craft items and works of folk art; and the Saturday- and Sunday-only outdoor markets, also general in nature, but with lots of crafts on display.

WHAT TO BUY: The range of Mexican craft items is very wide, but some tips on the high points of that range will help you in your browse through the capital's markets and shops. Here are some things to look for:

Baskets: Woven of reed or raffia, they come in dozens of shapes and sizes. The ones woven in Oaxaca of split reed or cane are very sturdy, and will last for years. Expect to pay 200 to 300 pesos ($4 to $6) for a good-quality, fairly large basket. If you're buying a market shopping basket, try to find one with a flattened handle easy for carrying, heavily laden, on the forearm.

Blankets: The dyes are often synthetic these days, but the wool of the best-quality ones is super-soft. Size, wool purity, and quality are what determine the price. The blankets, mostly from Oaxaca and nearby Mitla, come in small sizes (about a quarter of a full blanket, or less) to be used as wall hangings, in half sizes for use as throw rugs, or in full double-bed size. Warm! Beautiful! Pay somewhere between 1800 and 3000 pesos ($36 and $60) for a full-size blanket.

Ceramics: Pottery capital of Mexico is Tlaquepaque, outside Guadalajara, but other kilns swelter in Puebla (for faïence) and Oaxaca. The hand-painted dishes and bowls, and the glassware, come mostly from Tlaquepaque, the fantastically ornate and colorful candelabra from Oaxaca, and of course those marvelous Puebla tiles. Look also for the curious black pottery from Oaxaca. Prices vary with size, item, style, and quality—also rarity, for some items are one-of-a-kind.

Gorangos: These knitted wool pullover-ponchos are made in Santa Ana Chiautempan, about 30 miles north of Puebla. They come to about hip length and are more than hip these days. Prices vary widely, depending on the quality of the item, its weight, and also the class of the shop (designers' boutiques in the Zona Rosa will be much higher, natch), but a standard might be 500 to 1200 pesos ($10 to $24).

Guitars: Not up to the fine finished quality of Martins perhaps, but not priced so high either. Widely available for under $100.

Hammocks: These are real bargains down here, as they constitute the staple of the Yucatán "bedding" industry—in the hot and humid savannahs of Yucatán, everybody sleeps in one of these naturally air-cooled "beds" every night. In Stateside shops you may pay $50 for one; here the prices are more like $18 to $25, depending on quality and size. Note that a good *matrimonio* (the sleeping equivalent of a standard double bed) should have at least 100 pairs of strings at the ends; when held up by one hand above the user's head, the *body* (excluding completely the end strings) should stretch from the user's fist at least to the floor. Thus the body of a good, all-cotton *matrimonio* should be about eight feet in length, and have about 140 pairs of end strings. For this, expect to pay about $22. Cylindrical mosquito nets, which fasten around the hung hammock like a sausage casing, are available for the serious hammock sleeper, at about 250 pesos ($5) extra. Don't forget to pick up a set of end ropes.

Hats: Woven straw hats are everywhere, for every price. Real "Panama" hats are actually a Mexican product, made from maguey cactus fibers in the Yucatán. They keep their shape through just about anything, but cost 800 to 1000 pesos ($16 to $20).

Huaraches: Mexicans get at least 5000 miles more out of tires than do Norteamericanos, and the reason is the production of these attractive tire-soled sandals of woven leather straps. *Buy them small,* at least a size too small, for they stretch almost at once and will soon be too floppy-big to wear unless you've bought them very tight-fitting. First chance you get, rub them with mink oil, neat's-foot oil, or, in a pinch, neutral shoe polish. Pay 300 to 600 pesos ($6 to $12) the pair, depending on size and quality of work.

Lacquer Goods: Most of these wooden lacquered items come from Uruapan, 300 miles west of Mexico City. Many are well done but in execrable taste. Buy if you find something you, ah, like.

Leather Goods: Bags and suitcases, gloves and jackets are all to be had. Quality is generally good, but prices are not fantastically low, although they do constitute a saving over the similar products bought back home.

Onyx: Puebla and Queretaro have most of the carvers, but Mexico City has most of the eggs, ashtrays, and similar items. An egg, just for example, should cost 100 to 160 pesos ($2 to $3.20).

Rebozos: A rebozo is a rectangular cotton cloth to be worn around the shoulders or waist by either men or women. They come from various parts of Mexico, and are used more often by tourists as wall hangings or cloths for small tables. They are usually embroidered, and the price thus depends on the amount and degree of workmanship. You'll find them for 900 to 1600 pesos ($18 to $32).

Serapes: These heavy woolen blankets, with a convenient slit cut for the head, are part of the standard stereotyped Mexican costume. Once you've worn one, you'll find out why they're so popular. Judge the quality of the cloth, its weight, the amount and quality of the workmanship, and then expect to pay 900 to 1600 pesos ($18 to $32) for a small one, a good deal more for a large one of high quality. Serapes are the Mexican peasants' long-wearing, high-quality overcoats, and are priced accordingly.

Silver: The *conquistadores* came for gold, but they also found vast quantities of silver, many sources of which are still yielding the precious metal to this day. The silver craftsmanship of Taxco artisans is famed throughout Mexico. Prices depend on a base price for the weight of the metal, then for the workmanship involved, but prices for jewelry, vessels and utensils, and decorative items are much less than at home. Shop around, though. And before you buy *any* silver object, look for the mark "925" stamped into its surface. This government-controlled mark is to certify that the object is made from metal containing 925 grams of pure silver per kilogram, that is, the silver is 92.5% pure. This is the highest grade found in Mexico. Without this mark, you might end up paying top price for something that's mostly nickel, or even silver plate.

Stones, Precious and Semiprecious: Most people don't think of Mexico when talking of precious and semiprecious stones, but in fact the volcanic mountains and intermountain valleys here are filled with geodes, chalcedony, turquoise, lapis lazuli, and amethyst. Small objets d'art such as mushrooms and figurines carved from chalcedony are priced per item in the range of 150 to 300 pesos ($3 to $6), but the stones by themselves are sold by the carat, at so many pesos the carat.

Tortoise Shell: Combs, pins, and other curious and sometimes useful things are made from this attractive material around Veracruz and in other coastal areas where tortoise shell is a natural resource. Finding the stuff is not easy, though, and working it is tricky, and so a small pin may cost 200 to 350 pesos ($4 to $7), a comb somewhat more.

BARGAINING: Before you head out to shop, though, you should know a bit about bargaining. First and foremost, *never start bargaining unless you intend to buy.* Once you've looked around the shop or shops (at leisure and never showing too much enthusiasm over any one object, especially the one you're thinking of purchasing), ask the price. After he's answered, you might respond with *"es muy caro"* (it's very expensive), or better yet with no response at all. The owner will probably lower his price or ask you *"¿Cuanto quiere pagar?"* (How much do you want to pay?). Don't answer at this point, just keep looking around, asking prices of things you're interested in. Once you have an idea of his prices and have decided the price you're willing to pay, then you can begin to bargain.

There are two approaches I've used—the first is probably the best. I set a price I want to pay for the goods (never wanting it so much that I can't leave without buying it). I look around a bit more (perhaps there's something else, and it's always easier to bargain a "two for one" price), then I state my price *"á la mas, quinientos pesos"* (at the most, 500 pesos). Simple: no bargaining, just state the price you want to pay. This approach, of course, is good only if you're a fair judge of quality and know the going prices around town. Obviously, if he asks 1000 pesos for a hand-embroidered shirt and you tell him 100 pesos, then all you've accomplished is an insult!

The second approach is to halve or even quarter the quoted price (depending on the product) and work on up to a compromise. He asks 1000, you say 500, and you end up at 750—plus or minus 50 depending on who's more adept at bargaining.

Of course, not all places go in for bargaining. Government shops are fixed price, and boutiques in the Zona Rosa might call an ambulance if you started to haggle over price; but in large markets and lower-class shops bargaining is usually expected. If it's not, and if the prices are really fixed, the owner will soon let you know. But the fact that pricetags are affixed to some items does not necessarily mean that the shopkeeper is not open to bargaining. Try him and see—it can't hurt.

Large General Markets

Now that you've been briefed on what to buy and how to go about buying it, head out on your browsing and shopping spree. The markets and shops are found in various parts of the city, but I'll use the familiar Zócalo as a starting point for our explorations.

From the Zócalo, head down Pino Suarez, which is loaded with little *tiendas* selling everything from belt buckles to shoestrings, until you reach the broad divided boulevard which is Fray Servando Teresa de Mier. Beginning here and for about six blocks east along Servando, through side streets and alleys, is an exciting maze of vendors and craftsmen.

MERCED MARKET: Having had a brief lesson in haggling, try your skill at the Merced Market, the biggest in the city (Metro: Merced). Continue down Fray Servando about six blocks and take a left on the Avenida Anillo de Circunvalación. The market is three or four blocks up this street.

The Merced Market consists of several modern buildings. The

first is mainly for fruits and vegetables; the others contain just about everything you would find if a department store joined forces with a five and dime—a good place to go looking for almost anything.

The area to the north of the market is a tangled confusion of trucks and stores, in which cascades of oranges spill gloriously down onto sidewalks.

At the corner of Circunvalación and Calle Gómez Pedraza, a crowd has gathered to watch a street entertainer do his tricks. His rolled-up handkerchief lies on the ground and, as he beckons it toward him, in a cracked voice, interruptions come from a small figure in a battered fedora hat. The crowd roars, as much at the incongruity of the urchin's painted cheeks, oversize black mustache, and baggy pants, as at anything he says. Finally, feigning uncontrolled indignation, the entertainer seizes his straight "man" by the tie and drags him around the circle. But the boy (who can't be older than seven) has slipped out of the noose, which hangs limply from the entertainer's hand, and continues blithely on his way. A shower of coins testifies to the crowd's appreciation.

These street entertainers, the equivalent of Europe's age-old buskers, can be found everywhere in the capital. Many of them are strolling musicians or mariachis, but sometimes they are youthful crosswalk teams with amazing mass appeal. It isn't necessary to speak Spanish to appreciate the down-to-earth humor of, say, a pair who can sometimes be found doing a "Knock, knock, who's there?" routine at the head of the Calle Talavera, which goes into the Plaza Merced.

To return to the Zócalo or anywhere else within the city, take the Metro from the Merced station, which is just outside the enclosed market. You can change at Pino Suarez (first stop) to Line 2, which will take you to the Zócalo.

LAGUNILLA MARKET: A few blocks north of the Plaza de Garibaldi (Metro: Allende) is another market well worth visiting. The Lagunilla Market, whose two enclosed sections, separated by a short street, Calle Juan Alvarez, have different specialties, is noted for clothes, rebozos, and blankets to the north, and tools, pottery, and household goods, such as attractive copper hanging lamps, to the south. This is also the area for old and rare books, many at a ridiculously low cost, if you're willing to hunt and bargain. Most, however, are in Spanish.

The area around the Lagunilla Market is the site for the Sunday-only Thieves' Market (see below for details).

ARTESANOS de la CIUDADELA: A fairly new market (Metro: Balderas), large, clean, and with numerous little streets, it rambles on forever just off Balderas and Ayuntamiento in the Plaza de la Ciudadela. The merchandise is of good quality, well displayed, and bartering is a must. I think this is probably the best place for buying; anything you want is here. The shops don't really get going until 11 a.m. or noon so it's best to save your shopping in this area until the afternoon. Open until 8 p.m.

You might want to come for lunch before shopping; if so I can highly recommend the restaurant in the market called **Fonda Lupita,** just off the small plaza from the Balderas and Ayuntamiento entrance. It has Spanish decor, new and immaculately clean. A very handsome white-haired lady keeps the place shipshape and also prepares the very tasty food. The set-price lunch is only 65 pesos ($1.30); a plate of enchiladas a mere 50 ($1).

SAN JUAN BASKET MARKET (Mercado de Curiosidades): This is a large, rather modern building set back off a plaza on the corner of Ayuntamiento and Dolores (Metro: Salto del Agua). It's comprised of a number of stalls on two levels selling everything from leather to tiles. They have some lovely silver jewelry and, as in most non-fixed-price stores, the asking price is high but the bargained result is often very reasonable.

CENTRAL CRAFTS MARKET: Not far from Buenavista Railroad Station (Estación Buenavista) is the Central Crafts Market, a commercial concern with a lot of floor space and an uninspired collection of crafts at rather high prices. If you want a look, take a no. 17 bus north on Insurgentes to the railroad station. Get off and walk in front of the station—you'll be heading east. The first real north-south street you will come to is Calle Aldama, and the Central Crafts Market is at Aldama 187, just a few steps away.

Note: The Central Crafts Market employs undercover agents who prowl the length of Avenida Juárez and other tourist-frequented areas to tout the excellence of the market's wares. Offering "free tourist information" or "free guide service," they are friendly and helpful, but their goal is to persuade you to visit the market.

Arts and Crafts Shops

Mexico is famous the world over for the quality and variety of its arts and crafts. Several government-run shops and a few excellent privately run shops have exceptionally good collections of Mexico's arts and crafts. As fascinating as a fine art gallery, these shops deserve a visit whether you intend to buy or not.

ARTES POPULARES SHOPS: If the teeming Merced Market is a bit too fast for your blood pressure, don't fret, because the city is loaded with Artes Populares (handicrafts) shops. Two of the nicest shops with the most varied assortment of gifts are those run by the government, and the *prices are fixed* so you can avoid haggling. The **Exposición Nacional de Arte Popular** (Metro: Hidalgo or Juárez), located at Juárez 89, has simply everything! There are two floors of papier-mâché figurines, woven goods, earthenware, colorfully painted candelabras, hand-carved wooden masks, straw goods, beads, bangles, and glass. It's run by FONART, the quasi-governmental crafts organization.

When you're finished here, walk down a few blocks to the **National Museum of Popular Industrial Arts,** located across the street from the Benito Juárez statue in Alameda Park at Juárez 44. They have similar Mexican crafts from all over and because the prices are fixed you can get an idea of quality vs. cost for later use in market bargaining. Even if you don't buy anything you should visit the shop, as it displays an enormous selection of crafts. Both government shops are open every day except Sunday, 10 a.m. to 6 p.m.

The **Fondo Nacional para el Fomento de las Artesanías, or FONART,** is a quasi-governmental body set up to encourage production, quality control, and marketing of traditional crafts items. It operates the store described above at Juárez 89, and also the very attractive stores at Juárez 70 (in the Hotel Del Prado) and Juárez 92. You'll find yet another FONART shop in the Zona Rosa, at Londres 136.

VICTOR'S ARTES POPULARES MEXICANAS: This is a shop for serious buyers and art collectors. The Fosado family has been in the folk art business for over 50 years and is a reputable authority. The store is located near the Alameda at Madero 10, second floor, Room 305 (Metro: Juárez). They buy most of their crafts from the Indian villages near and far, and supply various exhibits with native craftworks. Hours are 11 a.m. to 7 p.m., Monday through Friday.

The Outdoor Markets

THE BAZAR SABADO (SATURDAY ONLY): The Bazar Sabado in San Angel, a suburb a few miles south of the city, used to attract artists and writers and out of this grew the famous Saturday Market, a fair for arts and handicrafts. See Chapter V for full details.

THIEVES' MARKET (SUNDAY ONLY): On Sunday mornings, you might enjoy a visit to the famous Thieves' Market, next to the Lagunilla Market on the corner of Allende and Libertad. To get there take the Metro to the Guerrero station and walk east on Mosqueta which intersects Reforma; just past the intersection is the market. Or, you can take a bus north along Avenida Lázaro Cárdenas—almost any bus will do.

Sunday mornings, the area is filled with stalls and sidewalk blankets piled with goods of every description. Principally, there are antiques, brass candlesticks, and weighing scales, but you'll also see such prosaic items as sunglasses and old magazines, furniture and jewelry, coins, extinct banknotes, and buttons. It's a place where bargaining is expected. If you want to buy anything, offer half the price asked and be prepared to forget the whole thing if the vendor won't lower his price. Best time to arrive is about 11 a.m. Watch carefully for pickpockets, or your wallet or handbag, emptied of its contents, might be among the items up for sale at next week's market.

Don't wear yourself down too much with daytime activities, for Mexico City has a lot to offer after sunset. Find out all about it, starting on the next page.

Chapter VII

MEXICO CITY
AFTER DARK

TAKE THE ELEVATOR to the top of a luxury hotel, or to the observatory of the Latin American Tower, just after sunset. A vast sea of glimmering lights will meet your eye as you take in Mexico City after dark.

Actually, although the view from the top is breathtaking, the real excitement is down in the city's streets and back streets. Whatever your favorite entertainment, from Folies Bergère-style reviews to simple people-watching, Mexico City can provide it for you in abundance.

Here, then, is a catalog of delights to be had in Mexico City after dark, but note that the clubs and nightspots located in the larger hotels have been mentioned under each hotel's name in Chapter III.

For further information on nighttime activities, be sure to pick up a copy of *Calendario Actividades*, put out by the Instituto Nacional de las Bellas Artes each month, and available from your hotel information desk or from the Palacio de las Bellas Artes. The *Calendario* lists art exhibitions, lectures, ballet, symphony, opera, and art film offerings currently available. Check also the entertainment listings in *The News*, Mexico City's English-language daily newspaper, on sale at most newspaper stands and kiosks.

Painting the Town Pink

Mexico City's "Pink Zone" (Zona Rosa) positively bustles with activity each evening—in fact, evening is the busiest time of day here. From sidewalk cafés and taco shops to sybaritic restaurants and exclusive clubs, every establishment is filled with the rich and beautiful, or not-so-rich but still beautiful. For a conventional night out on the town, the Zona Rosa is the place to go first.

The streets named **Genova, Copenhague,** and **Oslo** have been turned into pedestrian-only streets (save for the occasional car zipping in to the Aristos hotel), and sidewalk café-restaurants have sprung up making Copenhague one of Mexico City's most delightful in-places. Tables are usually packed unless you come early. Some establishments are selected by the cognoscenti as "in," and chairs are then at a premium, while other places do a slower business and have tables more readily available. On Oslo the attraction is the several coffeehouses with coffee, pastries, and fortune-tellers. Try, for instance, the **Elite Café Turco,** at no. 3, where coffee is 20 pesos, pastry 26, and a reading of the Tarot deck just-for-you costs 150 pesos ($3). The low, mod decor here draws mostly people in love and people who are looking to fall in love. At Oslo 10 is a tiny student beer hangout called **La Cavita,** where the guests make their own music for entertainment and the barman is zealous in the refilling of your mug.

Another such crossroads for live entertainment is in the arcade located at **Londres 104,** just off Genova. Half-a-dozen restaurants here (Alfredo's, La Trucha Vagabunda, Toulouse-Lautrec, Le Bistrot, La Cabaña) also serve as cafés, and Toulouse-Lautrec has live entertainment most evenings. Come for a margarita (100 pesos, $2), a shrimp cocktail, or a full meal—by sitting in the outdoor section of one restaurant, you get to enjoy what's going on in neighboring places as well.

FOR THE WELL HEELED: Make your way to Florencia 36 if you're well dressed, well heeled, and out for adventure, for this is where you will find a long stucco facade bearing the name **Marrakesh.** Actually, there are three separate clubs within these trendy walls, the newest of which is **Valentino's,** heavy on silent-film-era nostalgia. Don't go before 9:30 p.m., and don't plan to stay past 3:30 a.m. Bring about 500 pesos ($10) for the cover charge, per person. Closed Sunday.

Mexican Entertainments

For more traditionally Mexican entertainments, one must venture out of the Pink Zone to other locales. Mariachi music is always a big part of any Mexican night out, and most Mexicans—*Mexicanos* more than *Mexicanas*—are not averse to a drop or two of *aguardiente,* thinking perhaps that it adds to the enjoyment of the music. (Meeting the mariachi bands, one gets the distinct impression that it adds to the production of the music as well!)

MARIACHIS: At some time or other, everybody—Mexicans and turistas alike—goes to see and hear the mariachi players. The mariachis are strolling musicians who wear distinctive costumes, which make them look like cowboys dressed up for a special occasion. Their costume—tight spangled trousers, fancy jackets, and big floppy bowties—dates back to the French occupation of Mexico in the mid-19th century, as, indeed, does their name. Mariachi is the Mexican mispronunciation of the French word for marriage, which is where they were often on call for music.

In Mexico City, the mariachis make their headquarters around the **Plaza de Garibaldi** which is a ten-minute stroll north of the Palacio de las Bellas Artes up Lázaro Cárdenas, at Avenida Rep. de Honduras.

In the Plaza de Garibaldi, mariachi players swarm all over. Wherever there's a corner, guitars are stacked together like rifles in an army training camp. For music, see what there is of it in the square itself (hottest about 9 or 10 o'clock in the evening, especially on Sunday). Young musicians strut proudly in their flashy outfits, on the lookout for señoritas to impress. They play when they feel like it, or when there seems to be a good chance to gather in some tips, or when someone orders a song—the going rate seems to be around 250 pesos ($5) per song.

After all that singing, a man's got to wet his whistle, and so the plaza is surrounded with places for drinking-and-singing. Most famous of these is the **Tenampa,** once an all-male preserve but now open to men and women (no children, though), tourist and local alike. Across the plaza is the **Tlaquepaque,** a rather fancy restaurant where you can dine to strolling mariachis. But perhaps the most adventurous spot for newcomers to Mexico City is the **Pulquería Hermana Hortensia,** near the northeast corner of the plaza at the corner of Amargura and Rep. de Honduras. Unlike most pulque bars, La Hermana Hortensia is a *pulquería familiar* (a "family" bar, i.e., you can bring your wife—but not your kids). Pulque (that's POOL-keh) is a thick and flavorsome drink made by fermenting the juice of a maguey ("century") plant. Discovered by the ancient Toltecs and shared with the Aztecs, pulque was a sacred drink forbidden to the common people for centuries. One of the effects of the Spanish conquest was to liberate pulque for the masses. Was this good or bad? Ask your neighbor in La Hermana Hortensia as you quaff the thick brew. Pulque packs a wallop, by the way, although it's not nearly so strong as those other maguey-based drinks, tequila and mezcal. By the way, the pulque here can be ordered with nuts blended in for a different flavor.

In any of the eating and drinking establishments around the plaza you can enjoy the mariachi music that swirls through the air. But remember—if you give a bandleader the high sign, you're the one that pays the 250 pesos for the song, just like outside in the square.

Don't get the idea that you'll see only your countrymen in the Plaza de Garibaldi, for it is indeed a Mexican phenomenon. As evening falls, lots of people from the neighborhood come to stroll or sit, catching some of the music or trying their hand at one of the stands where they can bust a balloon with a dart to win a prize.

The **Plaza Insurgentes,** built above the Metro station of the same name, is another lively spot in the evening. The plaza, sunken below street level, is always full of young mods, mariachis, and rock groups. Cafés ring the plaza, and you can sit in one and enjoy a beer (45 pesos, 90¢) or a drink (100 pesos, $2) and watch the action. Day or night, this is a fun place to be, as business people, secretaries, and students hurry here and there. Music issues from the cafés to the outdoor tables; sometimes it's live rock, sometimes records. The beer costs money, but the show's for free.

Devotees of the best in mariachi music will want to spend the money for an evening at the upstairs (mezzanine) lounge in the **Hotel Alameda,** on Avenida Juárez at Calle Garcia Lorca. Called La Fería de la Música, the show here is an almost continuous succession of mariachi numbers, by bands of highest quality. The cover charge is 200 pesos ($4) per person, and drinks cost 140 to 200 pesos ($2.80 to $4) apiece. You certainly get your money's worth in music.

MARGARITAS: It make it a point, every time I come to Mexico City, to have at least one margarita (usually the first) in the **Muralto** bar of the Latin American Tower on Lázaro Cárdenas, at Madero. The observation deck costs 50 pesos ($1), but you get the same view from the Muralto with your drink at no extra charge. And what a view! Cynics will say you could be anywhere:

Top of the Hub in Boston, Top of the Mark in San Francisco, or any other skyscraper. But to me the feeling of gazing down at the Bellas Artes and the Alameda, Paseo de la Reforma out to Chapultepec and the Monument to the Revolution, is always a unique thrill. The late-afternoon thunderstorms are a sound-and-light show of great power, for from the Muralto you can follow the path of every lightning bolt to earth. You can dine here, too—see Chapter IV for full details. I note with some chagrin that margarita quality has been dropping although the price has been increasing—it's now 100 pesos ($2), and service is sometimes bad. But the view is still the best in town.

CANTINAS: Mexico City's cantinas are the last resort of male dominion, and will be the last to fall before the wave of equality of the sexes. Here is where the macho Mexican male comes to let loose and have a good time without having to be on his good behavior. Cantinas range from luxurious men-only taverns to frowsy boozeries, and each has its accustomed clientele. Indeed, there's even a sort of caste system in cantinas of this city whereby a government official wouldn't think of wandering into a place where newsboys and the like have their evening rum or tequila.

Cantinas get rowdier, and therefore more interesting, as one proceeds down the social scale. I've visited one in which barely anyone noticed when a man drew a pistol from his pocket and fired two rounds into the ceiling. (The only ones who complained were the ones who got covered with plaster chips!) The inexpensive places get around a liquor licensing law prohibiting liquor by the drink in certain places with a ruse: the law says "bottle sales only," and so they sell big bottles (for groups) and miniatures (for individuals). Locals and regulars buy a big bottle, have some, write their name on it, and leave it there for next time.

Although it helps to know some Spanish and to have a few Mexican friends to go cantina-hopping, you can share in the fun (women, too!) by visiting a few well-selected places. Try these:

For Men and Women

The **Bar Negresco,** on the corner of Balderas and Victoria/Morelos, is an authentic cantina and no tourist trap, but it admits—even welcomes—women. This all came about during the 1940s when an American newspaper correspondent named Alma Reed was told she couldn't come in, and decided then and there to put a stop to *that!* Ms. Reed was admitted, and ever since that early coup for equality, the Negresco has welcomed, or at least politely admitted, ladies as well as men. You will not find men firing revolvers into the ceiling here, as it's a higher-class place than that, and besides, with ladies present the regular patrons don't want to be *too* rowdy, although the attitude is one of we're-all-in-this-together. You'll enjoy it here. The drinks are 70, 80, and 90 pesos ($1.40, $1.60, and $1.80), and if you come in the late afternoon you may be treated to a few free plates of hors d'oeuvres, called *entremeses.*

For Men Only

To my knowledge, no Mexican legislator has yet proposed a Mexican Equal Rights Amendment, and even if one passed it is doubtful that things would change at **La Opera Bar,** a staunchly masculine drinking and dining establishment at 5 de Mayo 14, corner of Filomeno Mata, a block from the Bellas Artes if you're heading toward the Zócalo. Men may enter and enjoy the gilded baroque ceilings, the dark wood booths with patches of beveled mirror and exquisite small oil paintings of pastoral scenes, or sidle up to the heavy carved wooden bar for some tequila and lime. La Opera is the Mexican's equivalent of a Londoner's club, and men in shirtsleeves or dark suits will be playing dominoes or cards, drinking beer (40 pesos, 80¢) or *copas* (hard liquor of whatever sort; 70 to 105 pesos, $1.40 to $2.10), and perhaps having supper from the selective menu. La Opera Bar is open every day, but it closes early (9 p.m.) on Saturday night. Women should at least take a look, as much of the interior can be seen from the sidewalk.

MUSIC: The plushest circumstances under which I've ever listened to a pianist were at the **Hotel Maria Isabel,** Reforma 325, near the "Angel" Monument. A split-level fountain tips you off as to the quality of this hotel even before you enter. Once inside, you'll sink ankle-deep into lush red or blue carpets, admire hunks of Mayan architecture spotlighted in corridors, and eventually find your way to an elegant, second-floor cocktail bar. Drinks here cost about 80 to 150 pesos ($1.60 to $3) each, and for this you'll hear some marvelous arrangements from whichever "musica romantica" group happens to be featured—usually dreamy Latin stuff.

For contrast and high decibels, try **Le Rendezvous** at Madero 29, across from the Ritz Hotel several blocks west of the Zócalo.

From about 7 p.m. until midnight the place has jazz and rock groups which change hourly. There is a 35-peso (70¢) cover. Drinks run about 90 pesos ($1.80); Cokes, 50 pesos ($1). You can also order food, which ranges from 190 to 250 pesos ($3.80 to $5). A popular place—I've returned on several occasions always to find a jolly atmosphere.

Movies and Theaters

MOVIES: You'll find many current first-run hits playing in Mexico City, usually in the original language version with Spanish subtitles, and usually under the same title (although the title will be translated into Spanish). Thus, if you see *Cazadores del Arca Perdida,* you'll know they're running *Raiders of the Lost Ark.*

The best place to check for what's currently being shown is in the entertainment section of Mexico City's English-language paper, *The News.* Note that various cinema clubs, and the National Museum of Anthropology, also screen films from time to time.

Tickets cost about 60 to 80 pesos ($1.20 to $1.60), even at the fancy movie houses along Reforma. At the gigantic Cine Diana there's a bonus: an enormous mural stretching the entire length of one wall, which is almost worth the price of admission alone.

THEATERS: Mexico City's theater district is near the Plaza de la República, centered on Calle Antonio Caso. Bright marquees advertise the plays or vaudeville shows currently running, and box offices sell reserved-seat tickets in advance. It's all in Spanish, of course, but still very entertaining. As ticket prices are low, you have little to lose by trying an evening at the theater. Check the entertainment listings in the daily Spanish-language newspapers for current theater offerings.

The English-language community in Mexico City sponsors plays and shows in English from time to time, and *The News* will always carry details.

The **National Auditorium** in Chapultepec Park, fronting onto Reforma, is usually the biggest bargain in town. International ballet, opera, and theater companies play here at prices as low as 20 pesos per seat. Often they are the same companies that played at the elegant Bellas Artes theater with a 215-peso ($4.30) minimum. The newspapers list performances at both, but it's worth walking past the National Auditorium once in a while to see what forthcoming events they are announcing.

The Ballet Folklorico

A combination of religious ceremony, can-can, pantomime, low comedy, and sheer beauty of color, design, and choreography—that's the **Ballet Folklorico de México.** There are two companies—three, if you count the one usually on tour—and their performances are given at the Palacio de las Bellas Artes (tel. 585-4888, ext. 29).

Performances are on Sunday at 9:30 a.m. and 9 p.m., and on Wednesday at 9 p.m.; you cannot buy your tickets before Monday for the Wednesday performance, or Thursday for Sunday. The box office is open 10:30 a.m. to 1 p.m. and 4 to 7 p.m.; tickets range from galleria seats at 215 pesos ($4.30; on the third floor) to 450 pesos ($9) for second-floor and 500 pesos ($10) for first-floor seats. The show is popular and tickets are bought up rapidly (especially by tour companies) so if you want a seat, go early, or book seats through a tour agency (at twice the cost). The box office is on the ground floor of the Bellas Artes, main entrance.

A typical program will include Aztec ritual dances, agricultural dances from Jalisco, a fiesta in Veracruz, a Christmas celebration—all welded together with mariachis, marimba players, singers, and dancers.

As many other events are held in the Bellas Artes—visits by foreign opera companies, for instance—there are times when the Ballet Folklorico is moved. Usually, it reappears in the National Auditorium in Chapultepec Park. Check at the Bellas Artes box office; if it's at the "Auditorio," catch an Expresso Reforma bus from the Juárez Monument on Avenida Juárez.

An alternative to the Ballet Folklorico de México is the **Ballet Folclorico Nacional Aztlan,** in the Teatro de la Ciudad at Donceles 36. Performances here are as good as the better known ones in the Bellas Artes, but tickets are much cheaper and easier to get hold of. Shows are at 9:30 on Sunday morning and 8:30 on Tuesday evening.

The National Lottery

Any Monday, Wednesday, or Friday, walk in the front door of the older National Lottery Building, where Juárez meets Reforma, go straight up the steps, and take a seat in the small auditorium that faces you. Sharp at 8 p.m. a dozen pages, clad in maroon uniforms, enter to begin the ceremony of picking small wooden balls from two revolving cages. One cage contains 50,000 balls (or more, depending on the number of tickets issued for the lottery), the other contains balls relating to the number of prizes with the total of each prize on it. As each ball is picked and dropped into cages, the pages keep up a sing-song patter of the winning numbers. The big-money winners are posted on a board at the end of the stage. The whole ceremony is broadcast, and the winning numbers are also printed in the papers next morning and listed at all the stands where lottery tickets are sold. Attendance at the lottery takes on a whole different element of suspense if you are clutching a 50-peso ticket in your hand as the numbers are called.

Jai Alai

Jai alai (pronounced "hi-lie") must be the fastest game in the world, and is exciting to watch even without prior knowledge of how it is played. Games take place most Tuesday, Thursday, Saturday, and Sunday nights throughout the year in the Fronton México, on the Plaza de la República, which is the plaza donated by the Monument to the Revolution. The plaza is a few blocks along Juárez west of Reforma. Any bus going west along Juárez will take you to the Juárez-Reforma intersection and it's a short walk from there, or you can take the Metro to the Revolución station, and walk three blocks down Arriaga (south) to the plaza. It doesn't much matter what time you arrive. The box office opens at 6:30, and there are several games on each night's card.

As you walk into the fronton, the ticket office is to your left; pay 20 pesos (40¢) at the *"Admission General"* window, then walk the length of the big lobby to a stack of small brown programs on a cigarette counter to your left. Take one, they're free. And then take a seat—the game will probably already be under way.

Jai alai players wear small baskets on their right arms, with which they catch and sling a fantastically resilient ball against the wall to the right of where you're sitting. In the best games, four players, two with blue armbands and two with red ones, are competing with each other in a fashion similar to tennis, but even more similar to squash. The member of one team throws the ball against the wall, the other team has to return it. The whole thing is done at an incredible speed, and how they manage to see, much less catch, a ball traveling at about 80 miles per hour is just marvelous.

The most fun, of course, is in the betting, you'd be amazed at how much more exciting a game seems to you when you have money riding on the result. Wait until the program announces a game of 30 points *(partido a treinta tantos)* and watch the bookies. These colorful gentlemen, who all wear white jackets and bright-red berets, carry little pads of betting slips edged in red *(rojo)* or blue *(azul)*, and when the game begins, they'll be offering only a slight edge on one team or another—say 95 pesos to 100. When the scoring starts, however, the odds will change. If you're as good a mathematician as most jai alai aficionados, you'll be able to bet with impunity on both sides at different points of the game—and still finish up ahead.

As you get to know Mexico City and begin to see its sights, you'll want to expand your horizons. Tomorrow, consider a short trip out of town for the day. Following are suggestions of the prime places to go.

Mariachis

Chapter VIII

DAY EXCURSIONS FROM MEXICO CITY

THE VALLEY OF MEXICO and especially the site of an ancient Lake Texcoco have seen so much history that the surroundings of Mexico City are particularly rich in possibilities for day trips and overnighters using the capital as your base. Your visit to Toluca should be planned for a Friday, which is market day in that market town. Should you be driving or busing from Mexico City to Acapulco, you might want to plan visits to Cuernavaca and Taxco along the way. Otherwise, it's a simple matter to visit these places on a day tour—admittedly a long one—from Mexico City. Tourist agencies will be glad to help you with arrangements, should you not want to bus-hop or rent a car. Many agencies run daily tours to both Cuernavaca and Taxco.

No matter which of the other sights in the surroundings you choose to see, there is one which *you absolutely must not miss!* This "wonder of the Western Hemisphere" is almost as famous as Mexico City itself, and should be the first stop on your out-of-town sightseeing schedule. Here's a description.

Pyramids of San Juan Teotihuacan

The pyramids of San Juan Teotihuacan were built about 300 B.C., the time when the Classical Greeks were building their great monuments on the other side of the world. Teotihuacan was the dominant city of its time, with its magnificent pyramids, palaces, and houses covering eight square miles. At its zenith around A.D. 500 there were 125,000 inhabitants, more than in contemporary Rome. But little is known about the city's inhabitants or about why they abandoned the place in A.D. 700. Today what remains are the rough stone structures of the three pyramids and sacrificial altars, and some of the grand houses. This is one of Mexico's most remarkable ruins, and you shouldn't miss it.

You may want to pack a lunch to take to the ruins. Restaurants exist, but they are expensive, or disappointing, or a long walk from the ruins, or all of the above. If you forget your box lunch, don't panic. Drinks and snacks are sold by vendors, so you needn't starve. For further recommendations on meals at Teotihuacan, see below.

GETTING THERE BY BUS: Don't let anyone tell you that it's difficult to get to the pyramids by bus, and that you should take a tour or a cab! It's simple, relatively fast, and very inexpensive to go by bus. Two different lines serve the route between Mexico City and San Juan Teotihuacan.

Buses leave every half hour (6 a.m. to 8 p.m.) every day of the week from the Terminal Central de Autobuses del Norte. Cost for a one-way ticket is 36 pesos (72¢), and the trip takes one hour. To get to the Terminal Norte take bus no. 17 ("Indios Verdes") going north on Insurgentes, or take the Metro (Line 5) to Terminal A. Norte.

When you reach the Terminal Norte, look for the Autobuses Teotihuacan desk, located at the far west end. Try to go early in the morning and give yourself plenty of time to wander around the ruins, for there is a lot to see.

Another way to get to the pyramids by bus is to walk from the Zócalo north on Rep. de Argentina, then right on Justo Sierra. Walk five blocks on Sierra (which changes its name to Mixcalco and then to Alarcon) and cross Avenida Vidal Alcocer. Buses ("Pyramides") leave from the "Garage Teotihuacan," on the right-hand side of Mixcalco, just before Calle Bravo, about every 15 minutes for the hour-long trip to the pyramids. The fare is 32 pesos (64¢). For the return journey, catch a bus at the traffic circle near the pyramids entrance close to the museum. The Mexico-Metro bus will drop you at the Indios Verdes Metro station, from whence it is a short ride to any other point in the city.

GETTING THERE BY CAR: Driving to San Juan Teotihuacan on the new toll road will take about an hour. Head north along the Insurgentes (returning to the same road again if you turn off for a side trip to Guadalupe). What you're looking for is Hwy. 85.

Actually, there are two Hwy. 85s, and both go to the pyramids. No matter which you choose, you'll probably get lost at least once, as traffic is fast and furious, intersections and turnoffs are badly marked (or not marked at all), and confusion reigns supreme. Don't be afraid to stop and ask directions frequently. But about those two roads to the pyramids: one (Hwy. 85) passes through picturesque villages and the like, but is excruciatingly slow, due to the surfeit of trucks and buses; the other (Hwy. 85D) is the toll road, which is a little duller but considerably faster. However, if you're in the mood for a leisurely drive, you might as well take the old two-lane road, slow as it is. And now I'll mention a few of the sights you'll pass.

About 15 miles from town, the village of **San Cristobal Ecatepec** looms off to the left. Note, also on the left, an old wall built centuries ago to keep what was then a lake from flooding the area. When the road forks a mile or so farther north, take the road to the right.

Three miles farther along this road, is the ancient **Convent of San Augustine Acolman** (1539-1560). For years the monastery was in ruins, the only sounds being the ticking of a modern clock, the faint braying of sheep from the fields outside, and the chatter of birds building nests on the roof. Now, however, the monastery and church are restored.

The next mile or so is as typically rural a slice of Mexico as can be found. Goats and horses graze beside the road outside gardens fenced in by giant cactus; bales of hay can be seen stacked high on a thatched farmhouse roof; women scrub their clothes in a small brook, spreading them out on the ground or on the trees and shrubs to dry.

SEEING THE PYRAMIDS: During your visit to the pyramids and temples of Teotihuacan, please keep in mind these important points:

—You will be doing a great deal of walking, and perhaps some climbing. It is a full mile from the Pyramid of the Moon to the Unidad Cultural (Museum) and Ciudadela; and there are 248 steep steps up to the top of the Pyramid of the Sun.

—Because the site is so vast, I'll describe it in sections. Whichever entrance you use to the site, locate the section nearest you and visit it first. Backtracking takes too much time and energy.

—Remember always that you're at an altitude of more than

7000 feet, and you will tire more easily than usual. Take it slowly. Also, the sun and heat can get you. Protect yourself.

—In the summer rainy season, it rains almost every afternoon. Plan to be in the museum or a restaurant when the showers come at 2 or 3 o'clock.

Admission

Teotihuacan is open every day of the week from 9 a.m. to 5 p.m. (you must be off the site by 6 p.m.); admission is 20 pesos (40¢), and there's a 15-peso (30¢) parking fee if you have a car. On Sunday and holidays you pay less for admission, but the same for the car.

The Layout

The grand buildings of Teotihuacan were laid out on a cosmic plan. The front wall of the Pyramid of the Sun is exactly square to (facing) the point on the horizon where the sun sets on the day it reaches its zenith. So if a line were drawn from the pyramid to the sun at noon on the day when the sun reaches its highest point (i.e., it seems to be directly overhead), and another line were drawn from the pyramid to the sun when the sun reaches the horizon later that same day, then the pyramid would be exactly square to these lines. The rest of the ceremonial buildings were laid out at right angles to the Pyramid of the Sun.

The main thoroughfare, called by archeologists the Avenue of the Dead, runs roughly north-south. The Pyramid of the Moon is at the northern end, and the Unidad Cultural (Museum) and Ciudadela are on the southern part of the thoroughfare. Actually, the great street was several miles long in its heyday, but only a mile or so has been uncovered and restored.

The Pyramid of the Sun is on the east side of the Avenue of the Dead.

Pyramid of the Sun

As pyramids go, this one is Number Three. The Great Pyramid of Cholula, on the Mexico City–Puebla road, is the largest structure ever built by man. Today it's so ruined that it appears as a muddy hill with a church built on top. Second largest is the Pyramid of Cheops on the outskirts of Cairo, Egypt. In third place is Teotihuacan's Pyramid of the Sun, which is almost—at 730 feet per side—as large as Cheops at the base. But at 210 feet high, the sun pyramid is only about half as high as its Egyptian rival. No matter. It's still the biggest restored pyramid in the Western Hemisphere, and an awesome sight.

Although the Pyramid of the Sun was not built as a great king's tomb, it does have secret tunnels and chambers beneath it. A natural grotto was enlarged and restructured into a four-room chamber which was used for some occult purpose—no one knows what. The tunnels are not open to the public.

The first structure of the pyramid was probably built a century before Christ, and the temple which used to crown the pyramid was finished about 400 years later (A.D. 300). By the time the pyramid was discovered and restoration was begun (early in our century), the temple had completely disappeared, and the pyramid was just a mass of rubble covered with bushes and trees.

If you're game, trudge up the 248 steps to the top. The view is marvelous, if the smog's not too thick.

Avenue of the Dead

As you stroll north along the Avenue of the Dead toward the Pyramid of the Moon, look on the right for a bit of wall sheltered by a modern corrugated roof. Beneath the shelter, the wall still bears a painting of a jaguar. From this fragment, build a picture of the breathtaking spectacle which must have met the eye when all the paintings along the avenue were intact.

The Avenue of the Dead got its strange and forbidding name from the Aztecs, who mistook the little temples which line both sides of the avenue for tombs of kings or priests.

Pyramid of the Moon

The Pyramid of the Moon faces an interesting plaza at the northern end of the avenue. The plaza is surrounded by little temples, and by the Palace of Quetzal-Mariposa (or Quetzal-Butterfly), on the left (west) side. You get about the same range of view from the top of the Pyramid of the Moon as you do from its larger neighbor, because the moon pyramid is built on higher ground. So if the prospect of dragging yourself up the sun pyramid was just too much, you can go up the 150-foot-high moon pyramid with less effort. There's a bonus, too: the magnificent perspective straight down the Avenue of the Dead.

Palace of Quetzal-Mariposa

The Palace of Quetzal-Mariposa lay in ruins until the 1960s, when restoration work began. Today it echoes wonderfully with its former glory, as figures of Quetzal-Mariposa (a mythical exotic bird-butterfly) appear painted on walls or carved in the pillars of the inner court.

Behind the Palace of Quetzal-Mariposa is the **Palace of the Jaguars,** complete with murals showing a lively jaguar musical combo, and some frescoes.

Ciudadela and Unidad Cultural

Along the southern reaches of the Avenue of the Dead, a 15-minute stroll from the Pyramid of the Moon, are two more important Teotihuacan sights.

The **Unidad Cultural** is the only modern building of any size on the grounds of Teotihuacan. It houses an entrance to the grounds, rows of little shops, a restaurant, a book and souvenir shop, and the museum, which is worth a look.

First thing you'll notice as you wander into the museum is an enormous statue (a copy, actually) of the goddess Chalchiuhtlicue. She stands in a small pool, which is appropriate as she was the goddess of water. Behind, around, and above her are various exhibits outlining the culture of Teotihuacan, as well as some artifacts found during excavations on the site. Useful in planning the rest of your visit is a scale model of the city of Teotihuacan.

Across the Avenue of the Dead from the Unidad Cultural is the **Ciudadela,** or Citadel, so named by the Spaniards. Actually, this immense sunken square was not a fortress at all, although the impressive walls make it look like one. It was the grand setting for a temple to Quetzalcóatl, the famed "plumed serpent" who appears so often in Mexican folklore. Once you've admired the great scale of the Ciudadela, go down the steps into the massive court and head for the ruined temple, in the middle.

The **Temple of Quetzalcóatl** was covered over by an even larger structure, a pyramid. As you walk toward the center of the Ciudadela's court, you'll be approaching the pyramid. Walk around to the right of it, and soon you'll see the reconstructed temple close behind the pyramid. There's a narrow passage between the two structures, and traffic is supposed to be one-way— which is why I directed you to the right.

It wasn't unusual for early temples to be covered over by later ones in Mexico and Central America. Rather, it was a very common practice. The Pyramid of the Sun may even have been built up in this way. As for the Temple of Quetzalcóatl, you'll notice at once the fine big carved serpents' heads jutting out from aureoles of feathers carved in the stone walls. Other featured serpents are carved in relief low on the walls. The temple provides a vivid example of pre-Columbian public decoration. The decoration at Chichén-Itzá, Uxmal, and Tikal is certainly more elaborate, but these sites are thousands of miles from Mexico City. Luckily, you can still get a good idea of the glory of Mexico's ancient cities from this temple. Don't miss it.

Where to Have Lunch

If you heeded my earlier advice to bring a box lunch, you can take a break wherever you like: in the shade of a tree or a palace, or atop a pyramid. Vendors sell soft drinks and various snacks, wandering with their wares throughout the ruins.

Outside the Unidad Cultural there are often primitive cookshops set up by local señoras, and you can sit at a rustic table under a shady tree and partake of whatever rough-and-ready fare is being served up. People prone to stomach grumbles had better head for a bona fide restaurant, however.

There is a restaurant in the Unidad Cultural, but more suitable places exist along the road which rings the archeological site. **La Gruta,** for instance, is a ten-minute walk east of the Pyramid of the Sun (go out the gate behind the pyramid and follow the signs). Open from 10 a.m. to 9 p.m. every day, La Gruta is just that—a huge, delightfully cool natural grotto filled with table and chairs, natty waiters, and the sound of clinking glasses. Soft drinks and beer are served till 3 p.m., and then the full bar opens. As for food, the set-price lunch of five courses will cost you about 300 pesos ($6) all in, although you can have lunch for about half that price if you order a hamburger and soft drink. La Gruta is exactly three-tenths of a mile from the Pyramid of the Sun, but after the blazing heat, the delicious coolness makes you think you're at the center of the earth.

Behind the Pyramid of the Moon, to the north, is the modest **Restaurant Tepantitla,** where your lunch will be a bit cheaper than at La Gruta, but without the delightful coolness. Next door to the Tepantitla are the fairly uninteresting ruins of Tepantitla. **El Chinanco,** on the ring road between the entrances at Pyramid of the Sun and Pyramid of the Moon, is a similar place.

Yet another classy place is **Pyramides Charlie's,** which has all the marks of a Carlos Anderson restaurant (you'll meet with others in various Mexican cities). Expect to pay 400 to 500 pesos ($8 to $10) for a good, full lunch here. Pyramides Charlie's is on the ring road between the two highways to Mexico City, the "Mexico Libre" (Hwy. 132) and "Mexico Cuota" (Hwy. 132D). It's not all that far from the Unidad Cultural.

SOUND-AND-LIGHT SHOW: The Mexican Tourist Office has organized a spectacle of sound and light nightly, except Monday, October to May, in English at 7 p.m. and in Spanish at 8:15 p.m. For 100 pesos ($2) you can relive some of the Aztec legends; it's splendidly engineered, very impressive, and features the National Symphony Orchestra and the voices of such notables as Charlton Heston (the sun), Vincent Price (a narrator), Ricardo Montalban (Tecuciztecatl), Agnes Moorehead (Black Ant), and numerous others. **Note:** Warm clothing is a must with that cold night wind howling around the pyramids! Phone 521-5602 for reservations. There is a bus which leaves from the Plaza de la República (by the Revolution Monument), but *only* for the 8:15 show (in Spanish). They have not found it worthwhile to provide a bus for the English performance.

Tula

In A.D. 900 or thereabouts, Teotihuacan was overrun by a people called the Chichimecs. Many Teotihuacanos, or Toltecs, fled northward to found the city of Tula, which flourished from 900 to 1156. In that year the Chichimecs caught up with their former enemies the Toltecs again, and wiped out Tula. But the one-time Toltec capital's impressive pyramids, giant statues, and curious three-legged pottery survived to be uncovered by modern archeologists.

The city's remains are memorably beautiful, although its history is a sad story. The peace-loving king of the Toltecs, Quetzalcóatl (the "feathered serpent" in later lore) sought to purge his people of such things as human sacrifice and to direct their efforts to peaceful agriculture. The warlike party in Tula disagreed with the king's aims, and forced him and a band of his followers to flee the city in about 987. They wandered as far as the Yucatán and Chichén-Itzá, spreading Toltec culture along the way and giving birth to the legend of Quetzalcóatl (see the brief history in Chapter I).

The Chichimecs seized Tula in 1156, but in 1200 a drought drove them out. They were succeeded by the Aztecs by 1325, and by the Spaniards in 1519, but Tula never regained its former glory.

Most striking of the city's remains are the 15-foot-high "Atlantean men," gigantic basalt figures mounted atop the Temple of Tlahuizcalpantecuhtli, (that Toltec mouthful means "Morning Star"). At one time, they supported the roof of the temple. The city's ball court, said to be the earliest ball court built on the continent, has been restored beautifully. To the west of the temple is the **Burnt Palace (Quemado)** where you'll be able to see several painted reliefs and a statue of Chac Mool, the reclining figure with head turned to one side. Between the temple and the ball court is a large wall with fantastic reliefs of the feathered serpent, skulls, eagles, and jaguars.

There's a small museum at the site containing a few Toltec artifacts as well as some Aztec pottery. Most interesting items here are the two stone figures once thought to be standard holders. The ruins and museum are open daily from 8 a.m. to 6 p.m.; admission costs 15 pesos (30¢).

GETTING TO TULA: Tula is about 50 miles due north of Mexico City along Hwys. 57D and 126.

By Car: Driving north on the fast toll road (57D), there are no less than three turnoffs for Tula, at km 58 ("Petrolera-Tula"), km 69 ("Tepeji del Río–Tula"), and km 84 ("Jilotepec-Tula"). Take the first, most southerly one at km 58 to avoid a toll.

When you reach the modern town of Tula, ask for directions to the Zona Arqueologica (there may be scattered signs), or follow signs to—get this—Tlahuelilpan. The ruins are about a mile from the center of town. Watch out for a sharp left turn just past a Pemex housing development.

By Bus: Buses leave every quarter hour from Mexico City's Terminal Central de Autobuses del Norte, reached by a no. 17 city bus ("Indios Verdes") going north along Insurgentes; or take the Metro to "Terminal A. Norte." When you enter the giant bus station, turn left and walk down to the far end to the Tula ticket counter, marked "Autotransportes del Valle del Mezquital." The trip takes about an hour and 20 minutes, and you should ask to get off the bus before it gets to the center of the town. Cross the railroad tracks and the junction of Hwys. 22 and 87, and, going along 87, follow signs as mentioned above. The walk will take about ten minutes.

You won't find any food or drink at the ruins, not even soft drinks, so you might want to have a bite or a sip in town before you hike out. The Café **"El Cisne,"** on Tula's tidy main street, can fill your light-lunch wishes admirably and cheaply. Assuming you won't eat heavily before walking to the ruins, you'll end up paying about 90 pesos ($1.80) for the daily set-price lunch, a bit more if you order à la carte.

Toluca

At 8760 feet, Toluca is the highest city in Mexico, and the hour-long trip there from Mexico City offers spectacular scenic views. Pine trees and icy-looking blue lakes dot the landscape, and only an occasional cactus plant or brightly colored painting, drying in the sun, will remind you that you're in Mexico. Toluca isn't a particularly exciting city, but it has an immense Indian market you'll want to visit on a Friday, early as possible in the day before the tour buses roll in.

It's easy to get to the market by bus from Mexico City. Take the Metro to the Observatorio station, and look for the Terminal Central de Autobuses del Poniente, the capital's western bus station. Enter the terminal, turn left, and look for the Toluca counter. Buses ("Toluca Directo") depart every 20 minutes on the hour-long trip.

Don't expect a small, backward Indian town at the other end of the bus trip. Toluca (pop. 150,000) is the capital of the State of Mexico, and has been an important town since Aztec times. You enter town along a beautiful parkway.

The gigantic **Mercado Juárez,** at the edge of town on the highway to Mexico City, has both market buildings and open-air grounds. Shops in the buildings are open all week, but it's on Friday that the people from surrounding villages come and crowd the plaza. The bus from Mexico City pulls into a terminal right across the street from the Mercado Juárez. You'll recognize the market by the twin slender concrete slabs which tower above it to serve as a landmark.

Because of the natives' bargaining powers, a peaceful walk around the market is not an easy matter. Every time you pause to admire such unfamiliar sights as a boxful of chattering chickens, a two-foot-high pile of assorted shoelaces, or an array of framed saints' pictures, some man or young boy will accost you with cries of *"Serapes, rebozos, Señor, very cheap."* And sooner or later the heat and crowdedness of the market will begin to get you down; you will barely raise your head as the man with the pig under his arm or the woman with a turkey sticking its head from the back of her shawl brushes past.

Some sights will make you pause—a marimba band banging away cheerfully between the stalls, and a little, open-fronted bakery where chains of tortillas can be seen pouring off a conveyor belt into a basket.

Finding a place for lunch is never a problem in such a huge market, but if none of the little market eateries appeals to you, there is an alternative. Search the skyline for the red-and-yellow star-sign that identifies the local branch of VIPs (pronounced "beeps"), a clean, bright, and cheery American-style restaurant.

The Volcanoes

One of the nicest picnic spots in all of Mexico is the Ixta-Popo National Park, whose *raison d'être* is the volcanoes of **Popocatepetl** and **Ixtacchihuatl**. These snow-capped peaks are usually associated with the city of Puebla, a three-hour trip from Mexico City, but it is by no means necessary to go all the way to Puebla to see them.

Take Metro Line 1 east, in the direction of Zaragoza, to the San Lazaro stop. As you come to the surface, you'll see the green-domed **TAPO** ("Terminal de Autobuses de Pasajeros de Oriente"), Mexico City's eastern bus terminal. Walk along "Tunel 1," the corridor to the central domed area, and look for "Lineas Unidas–Cristobal Colón" buses to Amecameca and Popo Park. Buses leave every half hour, every day, on the two-hour trip.

The bus will take the Puebla road (Route 190) out of Mexico City, turning off to the right (Route 115) at the village of Chalco. A few miles farther on is Amecameca (pop. 22,000) from where the best view of the volcanoes can be obtained. Situated at a height of 7500 feet, Amecameca is a fresh, clear town, with a big square and a 300-year-old parish church. Behind it are the two lovely mountains, neither of which has erupted in this century.

About the best hotel in Amecameca is the very plain but clean **Hotel San Carlos,** right on the main square to the right of the church, at Plaza de la Constitución 10 (tel. 80344). A room with one double bed costs 300 pesos ($6); with twin beds, 350 pesos ($7). All rooms have baths and—so I'm told—hot water. The San Carlos's restaurant serves light meals.

Getting to Ixta-Popo National Park from Amecameca takes some doing. You can hitchhike, or try to catch one of the rickety old village buses which leaves from the main square—look for the *camioneta azul* (blue minibus) marked "San Pedro–Los Volcanes." Otherwise, to get to the mountain lodge at Tlamacas you'll have to hire a taxi for about 650 pesos ($13) one way. Check at the Hotel San Carlos for other passengers, and perhaps you'll be able to split the cost. Make a deal with the taxi driver to come pick you up at a later time as there's no telephone at the lodge; or you can take a chance and try to thumb a ride down the mountain, which is often easily done.

THE LODGE: The **Albergue Vicente Guerrero,** at Tlamacas (elev. 12,800 feet, 3900 meters), Parque Nacional Ixta-Popo, was opened in 1978. It's beautiful: an ultramodern mountain lodge done in native stone and natural wood, complete with bunk-rooms, showers, a cafeteria, and a restaurant. If you want to stay the night, especially on a weekend, it's best to call or drop by the Mexico City office of the lodge for a reservation: the address is Avenida Lázaro Cárdenas 661 (tel. 590-7694). A bunk with sheets, blankets, and pillow costs 200 pesos ($4).

Outside the Albergue is the snow-covered summit of Popocatepetl, 17,887 feet (5452 meters) at the rim. In the morning the clouds may drift away for an hour, yielding an incomparable closeup view. Across the valley, Popo's sister volcano, Ixtacchihuatl, may be exposed as well. When you see them gleaming in the morning sun, surrounded by the chilly morning air, you'll remember the moment for a lifetime.

THE TRAILS: Please take me in dead seriousness when I say that Popocatepetl is no mountain for rookie climbers, or for any expert climber who's not in top shape. Even at the lodge trail-head, the air is so thin that even walking makes a normal, healthy person dizzy—and the air's considerably thinner at 17,887 feet! And it's *cold* up here, even in the sweltering heat of summer. But if you're an expert climber, pack your down sleeping bag, pitons, and what-not, and check in at the rescue hut next to the lodge. You'll have to pass an equipment check, and sign your name in the hikers' register, before you set out. Maps of the various trails to the summit, showing the several huts and shelters, are on view in the rescue hut. The trek to the summit takes from 9 to 12 hours, depending on what shape you're in and which trail you choose. You must camp at the summit that night, and return the next day.

When you return to the lodge, if all the bunks are taken, no one will mind if you pitch your hiking tent in the pine grove just below the lodge.

Cuernavaca

Cuernavaca (elev. 5058 feet, pop. 360,000), capital of the State of Morelos, has been popular as a resort for people from Mexico City ever since Emperor Maximilian built a retreat here over a century ago. Mexicans say the town has a climate of "eternal spring," and on weekends the city is crowded with day-trippers from surrounding cities, especially from the capital. On weekends the roads between Mexico City and Cuernavaca are jammed, and so are restaurants and hotels in this city. Cuernavaca has a large American colony, consisting mostly of well-to-do retired people, plus students attending one of the myriad language and cultural institutes which crowd the city. Despite its reputation as an educational fount, Cuernavaca has in recent years lost much of the colonial charm it once had. The downtown area is not nearly so attractive as similar sections of cities such as San Luís Potosí, Veracruz, or even Puebla, and burgeoning industry—notably the CIVAC complex on the outskirts—has created pollution problems and tarnished Cuernavaca's image as a haven for clean air and the simple life of plain living and high thinking.

GETTING TO CUERNAVACA: The Mexico City–Cuernavaca train no longer carries passengers, so those without a private car have little choice: you go to Cuernavaca by bus. The Mexico City **Central de Autobuses del Sur**'s reason for being is the route Mexico City–Cuernavaca–Taxco–Acapulco–Zihuatanejo: 90% of the buses leaving that terminal ply this route, and they do it with great frequency, so you'll have little trouble getting a bus.

Several lines serve the city, including **Estrella de Oro** and **Lineas Unidas del Sur–Flecha Roja,** but the line with the most convenient downtown terminal in Cuernavaca is **Autobuses Pullman de Morelos.** When you arrive in Cuernavaca after the hour-long ride, you'll alight at the last stop (don't get off at the "La Selva" stop north of the city!), in the bus station at the corner of Abasolo and Netzahualcóyotl. Walk up the hill (north) on Netzahualcóyotl two blocks to Hidalgo, then turn right onto that street to reach the center of town. If you'd like to pick up some maps and brochures before you set out sightseeing, turn left onto Hidalgo and walk straight to the Jardín Borda. Just inside the entrance from the street is a small Tourist Information Office or Información Turística (tel. 21815).

Cuernavaca has two centrally located squares, the smaller and more formal of the two being the Jardín Juárez (sometimes called the Zócalo); the larger of the two being the Alameda, or Jardín de los Héroes, which is southeast of the Jardín Juárez.

WHAT TO DO: First sight to see here is the ancient **Cortes Palace,** just off the Alameda to the south across the traffic circle. Begun by Hernan Cortes in 1530, it was finished by the conquistador's son Martin, and later served as the legislative headquarters for the State of Morelos. It now houses the **Museo de Cuauhnahuac** (that's the original Aztec name for the town), open from 10:30 a.m. to 6 p.m. weekdays except Thursday, and 11:30 a.m. to 7 p.m. on Saturday and Sunday. Besides the historical exhibits, you should be sure to see the chamber where the state legislature met until only recently, presided over by a huge painting of Morelos. Also on the second floor, on an open loggia, are murals by Diego Rivera presented to the city by Dwight Morrow, former U.S. ambassador to Mexico. One panel is of Morelos, whimsically painted with Rivera's face, leering at Zapata directly opposite. Other panels are of Cortes extracting gold from the Indians, of the Spaniards crossing the *barranca* (ravine) on their arrival in Cuernavaca, using a bent tree for a bridge, and of the Aztecs in tiger and eagle masks doing battle with the armored Spaniards.

Cuernavaca offers excellent sport for the shopper. You'll have no problem finding things to buy. The main market is just to the right of Calle Guerrero, across the *barranca*. You'll find the best prices here, but bargaining is necessary.

The **Jardín Borda** (Borda Gardens), at Avenida Morelos and Avenida Hidalgo, used to be the summer retreat of one-time Emperor Maximilian and Empress Carlotta. The place was built by one José de la Borda, a Taxco silver magnate (see the next section in this chapter), in the mid-1700s, and later taken over by the Hapsburg couple. In recent times it had become pretty rundown, but now it's been fixed up and an admission charge has been tacked on to what, in its unredeemed state, was a free place to wander. Handicraft and art shops in the rooms off the entry court can be visited for free, but to get into the small preserve of the gardens proper costs 15 pesos (30¢) per person, 8 pesos (16¢) for students.

Since Borda started the trend, and Maximilian promoted it, many other well-to-do outsiders have moved to Cuernavaca in search of the perfect climate and a lavish garden. Cuernavaca thus became a "city of gardens," but virtually all of these are hidden away from the casual visitor behind high walls. What you're liable to see most of downtown is buses and people, although the two central parks have been nicely fixed up in recent years, and a few streets closed to vehicular traffic.

For a glimpse of what the "other" Cuernavaca is like, stroll down Morelos south of 20 de Noviembre, down the hill from the Jardín Borda. Ignore the thundering buses if you can, and peek through gates and doorways, and over walls, to get some idea of why the former Shah of Iran chose this town as his first home-away-from-home. Many estates on the outskirts are even more sumptuous—but even more inaccessible.

INCIDENTAL INTELLIGENCE: Now down to some serious business. There are a number of language schools in Cuernavaca which offer scheduled or private instruction as well as summer sessions at the university with college credits. For information on schools, schedules, and fees, drop in at the Tourist Office in the Jardín Borda.

The **National Institute of Fine Arts,** Degollado and Obregon, houses some interesting murals and paintings by Mexican painters. This is also a school of art and there are several rooms exhibiting some of the student art.

The **post office** is on the south end of the **Palacio de Gobierno,** which is just to the west of the Alameda Park.

FOR LUNCH: Because of the huge influx of visitors from out of town, Cuernavaca is well equipped with places to dine. Here are my favorites, starting with an elegant patio restaurant and ending with a little ma-and-pa eatery.

Cuernavaca can boast of many extremely elegant garden restaurants, but oftentimes these places will have such a steady stream of local, regular customers that they become virtual private clubs. Service to "nonmembers" from out of town suffers accordingly. But everyone is treated equally, and treated well, at **Lancers** (tel. 20132), Calle Dwight Morrow 13, near the corner with Comonfort. The restaurant and bar are ranged around a central garden plot of emerald grass and well-kept verdure, far (it seems) from the bus-choked streets nearby. Service is polished and pleasant, and prices are in the moderate-to-high range. Although steaks are the specialty, seafood and chicken are served as well. Start with sopa Lancers, made with garlic bread and cheese, and pass on to filet mignon cooked any way you like. Finish with pastry or a fancy dessert, and coffee, and the bill for one will be about 800 pesos ($16), tax and tip included. Add 125 pesos ($2.50) per drink or 500 pesos ($10) for a bottle of wine. Lancers is open from 1 p.m. to 1 a.m. seven days a week.

Very different in cuisine, atmosphere, and price is the **Restaurant Vienes,** at Lerdo de Tejada 4, near Comonfort. Open from 11 a.m. to 10 p.m., the Vienes tries hard for a Central European ambience, although it has the convenience of an English-speaking manager. You can order an excellent quiche with vegetable and salad (200 pesos, $4), or the chef's special, a "Farmer's Plate" consisting of pork ribs, roast veal, frankfurters, sauerkraut, and potatoes for 280 pesos ($5.60). Other plate dinners are between these two in price. Closed Tuesday.

Next door to Las Plazas, across from the Jardín Juárez, is the similarly named **Viena Cafeteria,** Guerrero 104, whose specialty —besides being an excellent spot from which to people-watch— is its excellent pastries and ice cream. Coffee (the cappuccino here is reputedly the best in town), and ice cream or pastries, will run about 40 to 70 pesos (80¢ to $1.40); club sandwiches or hot and cold plates sufficient for a light lunch are priced from 100 to 175 pesos ($2 to $3.50).

A few doors down from the Viena Cafeteria is **La Parroquia,** off the Jardín Juárez, at Guerrero 102. They have an open-air restaurant as well as a few outdoor café tables. This place does a teeming business, partly because of its great location right off the jardín and partly because they have fairly reasonable prices for Cuernavaca. Four quesadillas con pollo (with chicken) go for 75 pesos ($1.50), or you can just sip a beer for 28 pesos (56¢).

Rosticeria Cuernavaca, Matamoros 100, on Jardín Juárez is a cheerful place, with green-checked tablecloths. As it's open from 8 a.m. to midnight daily, you can have breakfast here. Try an omelet á la francesa for 65 pesos ($1.30). Add juice and café con leche for a 125-peso ($2.50) total. Later on, chicken, cheese, and ham enchiladas cost 95 pesos ($1.90).

There are two restaurants right next to each other at no. 2 Galeana, corner of Rayón: **La Cueva** and **El Portal.** I put them together because there seems to be stiff competition between them with each other vying daily to offer the lower prices.

Both are clean with friendly service and good food. They both offer four-course *comidas* between 90 and 130 pesos ($1.80 to $2.60) which include soup, rice, fish or meat filet, dessert, and coffee. They also have à la carte items which range from 60 to 150 pesos ($1.20 to $3). The *comida* menus are written on blackboards in front of the restaurant, so your best bet is to check to see which menu and which price agrees with you.

Going down the price scale a bit, there are several hole-in-the-wall eateries which offer 50-peso ($1) *comidas,* consisting of four courses, which are not as fancy as you'll get elsewhere (for a higher price) but substantial. There are two such on Aragon y Leon between Morelos and Matamoros: **Mary** and **San Miguel,** which served soup, omelet, frijoles, and salad the last time I was there for a mere 70 pesos ($1.40).

CUERNAVACA NIGHTLIFE: This town has a number of cafés right off the Jardín Juárez where people gather to sip coffee or drinks till the wee hours of the morning. The best of the cafés are **La Parroquia** and the **Cafeteria Viena,** previously mentioned in the restaurant section. There are band concerts in the Zócalo (Jardín Juárez) on Thursday and Sunday evenings.

Another branch of the Carlos Anderson chain (Anderson's Bar & Grill in Mexico City, Carlos 'n Charlie's in Acapulco) is **Harry's Bar,** Gutenberg 3 (tel. 27679). Their with-it atmosphere includes stereo, long-haired waiters, and Mexican revolutionary posters. Although they serve full dinners here, I'd recommend that you go for drinks (60 to 130 pesos, $1.20 to $2.60). Open Tuesday to Thursday from 6 p.m. to 1 a.m., on Friday and Saturday from 1:30 p.m. to 1:30 a.m., and on Sunday from 1:30 p.m. to midnight.

ONWARD (AND BACKWARD) FROM CUERNAVACA: Those returning to Mexico City from Cuernavaca need only make their way back to the terminal of **Autobuses Pullman de Morelos.** But to catch a bus onward to Taxco or Acapulco, head for the terminal of **Autobuses Estrella de Oro** (first class, tel. 23035) at Morelos 900; or **Autobuses Unidas del Sur–Flecha Roja** (tel. 20066) at Morelos 503.

Taxco

Taxco (pronounced "TAHS-ko"; elev. 5850 feet, pop. 70,000), famous for its silver, sits on a hill among hills, and almost everywhere you walk in the city there are fantastic views.

The famous **Church of Santa Prisca,** with its twin spires (recently repointed and repaired), was built by a French miner, José de la Borda, who made a packet in the 18th century. It is illuminated at night.

Taxco's renowned silver mines, first worked in the time of Cortes four centuries ago, were revived, for all practical purposes, by an American, William Spratling, about 30 years ago. Today, its fame rests more on the 180 silver shops, most of them little one-man factories, which line the cobbled streets all the way up into the hills. It is no place to come for bargains, with some silver prices actually higher than in Mexico City because of the magnitude of the tourist trade. In some cases, though, the bracelets and other items are heavier and this accounts for the difference in price.

You can get the idea of what Taxco's like by spending an afternoon there, but there's much more to this picturesque town than just the zócalo and the shops surrounding it. You'll have to stay overnight if you want more time to climb up and down its steep streets, discovering little plazas and fine churches.

GETTING TO TAXCO: The ride from Mexico City takes about 3½ hours, with a toll road at each side of Cuernavaca, the halfway point. From Cuernavaca, the trip takes less than two hours.

By Bus: Estrella de Oro (Calz. de Tlalpan 2205, at the Central de Autobuses del Sur in Mexico City—Metro Taxqueña—tel. 549-8520) has five buses a day to Taxco, both first class and deluxe. **Lineas Unidas del Sur–Flecha Roja** also has several buses a day from the Central de Autobuses del Sur, but is a second choice to Estrella de Oro. From Cuernavaca you can catch an Estrella de Oro bus as it passes through, if there are seats. It is also possible to stop in Taxco on your way back from Acapulco; two buses per day will drop you in Taxco.

GETTING AROUND TAXCO: The main part of town stretches up the hillside from the main highway, and although it's a steep walk it's not a particularly long one. But you don't have to walk: vehicles make the circuit through the town, up the hill and down, picking up and dropping passengers along the route. There are *burritos* ("Servicio Urbano"), VW minibuses which run the route, and small city buses as well. Both run from about 7 a.m. until 9 p.m.

Beware of self-appointed guides, who will undoubtedly approach you in the zócalo and offer their services—they get a cut (up to 25%) of all you buy in the shops they take you to. Should you want a guide, however, ask to see his Departamento de Turismo credentials. Call 732/205-79 or go to the Department of Tourism office on the highway at the north end of town to engage a licensed guide (at about 200 to 300 pesos—$4 to $6— per hour).

WHERE TO STAY: Although Taxco can be visited in a day's excursion from Mexico City, you may want to stay the night in order to take in more of this beautiful town's charm. Those heading on to Acapulco can use Taxco as an overnight stop— indeed, it's the prettiest and most interesting town along the Mexico City–Acapulco road.

For location, luxury, and moderate price, you can hardly do better than the **Hotel Rancho Taxco Victoria** (tel. 732/210-14 or 200-04). Perched on the hillside above the center of the town, the Victoria provides breathtaking views while still being walking distance from the main plaza. It's on a cobbled, winding street named Calle Carlos J. Nibbi, at no. 14—to find it, look for the street climbing steeply uphill out of the Plazuela de San Juan.

The Victoria's 150 rooms can be rented with or without three meals a day in most seasons. Base price is 885 pesos ($17.70) single, 1015 pesos ($20.30) double, without meals; if you want three meals a day, you'll pay 1820 pesos ($36.40) single, 2860 pesos ($57.20) double. Some rooms have fine views, but if you don't get one of these, just spend your time on the hotel's various patios and terraces, or by the pool, or in the restaurant, taking in the magnificent view. The Victoria's Spanish colonial decor, festooned with plants and founded on quaint cobbled paths, fits in well with Taxco's scenery.

Many of the most comfortable places to stay are right on the main highway through town, Hwy. 95, which has the street name here of Avenida Presidente John F. Kennedy. For instance, the **Hotel de la Borda** (tel. 732/200-25) was one of the first hostelries to be built outside the center of town. The emphasis is on colonial style in this eminently colonial town, with many of the 150 guest rooms having balconies or terraces. Modern comforts include a swimming pool, and a restaurant/bar with live entertainment most evenings. Prices for the rooms, *three meals included,* are 3000 to 3300 pesos ($60 to $66) single, 3570 to 3760 pesos ($71.40 to $75.20) double. Subtract 995 pesos ($19.90) per person if you don't want the meals.

Taxco is so popular with sightseers that it now has its own **Holiday Inn** (tel. 732/213-00), which is the most luxurious place in town. The inn overlooks the rocky hills and the town itself and has one of the best views (in a town of fantastic views), plus such luxury accoutrements as a golf course, heated pool, tennis courts, and even a riding stable. All rooms are air-conditioned and equipped with televisions, and some rooms have little servi-bars filled with beverages. The location is somewhat remote—three miles from town up a very steep road—but an aerial tramway glides between the hotel and the main highway. Rates at the Holiday Inn are quoted in U.S. dollars: $63 single, $67 double. Have reservations if you plan to arrive on a weekend.

A smaller hotel on the outskirts (but still not small, really—almost 100 rooms and a fairly lavish layout) is the **Posada de la Mision** (tel. 732/200-63), on Hwy. 95. Here the rooms are again colonial, and come to you for 1145 pesos ($22.90) for single, 1430 pesos ($28.60) double, but for this fairly high price you get a restaurant and bar, a tennis court, a heated swimming pool, servi-bar refrigerators in each room, and a play area for the kids.

Although not often as luxurious and spacious as some of the hotels on Hwy. 95, the hotels in the center of Taxco offer the distinct advantage of having the cobbled streets and silver shops of Taxco right outside their front doors. Prices are generally lower for these "downtown" hotels.

One of the older and nicer hotels in town is the **Hotel Santa Prisca** (tel. 732/200-80) in Plazuela de San Juan. There are 59 cozy, comfortable rooms with couch, tile floors, wood beams, and a colonial atmosphere. There are two lush patios with fountains, and a lovely dining room done in mustard and blue. They offer the American Plan (three meals) with singles at 948 pesos ($18.96), doubles at 1595 pesos ($31.90); the Modified American Plan (two meals) costs singles 756 pesos ($15.12) and doubles 1212 pesos ($24.24); and rooms without meals are 495 pesos ($9.90) single, 727 pesos ($14.54) double. An excellent choice.

On a quiet side street just down the hill from the zócalo are two charming hotels with very reasonable rates. The **Posada de Los Castillo** (tel. 732/213-96), at Juan Ruíz de Alarcon 7, is a beautiful colonial mansion completely restored in 1980. Boasting lots and lots of plants (some even in planters in the bathrooms), its "new colonial" rooms surround a courtyard on four levels—like a 17th-century Hyatt Regency, let's say. All 15 rooms are small, but equipped with private baths, some with tubs. One person pays 435 to 558 pesos ($8.70 to $11.16); two pay 576 to 678 pesos ($11.52 to $13.56), whether in one bed or two.

Right across the street from Los Castillo is its more luxurious and expensive sister hotel, the **Hotel Los Arcos** (tel. 732/218-36), Juan Ruíz de Alarcon 12. Larger and more sumptuously fitted out, Los Arcos is in fact a converted monastery (1620), and the monks never had it this good: swimming pool (small but nice), a courtyard restaurant-bar, and a maze of little courts and passages hiding 28 very comfortable rooms-with-bath. Prices are 630 pesos ($12.60) single, 770 pesos ($15.40) double, 910 pesos ($18.20) triple. Whichever of these two hotels you pick, you'll be immersed in colonial charm, blissful quiet, and you'll still be only a five-minute walk from the zócalo.

Best known of the inexpensive hotels (there aren't many) is the **Hotel Melendez,** Cuauhtemoc 6 (tel. 732/200-06), which has 42 rooms with baths, all renting at 370 pesos ($7.40) single, 510 to 595 pesos ($10.20 to $11.90) double. It's a nice hotel just off the zócalo, and its airy bedrooms have blue-tiled walls and ornate glass and metalwork doors on the bathrooms. Several have terrific views. The hotel's restaurant has fairly reasonable prices—a complete dinner for 195 pesos ($3.90), or a breakfast of fruit, soft boiled eggs, coffee, and toast for about 150 pesos ($3).

The **Hotel Jardín,** Celso Munoz 2 (tel. 732/200-27), on the north side of Santa Prisca church just off the main square, is also a fine choice. The hotel is marked only by a small sign above the door, and very much resembles a European pension. It's surprisingly peaceful inside, with a fine view of the mountains from the flower-filled balcony patio. Clean, large rooms rent for 195 pesos ($3.90) per person, each of the seven rooms having a private bathroom.

The **Hotel Agua Escondida,** Spratling 4 (tel. 732/207-26 or 207-36), on one corner of the zócalo, is an exceptionally clean and well-tended establishment. Its 40 rooms are provided with extra touches such as vases of fresh flowers and bottles of mineral water at each bedside. Prices are good: 280 to 390 pesos ($5.60 to $7.80) single, 490 pesos ($9.80) double. An extra bed costs 90 pesos ($1.80) in either section.

WHERE TO EAT: Taxco gets a lot of people down from the capital for the day, or passing through on their way to Acapulco, and so there are a lot of restaurants to fill the demand for lunch.

But the demand is so great that prices are high for what you get. If you only need a snack, try this: in the building called El Patio de las Artesanías you'll find a small pizza parlor called the **Pizzaria Dama.** Walk through the courtyard and to the left. The small outdoor tables enjoy a fine Taxco view, plus lots of peace and quiet. The medium-size pizza will feed two people, if you're not terribly hungry, for 160 to 225 pesos ($3.20 to $4.50). A *grande* (large) will feed two hungry souls for 210 to 260 pesos ($4.20 to $5.20). Beer and soft drinks are served. For a soft drink that's not cloyingly sweet, order *manzanita,* a carbonated apple soda pop.

Perhaps the best *comida* bargain these days is the 195-peso ($3.90) lunch at the **Hotel Melendez,** served in an attractive tiled dining room overlooking the town and the valley. You ladle the soup from the tureen yourself (no need to skimp!). There follows rice and vegetables, a meat-and-vegetable plate, melon or pudding, and coffee or tea. For Taxco, you get your money's worth here.

Restaurant Arnoldo's overlooks the main square (it's directly across the square from the Santa Prisca church, but you enter by a little side street which runs around back of the restaurant), and offers a 180-peso ($3.60) *comida* as well as à la carte items like a hamburger, roast chicken, or a pork chop for 100 to 140 pesos ($2 to $2.80), other choices for slightly more. The señora who runs it is interested in pleasing her customers and will make sure everything is up to expectations.

You'll find atmosphere at **Restaurant de la Rosa,** Calle Bailar, around the corner from the Hotel Agua Escondida, just off the zócalo, where there are open arches, flagstone floors and stone walls, hand-carved wooden tables with colorful covers and napkins, all lit by wrought-iron lamps. The best time to be here is on Sunday afternoon when there's music from 1:30 to 4. The 190-peso ($3.80) *comida* is available daily, and may consist of, for instance, a choice of mushroom or asparagus soup, broiled filet mignon, T-bone steak, broiled pork chops, or a Mexican plate, lemon cream pie or peaches in cream, coffee or tea. A full breakfast costs 98 pesos ($1.96). Open 8 a.m. to 11 p.m. daily.

Hotel de la Borda, out on the highway but reachable by burrito, or a 65-peso ($1.30) taxi ride, has exceptionally good food, worthy of the 650-peso ($13) price for lunch or dinner. I suggest doing it for dinner, then staying for the show and making an evening of it.

On the attractive Plazuela de San Juan (the one with the

fountain) you'll spot the **Restaurante Ethel.** A family-run place, it's kept clean and tidy, with cloths on the tables and a hometown atmosphere. The hearty daily *comida corrida* consists of soup or pasta, meat (perhaps a small steak), dessert, and coffee for 170 pesos ($3.40), tax and tip included. And if that modest amount seems like too much, you should check out the **Restaurante Santa Fe,** just down the street from the Ethel, and even less expensive.

Carlos Anderson's Taxco eatery is called **Sr. Costilla's** (that's "Mr. Ribs"), on the upper floor of the Patio de las Artesanías facing the zócalo. As at the Mexico City branch (Anderson's Bar & Grill) and the one in Acapulco (Carlos 'n Charlie's), you're greeted upon entering by the completely unexpected: a marvelous antique jukebox, a fake skeleton, and a ceiling festooned with all sorts of flotsam and jetsam. A few tiny balconies hold a few even tinier tables with views of the square and the Santa Prisca church, but if you don't happen to get one of these, the room abounds with places to sit. The menu is vintage Anderson, with a large selection of everything: for soup, a small steak, dessert, and coffee, expect to pay about 630 pesos ($12.60) per person.

Busiest restaurant in town the last time I visited was the **Cielito Lindo,** on the main plaza at the corner near where the Calle San Agustín begins. The tables clad in white were packed on this weekend afternoon, and plates of food were disappearing as fast as the waiters could bring them. For an à la carte feast of soup, roast chicken (with two vegetables), pineapple pie, and coffee, tax, and tip, expect to pay 350 pesos ($7).

DAYTIME ACTIVITIES: In a word—shopping! When you're tired of that, perhaps you'd like a snoop through some colonial houses. **Casa de las Lagrimas** (House of Tears), also known as Casa Figueroa, above the zócalo, has been turned into a private art gallery and charges 5 pesos for a look around. Next door, incidentally, is the local art school.

Or you might sneak in for a look at Juan O'Gorman's mural beside the swimming pool at the **Hotel Posada de la Mision** (on the highway, go via burrito).

Taxco now has a fine little museum, called the **Museo Guillermo Spratling,** almost directly behind the Santa Prisca church (open every day but Monday from 10 a.m. to 2 p.m. and 3 to 6 p.m.; admission 10 pesos, 20¢). Don't write it off. The building and displays are of the high quality that's normal in Mexico. The entrance floor and the one above display a good collection of pre-Columbian statues and implements in clay, stone, and jade; the lower floor has a display on the history of Taxco. Documents, clippings, letters, engravings, and photographs give you an idea what it was like a century or two ago in this mountain mining town: miners' implements, helmets, lanterns, and such add a touch of realism to the display. Look for the samples of silver ore, Taxco's *raison d'être.* A plaque (in Spanish) explains that most of the collection and the funds for the museum came from William Spratling, an American born in 1900 who studied architecture in the U.S., later settled in Taxco, and organized the first workshops to turn out high-quality silver jewelry. From this first effort in 1931 the town's reputation as a center of artistic silver work grew to what it is today. In a real sense, Spratling "put Taxco on the map." He died in 1967 in a car accident.

After your visit to the museum, stroll along Ruíz de Alarcon street right near the museum, looking for the richly decorated facade of the **Von Humboldt House.** The renowned German scientist and explorer Baron Alexander von Humboldt (1769–1859) visited Taxco and stayed in this beautiful house in 1803. Besides the beauty of the house, and the lingering fame of its illustrious guest, you're here to see the **Exposición Nacional de Platería.** A collection of fine craft items, particularly silverwork, fills the main hall. Everything you see is for sale.

After shopping, a walk around town, and a visit to the museum, drag yourself back to the zócalo and up the flight of cobbled steps lined with geraniums to **Paco's Bar,** overlooking the zócalo. Drinks are anywhere from 24 pesos (48¢—soft drinks), through beer at 30 to 50 pesos (60¢ to $1) and rum or tequila at 75 pesos ($1.50), to more sophisticated concoctions costing up to 100 pesos ($2). The celebrated "Berta," which originated across the square in another bar (see below under "Nightlife"), is only 50 pesos ($1) here. In the summer a trio plays at Paco's from 5 to 9 p.m.

The Flower Festival

In 1978, Taxco's city fathers held the first annual **Festival de la Flor en Taxco** at the end of May and beginning of June. This gala event packed the city's hotels and restaurants, and there was not a parking spot to be had for miles. The president of the republic himself opened the festival, which included art exhibits, concerts and performances, discussions and conferences. The

·date of the festival's principal activity, May 30, was the bicentennial of the death of Taxco's first silver king, José de la Borda (he died in 1778), and the festival will no doubt center on this date in years to come. At festival time, have an ironclad hotel reservation, or plan to come just for the day.

TAXCO NIGHTLIFE: Possibly the pleasantest place from which to view Taxco at night is the terrace of the luxurious **Hotel de la Borda,** off Hwy. 95, at the entrance to town (attainable before 10 p.m. by burrito). This is one of those hotels with heated swimming pool, illuminated at night with colored lights set into the glass-covered patio floor for dancing. La Borda's nightclub, El Bocanal, operates on a two-drink minimum (most 60 to 150 pesos, $1.20 to $3), features a marimba orchestra from 6:30 to 11 p.m., and a show, part of which is usually a cockfight exhibition, and which, in season, features flamenco dancing.

Completely different in tone is **Berta's,** right next to the Santa Prisca church. Open since the early 1930s by a lady named Berta who made her fame on a drink of the same name (tequila, soda, lime, and sugar syrup), Berta's is traditionally the gathering place of the local gentry. Spurs and old swords decorate the walls, a saddle is casually slung over the balustrade of the stairs leading to the second-floor room where tin masks leer from the walls. A Berta costs 60 pesos ($1.20), rum the same, scotch 130 pesos ($2.60), and beer 45 to 60 pesos (90¢ to $1.20). Open 9 a.m. to around midnight.

On the road again after your Taxco sojourn, your next stop to the south is the one with that magic name among resorts: Acapulco.

Chapter IX

INTRODUCING ACAPULCO

EVERY FIRST-TIME VISITOR to Acapulco finds a unique place, for in a very real way Acapulco is what you make of it. The breathtaking sweep of bay, the vivid blue of the water, the padded and gleaming luxury of the hotels, the pumped-up decibel levels in the discos are all there waiting to be enjoyed, but it takes the initiative and interest of the visitor to bring them to life. This is the sort of place in which to let yourself go lively, not let yourself go slack.

This is all the more true as Acapulco is not simply a resort town, but an important port and commercial city of almost three-quarters of a million souls. Unlike shiny new megadevelopments like Cancún and Ixtapa, Acapulco has lots of "real life": Lions Clubs, banks and offices, small factories and workshops, middle-class neighborhoods and slums. Manicured golf courses alternate with the unformed rubble of a construction site; itinerant peddlers are right outside the doors of the luxury hotel towers. With an active outlook and the determination to be adventurous, Acapulco is a real Mexican microcosmos, rather than just a playground for Beautiful People and jet-set types.

And it's not just foreigners who enjoy the pleasures of this widely acclaimed resort: Mexicans by the thousands flock here during vacation times for swimming, sunning, and evenings on the town. In fact, you're more likely to make some interesting Mexican friends than you are to cross paths with the rich, famous, and powerful headline-makers, most of whom rarely set foot outside their private compounds or the drawing rooms of a very exclusive society. The real Acapulco belongs not to them, but to you. Whatever you do, try not to arrive with preconceived notions bred of publicity hype or society-column gossip which can keep you busy hunting for an imaginary Acapulco while the real one awaits your discovery at every moment and around every corner.

Part of the real Acapulco, it must be admitted, is overpriced and underserviced, a classic case of "resort syndrome." Don't be surprised to find service slow and indifferent or to encounter such dizzying prices as 35 pesos (70¢) for a small bottle of plain drinking water. Sometime in your trip you're going to get the feeling that the natives see you as the possessor of boundless money and patience, and that you're in Acapulco for their benefit, rather than vice versa. Usually, all you have to do in order to shrug off such disappointment is to trot down to the beach or stretch out by the pool. There's nothing like surf and sun to smooth ruffled nerves.

The city fathers are taking steps to polish up Acapulco's image, tarnished in recent years by rubbish in streets and streams, by beach peddlers who never let you alone, and by bad service and high prices. They're working hard, and results are beginning to show.

Acapulco's climate deserves a note. This city has the dubious distinction of being Mexico's rainiest place. The rainy season starts in late May or early June, and the town can be pretty wet just after it starts, with dark clouds and blustery storms several times a week. July and August are hot and muggy, but there is less rain than at the onslaught of the rains, and most days are sunny. September and October see the coming of more rain, up to the beginning of the dry season. From mid-November through mid-May there is little rain, less humidity, more moderate temperatures, and generally perfect weather for water sports. For obvious reasons, winter is the busy season here, when reservations get scarcer, hotel prices rise, and rental cars get booked up in advance. The Christmas/New Year's holiday is always very busy, and in general the month of February, too. While an off-season (that is, summer) Acapulco vacation can be very enjoyable, there's nothing to beat flying down to Acapulco to escape the northern cold of winter.

GETTING TO ACAPULCO: This is an easy task because Acapulco is well served by public transportation. What follows is a brief listing of the major means of conveyance.

By Bus

Remember that buses from Mexico City to Acapulco leave from the Terminal Central de Autobuses del Sur (Metro: Taxqueña). The trip to Acapulco takes about seven hours.

Estrella de Oro (tel. 905/549-8520) has almost hourly buses from Mexico City to Acapulco, but you should definitely reserve your seat a few days in advance. Deluxe service costs a few pesos more than express service; the difference is a larger bus of equal comfort. I suggest you pick your bus by departure time (that most convenient for you) and ignore the deluxe or express part of it. All the buses are air-conditioned and have toilets.

Lineas Unidas del Sur–Flecha Roja also runs frequent buses to Acapulco from the Central del Sur, but their equipment is not generally up to the same standards as that of Estrella de Oro.

By Air

Acapulco has a *very* busy airport, and there are direct flights between this city and Los Angeles (daily), Atlanta (Eastern Airlines, two per weekend), Chicago (two a day), Dallas/Fort Worth (two a day), New York (two a day), and Guadalajara (daily). All these flights offer special low excursion rates. Operators are AeroMéxico, Mexicana, American Airlines, Eastern Airlines, and Western Airlines. There are a dozen flights daily to Mexico City, mostly by AeroMéxico, a few by Mexicana. By the way, Taxco has no airport, so you can't fly to or from that town.

THE LAYOUT: Acapulco Bay, shaped roughly like the cap of a mushroom, has got to be one of the world's best for resort activities. Protected by Punta Bruja to the southeast and La Roqueta Island to the southwest, the surf is kept from pounding the beach in towering walls, but is still great enough to make swimming interesting and challenging. North of the mushroom cap of the bay are mountains, past which lies the Mexican highland. The town of Acapulco started life as a fishing village and port with docks in the excellent natural harbor formed by the foothills and a peninsula which hooks around to shelter the westernmost portion of the bay. The center of town is the main square, or zócalo, with its regulation church, benches, and trees —a pretty spot. Around this are the main shopping streets and streets lined with little hotels and restaurants, banks and businesses, garages and light industry. The peninsula, due south of

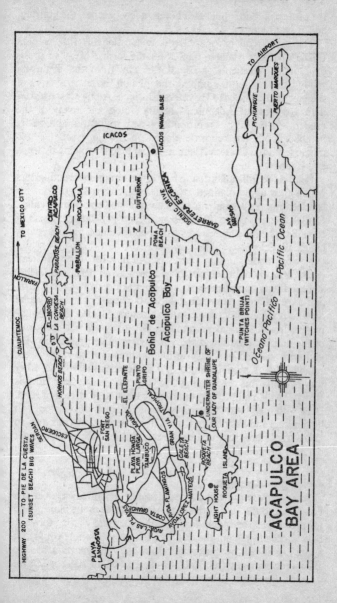

the center, is residential, with hotels, a few beaches, the bullring, and private houses.

The main road in Acapulco is unquestionably the **Avenida Costera Miguel Aleman,** named for the former Mexican president. This "corniche" goes all the way from the peninsula around the bay until, climbing the hills on the eastern shore of the bay, it becomes the Carretera Escenica. Along Costera Aleman are most of Acapulco's luxury hotels and many of the moderately priced ones. Nowadays, new residential and resort neighborhoods are being developed on the slopes of the hills inland from the Costera Aleman—Acapulco is growing by leaps and bounds.

Behind the hills inland, north of town, are the poorer quarters which grew up, unplanned, over the years. The city government is relocating these residents to a new, planned community called Ciudad Renacimiento ("Renaissance City") on flat land north of the hills. The hills themselves will soon become a national park, called El Veladero.

A word about finding addresses: As in most other Mexican cities, little thought seems to have been given here to a logical street naming and numbering system; the streets twist and turn, and have different names on different portions or the same name on totally different streets. On the Costera Aleman, each building is supposed to have a number, but many are not conscious of the number, and few display it anyway. I've tried to provide you with specific and easy-to-follow directions to each of the establishments recommended, but sometimes there is no other way of doing this than saying "on Costera Aleman near Hornos Beach," which admittedly takes in a rather large stretch of road. Bear with me. Soon the various locations along the Costera will be familiar and easy to find. And if you set out on your own to find a friend or a rumored new restaurant or club, be sure to get *detailed* instructions before you set out.

Arriving in Acapulco

Acapulco's airport is a good distance out of town, over the hills lying to the east of the bay. After you leave the plane, head for the baggage area, but don't just hang around waiting for your bags. Instead, step out the exit door to the curb, where you'll find a desk manned by personnel from the **Transportaciónes de Pasajeros company** (tel. 748/267-00, -01, -02, or 204-16, 222-75, 213-36). Buy your ticket and reserve your seat into town while the rest of the planeload is standing around waiting for the baggage to arrive. The exact price of your ticket will depend on where your hotel is—they operate on a zone system—but it should be around 300 pesos ($6), *round trip*. For your return to the airport at the end of your stay, call one of the numbers listed above at least a day (24 hours) in advance of your departure, and make a reservation for a seat back to the airport. The bus, minibus, or car (depending on demand) will pick you up about 90 minutes (domestic flights) or 120 minutes (flights to other countries) before your flight's departure time, and whisk you back to the airport.

As you head into town, the airport bus will take you over the hills, through the Hotel Las Brisas complex, and along the Costera Aleman passing virtually every one of the major hotels, making dropoff a matter of signaling the driver.

Arriving by bus from Taxco or Mexico City, you come past the new development called Renaissance City, through the seamier parts of town to the north of the hills ringing the bay, but then rise to a pass in these hills for a glorious change from squalor to magnificence. The bus then descends the hills to the station: in the case of Lineas Unidas del Sur–Flecha Roja, the bus station is in the market area only about six blocks from the zócalo; the Estrella de Oro bus station, however, is at Avenida Cuauhtemoc 1490. Cuauhtemoc is the major artery inland from and roughly parallel to the Costera Aleman. A taxi from the bus station of the Estrella de Oro line to the zócalo will cost about 75 pesos ($1.25); to any of the larger hotels, about the same amount. Local buses pass the terminal in both directions, and are a very inexpensive way of getting to your hotel.

Important Note: Acapulco's master development plan calls for construction of a brand-new bus station for intercity buses near Renaissance City (Ciudad Renacimiento) on the north side of the hills. It may be completed by the time you read this. At the new station, switch to a city bus for the ride downtown, or take a cab.

Public Transportation

Acapulco's city buses are sometimes the modern and comfortable behemoths which ply the streets of Mexico City, and other times they're well-used and fairly battered old Fords and Chevies, often pretty crowded, but dependable and very, very cheap.

You might just want to resort to the buses when the taxi drivers, always ready to haggle so it seems, start to get you down.

Two major lines will provide for most of your needs. From the zócalo, buses go southwest to Caleta and Caletilla beaches, and bear signs reading "Caleta Directo" and "Caleta Flamingos," this latter going via the "back" road of Avenida de los Flamingos. Going east from the zócalo, buses fill up by the moviehouse called Cine Río and go all the way to the eastern end of the Costera Aleman, where it meets the Mexican naval base, "La Base." Other buses, less frequent, make the run to Puerto Marqués—which is even farther east on the way to the airport. Finally, city buses bounce and rumble along the bumpy road over the hills west of town to the peninsula called La Pie de la Cuesta. These buses fill up next to the post office ("Correos") near the zócalo.

Taxis

Taxis are easy to find, with ranks near the zócalo, the parking lot at La Quebrada next to where the high divers do their thing, and throughout the town next to every major hotel. Prices are fixed and printed on an official card by the city government (there are no meters in the cabs). Normal rides in and around the center of town cost 65 to 95 pesos ($1.30 to $1.90), with longer journeys—say, from the zócalo to the Diana Circle, halfway around the bay—being proportionately more expensive. Always ask the fare *before you get into the cab*, and if you're in doubt, ask the dispatcher in the booth (if there is one) to show you the price list. Any trouble with taxis should be reported to the Tourism Office on Hornos Beach (tel. 748/221-70).

Car Rentals

Although there's not a lot of need for a rental car in Acapulco, you may find one will come in handy in your daily scooting around from beach to beach as this resort is so long and strung out. Competition is fierce, with virtually everyone, including each hotel and travel agency, ready to rent you a standard car, or more often a Jeep or Volkswagen Safari (sometimes called "The Thing" in the U.S. and Canada). Because the climate is so mild and the distances so short (I doubt you plan to drive to Mexico City), a Jeep or Safari will do fine. See Chapter XIV, "Travel Tips," for full details on renting a car.

Those planning to come down to Acapulco in the press of the

winter season, particularly in February, would do well to reserve a car in advance through one of the big international car-rental companies.

Tourism Information

The city, the State of Guerrero, and the national tourism organization are all represented through the Tourism Information Office on Costera Aleman at Hornos Beach (tel. 748/221-70). Drop in or call them for information on things to see and do, or complaints about goods or services. They're open Monday through Friday from 9 a.m. to 8 p.m., on Saturday and Sunday from 10 a.m. to 5 p.m.

Arrival matters aside, now that you're here you're ready to seek out a place to stay. Acapulco has everything from incredibly sumptuous to the unbelievably cheap.

The Ballet Folklorico

Chapter X

WHERE TO STAY IN ACAPULCO

FEW PEOPLE can comprehend the truly amazing range of hotel prices and accommodations available to a vacationer in this world-famous resort town. Depending on what you are willing to pay, you can bask in the sun by your own *private* swimming pool, while a multilingual waiter brings you a cool drink to help you pass the time as you survey the blue swath of Acapulco Bay; or, for the price of what one day in such a sybaritic situation costs, two people can stay at a modest Acapulco hotel just minutes from the famous beaches for over two weeks. It all depends on your style and your vacation budget, and on the length of time you intend to stay. It is certainly true to say that almost everyone can afford an Acapulco vacation of one style or another.

In making arrangements, remember that a travel agent will be able and willing to help you with reservations at any of the luxury or moderately priced hotels mentioned below, at no additional cost to you. As for the budget hotels, you can write ahead, or take pot luck on your arrival, in which case it's best to plan to arrive as early in the day as possible in order to get the first chance at a vacancy. Most of the year, budget rooms are fairly easily available in Acapulco, especially if you arrive on a weekday.

Rooms prices quoted below are for the *entire room*, and not for each person, unless otherwise indicated. The 10% IVA tax has been added to the room rates given here.

Acapulco's Luxury Hotels
(doubles $60 to $150 summer, $112 to $330 winter)

The row of gigantic hotels along the northern shore of Acapulco Bay has been photographed over and over for travel bro-

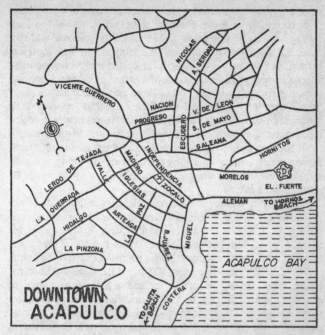

DOWNTOWN ACAPULCO

chures and posters, and at dusk as the lights twinkle on, these giants certainly do offer a romantic vista. A good number of the big hotels require that you purchase breakfast and dinner with your room during the busy winter season (usually mid-December through mid-April), and, while you'd have to pay to eat anyway, you could save some money dining in more modest restaurants than the hotels', if they allowed it. The hotels which don't require "MAP" (Modified American Plan," or the obligatory purchase of breakfast and dinner) have prices just as high as if the meals were included.

If you can plan your vacation in summer, you'll save a bundle as room prices are cut in half, and no meals need be purchased unless you choose to do so. Here, then, are descriptions of Acapulco's delights.

Hotel Las Brisas, Carretera Escenica, Las Brisas (tel. 748/415-80). Doubtless the ultimate hostelry for an Acapulco vacation is the fabulous Hotel Las Brisas, in Guitarron up on the hillside overlooking the bay. Although its location on the airport road south-east of the bay means that Las Brias is a long way from the center of town, guests at this posh resort tend to find that an advantage rather than a drawback. The reason is that the hotel is a community unto itself: the "rooms" are like separate little villas built into a terraced hillside, and each is luxuriously appointed and equipped, even to the extent of having a private (or semiprivate) swimming pool. From poolside, there's a panoramic view of the bay. All in all there are 250 "rooms," 200 swimming pools, new condominium units, tennis courts, a cocktail lounge, a restaurant, a travel agency, and a gas station.

Should you tire of your private pool and get used to the fresh flowers which are floated in it by the staff every morning, you can wander down to the private beach club for a swim or some snorkeling or diving.

Prices for the spectacle (and wait till you see the lights of all Acapulco twinkling across the bay!) depend on whether you want a room with a private swimming pool, or are content to share a pool with another room. Winter rates (November through April) are as follows: single rooms, 6750 to 8750 pesos ($135 to $175); double rooms, 7250 to 11,250 pesos ($145 to $225). Note that these prices include a $10-per-day service charge in lieu of all tips, and 10% tax. In summer, prices are about 35% lower. Remember that two children can stay in their parents' room free of charge. A travel agent will have all the details, or call Westin Hotels toll free from the U.S. at 800/228-3000; from Canada, 800/261-8383.

Acapulco Princess (tel. 748/431-00) and **Pierre Marqués Princess** (tel. 748/420-00), El Revolcadero Beach. The first luxury hotels most people see on arriving in Acapulco are the Acapulco Princess and the Pierre Marqués Princess, on El Revolcadero Beach just off the road to the airport. Set apart from the Manhattan of skyscraper hotels downtown, the Princess complex reminds one of a great Maya ceremonial center, its pyramid-like buildings dominating the flat surrounding land.

The sister hotels have superb luxury facilities: four swimming pools, two 18-hole golf courses, plenty of floodlit tennis courts, restaurants, and bars. Over 1000 guest quarters (rooms, suites, villas, etc.) are spread through the complex, and Princess is spending $28 million on 312 more. Winter rates require that you buy breakfast and dinner with your room, and so (10% tax included), one person pays 9250 to 9750 pesos ($185 to $195); two pay 12,000 to 16,500 pesos ($240 to $330), the last price being for the deluxe bungalow. Summer rates are about 40% lower, and include no meals (they're optional).

Princess International Hotels reservations can be made through any travel agent, or by calling toll free in the U.S. 800/223-1818.

El Presidente, Costera Miguel Aleman (tel. 748/417-00). Acapulco's Hotel El Presidente is one of three hotels near one another on the bay which are part of the Americana Hotels group, and guests at any one of the hotels are free to use all the facilities of any of the other hotels in the group. In effect, this means that you can try out any of three swimming pools (plus another three for children), five tennis courts, and two stretches of hotel beach, not to mention a dozen assorted bars, poolside and otherwise. Although most of Acapulco's luxury resort hotels accept nonguests in the use of their facilities (usually for a fee), the Americana trio is the only situation in which guests of one hotel are *encouraged* to look into what the others have to offer. In fact, guests who have prepaid meals (usually this means breakfast and dinner) are given a list of nine restaurants in the three hotels where they can have dinner (and three restaurants for breakfast), and no matter where you dine within the three-hotel complex, the meal tab is registered on your prepaid account.

El Presidente's twin towers hold 400 rooms and suites, each with individually controlled air conditioning and little balconies, some with views of the bay or the beach. El Presidente is actually the mid-range hotel as far as the other two Americana giants are concerned. In the summer season (mid-April to mid-December), rooms cost 3000 to 3700 pesos ($60 to $74), single or double. Children under 12 stay free with their parents. In winter, rates go up to 5750 to 6500 pesos ($115 to $130), single or double, and these rates do not include any meals, which you may be required to take. Look into package rates when you plan—sometimes there are special offers, particularly at the beginning and end of the winter season. You can call to make toll-free reservations at El Presidente and the other Americana hotels in Acapulco (see below).

Condesa del Mar, Costera Miguel Aleman (tel. 748/423-55). The Americana's Condesa del Mar is the pride and joy of the company's three Acapulco hotels. Larger (500 rooms) and more luxurious than the other two, the "Countess of the Sea" really makes you think there is "water, water everywhere": in the lobby-reception area are two giant toadstool-shaped fountains, and you must cross a little flagstone path through a big reflecting pool to get to the front desk. Elsewhere in the maze of terraces are groves of bamboo, and graceful jacaranda trees, plus the occasional rubber tree, huge and healthy, like nothing you've ever seen in a doctor's office.

The Condesa del Mar also seems to have the best entertainment. In the evenings the lobby bar becomes a performance area, with some of the best local and imported groups holding forth to a constantly changing audience. During the day, the Condesa's swimming pool has the best view of Acapulco Bay of any *swimming pool;* that is, immersed in its waters you can survey all of Acapulco. Lunchtime snacks are served from the poolside restaurant/bar, and in the evening, the Parrillada Los Faroles, an outdoor grill-restaurant, offers a buffet dinner to guests and nonguests alike for 750 pesos ($14), drinks extra, of course. (If you're staying at an Americana hotel and have paid for two meals a day, you can share in the buffet at no extra charge.)

The Condesa del Mar is the most expensive of the Americana hotels, with rooms in summer priced at 3700 to 4400 pesos ($74 to $88), single or double. Children under 12 stay free with their parents. In winter, a single or double room costs 5750 to 6500 pesos ($115 to $130), with the same provisions for children. (Remember, these rates do not include meals.)

For reservations at any of the Americana hotels, you can call 800-ACT-FAST, that's 800/228-3278 anywhere in the continental U.S. except Nebraska; in Canada, dial 800/261-9328.

Hotel Fiesta Tortuga, Costera Miguel Aleman (tel. 748/424-07). Of the three Americana hotels, the Fiesta Tortuga is the smallest and most economical. But "smallest" does not mean that this is in any way a small hotel. It holds 250 rooms and suites, each with a balcony, individually controlled air conditioning, and a servi-bar (little refrigerator filled with beverages—pay as you consume). Besides the Fiesta Tortuga's own swimming pool—in which you can plop down on a bar stool and be served right there in the water!—guests here are entitled to use any and all the facilities at the other two Americana hotels. In summer, rooms at the Fiesta Tortuga cost 2500 to 3000 pesos ($50 to $60), single or double. Children under 12 stay free. In winter, rates are 3500 to 4200 pesos ($70 to $84), single or double, the price differential coming from the difference in view (sea view or mountain view).

You're not on the waterfront if you stay at the Tortuga; you're on the land side of Costera Aleman. But the other hotels' beaches are a few minutes' stroll across the road, no great inconvenience.

Exelaris Hyatt Regency Acapulco, Costera Miguel Aleman 666 (tel. 748/428-88). Besides having the longest name of any Acapulco hotel, the local Hyatt Regency also has one of the longest lists of extra things to do: tennis courts, yacht trips, tours of the town and of Taxco—even of Mexico City—a day's fishing, a half-day's diving, a voyage in a glass-bottomed boat, a bullfight, even a round of golf are all offered to guests, although at an extra charge. For the price of your room alone, however, you receive a modern, luxurious room, the hotel's private beach, and the ambience of one of Acapulco's largest and poshest hotels. Also, in winter the price of your room includes breakfast and dinner each day, as it well might at these rates: single room, 10,000 pesos ($200); double room, 13,000 pesos ($260). In summer, the rates are for the room only, and are strikingly lower: 4750 pesos ($95) single, 5250 pesos ($105) double.

Note that the Hyatt Regency is located near the northeastern end of the bay near the naval base ("La Base"), a long way from downtown, Caleta and Caletilla beaches, and the high-divers. But this location has its advantages, being out of the noise and press of traffic, and near the Centro Acapulco along with many of the prime nightspots.

Paraiso/Marriott Hotel, Costera Aleman, Apdo. Postal 504 (tel. 748/241-40 or 247-41). You simply can't go wrong staying at Acapulco's luxurious Paraiso/Marriott, located about midway between the quaint downtown section and the Diana Circle. Prices are in line with those of other resort hotels, but the little touches of luxury are common sights here. For instance, even the tables under the *palapas* (palm thatch huts) in the beachfront restaurant have fresh tablecloths, and no matter what you buy in the hotel you can just sign for it. The surf roars on the beach, and the sea breeze wafts through the dining room as you sip your coffee and take in the sweeping view of the bay.

The rooms all have venetian blinds for good sun control, plus little balconies, each with its potted palm. Rates are based on season and on the view you choose, and of course the "mountain view" is a little less expensive than the "ocean view." In summer, singles are 2900 to 3300 pesos ($58 to $66) doubles are 3300 to 3800 pesos ($66 to $76). Children under 12 stay free with their parents. In winter, you are required to have breakfast and dinner in the hotel, and rooms then are priced at 6750 to 7700 pesos ($135 to $154) single, 8400 to 9700 pesos ($168 to $194) double, with those two meals and the 10% tax included in the price. For toll-free reservations in the U.S., call 800/228-9290.

Exelaris Hyatt Continental Acapulco, Costera Miguel Aleman, Apdo. Postal 214 (tel. 748/409-09). The Acapulco Continental, sister hotel to the deluxe Exelaris Hyatt Regency Acapulco, prides itself on having a swimming pool which is said to be the biggest in Acapulco. It's a ring of blue water surrounding a "tropical island" of the architect's own devising. The island is filled with a bar, restaurant, and lounge chairs for sunning and sipping. The atmosphere around the pool is so luxuriously sybaritic that you tend to forget the beach is right on the hotel's doorstep. Hyatt has just spent millions on renovations.

Almost a dozen places to eat and drink, a full range of shops and services, and facilities for arranging fishing trips and such are all part of the Continental's luxury lineup. Prices are set accordingly: in the winter season you pay 5600 pesos ($112) single, 6200 pesos ($124) double; in summer room prices are 3600 pesos ($72) single, 4200 pesos ($84) double, the difference in room prices being the difference between a room with an ocean view and one with a mountain, or city, view. The Continental adheres to the standard family plan: children 12 and under can stay free with their parents. For toll-free reservations, call Hyatt Reservations at 800/228-9000 in the U.S.

Holiday Inn Acapulco Beach, Costera Miguel Aleman 1260 (tel. 748/404-10). Of course there's got to be a Holiday Inn in Acapulco. (Actually, there are two.) No roadside motel this, it stands tall and cylindrical right on the beach on the way to the eastern end of the bay (Condesa Beach). Each room has two double beds, and since the rules allow children under 12 to share their parents' room for free, this money-saving double-up is both easy and extremely comfortable. All rooms have television sets (Norteamericanos use them for Spanish practice). Modern baths, FM radios, and balconies with a view are all included. Two freshwater swimming pools are available, as is the *palapa*-dotted beach right in front of the hotel. (You'll soon see that one pool is best for morning dips, and the other for the afternoon; the beach is great anytime.)

When it comes to rates, the management is particularly aggressive, its aim being to keep the hotel as full as possible, even if it means cutting rates substantially. In your case, when you call for reservations, ask what special discounts or packages might be offered. Normal summer rates are 3150 pesos ($63) single, 3450 pesos ($69) double (your children under 12 stay for free).

In winter, rates are 4850 pesos ($97) single, 5600 pesos ($112) double. Winter rates *do not* include breakfast and dinner, which are compulsory; many rooms have two double beds, and if another person (except a child 12 or under) stays with you, he or she pays 600 pesos ($12) for the bed. Minimum-stay requirements are imposed during holiday periods.

Holiday Inn is developing a vast new three-tower complex on the beach near the Glorieta Diana, the **Acapulco Plaza Holiday Inn.** The first building, of 400 suites, is already open, and the other two (hotel and condos) will open soon. When completed, the complex will have its own tennis club, 12 restaurants and bars, and two swimming pools. Fantastically low introductory rates are usually offered when a new hotel opens, so you should call and see what the situation is.

You can make reservations at the Holiday Inn Acapulco through any other Holiday Inn in the world, or by dialing, toll free from the U.S., 800/238-8000.

Ritz Acapulco Hotel, Costera Aleman, Apdo. Postal 259 (tel. 748/408-40). Not quite in the range of the truly tremendous luxury hotels, the Ritz is still very comfortable, as befits a member of the big Marriott chain, and the rooms are a bit larger than one normally finds in a luxury hotel these days (this is particularly true in the building's West Tower, or older section). The Ritz boasts its own nightclub, of course, and a restaurant called La Nina which has the most unusual "centerpiece" of any Mexican restaurant: a scale-model mock-up of Columbus's flagship, from which the restaurant takes its name. Next to La Nina is the Bar Navio, which sponsors a "happy hour" between 5:30 and 7:30 p.m. on summer evenings (i.e., *not* in the hectic winter season) when you can get two drinks for the price of one. As for room prices, no meals are included most of the year, although if you stay at the Ritz during the Christmas holidays or in the month of February you *must* purchase breakfast and dinner, which will add about $28 per person to your daily bill. During the winter season, single rooms are 3000 to 3900 pesos ($60 to $78), and double rooms are 3800 to 4700 pesos ($76 to $94), plus the meal tab; an extra person pays $12 but children under 12 stay free with parents. In summer, prices are about 34% lower, without meals. Lower prices are for the slightly older (and, actually, in some ways preferable) West Tower. You can get advance reservations in Mexico City by calling 525-1665, or in the U.S. by calling, toll free 800/228-9290.

Acapulco's Moderately Priced Hotels
(doubles $30 to $60 in summer; $50 to $122 in winter)

The moderately priced hotels in this resort town constitute very good vacation bargains, as you can stay in one for a very reasonable amount of money and yet enjoy the same beaches (not right outside your front door, but very nearby), nightspots, and restaurants frequented by those paying twice as much or more for their rooms. In only one or two cases do the establishments listed below require that you purchase breakfast and dinner during the winter season (again, mid-December to mid-April, varying a few days either way from year to year), and even those that do require this have room rates low enough to offset this (necessary) expense. Again, these prices constitute the entire price two people pay for the room, and *not* the price per person.

Of the smaller hotels in the row of giants, the **Hotel Maralisa** (tel. 748/409-76), Apdo. Postal 721, is one of the most congenial. It's got all the things the huge hotels have without the tremendous size: a fine palm-shaded swimming pool, a private stretch of beach, a bar called La Mar in between the beach and the swimming pool, and a dining room overlooking the bay. In addition, the Maralisa has its own sauna and massage room. Winter high-season prices include two meals, and run 5700 pesos ($114) single, 6100 pesos ($122) double. Off-season summer prices are drastically lower, although you don't get the meals: singles cost 2400 pesos ($48), doubles go for 3000 pesos ($60). Whichever accommodation you choose, you'll have a comfortable, modern, air-conditioned room with sliding glass doors (in most cases) opening onto a balcony-walkway. To find the Hotel Maralisa you must find the little side street called Enrique El Esclavo, which stretches between the beach and the Costera Aleman next to the restaurant called La Ballena.

Nestled among the giant resort hotels is an unpretentious but definitely comfortable hostelry called the **Hotel Sand's** (tel. 748/422-60), Costera Aleman 178 at Juan de la Cosa, across the Costera from the Hyatt Continental. From the road, you enter the hotel lobby through a stand of umbrella palms and a pretty garden restaurant. The Sand's rooms are light and airy in the style of a good-quality modern motel, with fairly dressy furniture, wall-to-wall carpeting, yellow tile bathrooms with showers, and individually controlled central air conditioning. Singles here are 1200 to 2000 pesos ($24 to $40), doubles are 1500 to 2750 pesos ($30 to $55), the higher figures being those charged in winter. The Sand's has two swimming pools (one of them for children), and a squash court as well. The price here is very reasonable, the accommodations quite satisfactory, and the location excellent. If you send a letter for reservations, note that the hotel's postal address is Apdo. Postal 256, Acapulco, Gro.

Want to try something different? Rather than booking a room in one of the Empire State Buildings arrayed along the eastern beaches, head for the **Hotel Boca Chica** (tel. 748/260-14), overlooking Caletilla beach at the end of the Costera Aleman. The five-story hotel fits into the hillside fairly unobtrusively. Lawns, terraces, the pool, the bar, and restaurant are on different levels. The hotel's location on the headland of the beach allows for 180-degree panoramic views. All the air-conditioned rooms have little verandas, fine marble-and-tile baths, lots of windows, and room to unfold in. The hotel can also provide facilities for water-skiing, sailing, scuba diving, deep-sea fishing, surfing, golf, and tennis. During the winter you must take breakfast and dinner in the hotel, and the cost is 2250 pesos ($45) single, 2850 pesos ($57) double. During the rest of the year you need only take the room, although meals are always available. Mid-April through June and September through mid-December, prices are about 18% lower. In July and August, rates rise to near winter levels.

If you like all this so far, be advised that the Boca Chica has a toll-free reservations number in the U.S.: 800/223-5695 (in New York City, dial 730-8100).

Although you may not have the bucks to stay at the Ritz, you may be able to swing a few nights at the **Auto Hotel Ritz** (tel. 748/219-22), just off Costera Aleman inland a half block from its high-rise namesake on Avenida Magellanes. Over 100 rooms here, in an L-shape around a swimming pool itself surrounded by trees and green arbors and set with tables which constitute the hotel's restaurant, called El Jardín. Elevators take you up to the comfortable, almost luxurious modern motel rooms which feature flower boxes on the little balconies (a few of which have sea views—ask for them on the seventh floor). Prices are 1600 to 2800 pesos ($32 to $56) single, 2000 to 3400 pesos ($40 to $68) double, the higher prices being for the winter season.

The **Hotel De Gante** (tel. 748/501-03; in Mexico City, 535-2446) Costera Aleman 265 at Playa Suave, is one of the older "new" hotels in Acapulco, but decoration and facilities are kept well up to date, as can be seen by the great amount of gleaming marble in the lobby. Rooms are all light and modern, with good beds and bright orange-flowered drapes, plus tiled bathrooms. Those on the front have little balconies and views of the bay; the second-floor restaurant has a bay view, too. Price for a single room is 1100 to 1800 pesos ($22 to $36), for a double 1350 to 2000 pesos ($27 to $40), the higher prices being the in-season (winter) ones.

A few blocks back from the beach up on the hillside is the new and shiny **Hotel Villa Rica** (tel. 748/480-40), Avenida Universidad at the corner of Avenida Dr. Chavez/Reyes Católicos. Front rooms have balconies with grand bay views, all rooms are spacious, tasteful, modern, and air-conditioned. Good, firm beds, a few parking spaces inside the gates, and a quiet location are extras, but the biggest extra of all is the beautiful swimming pool. Prices are a bit high, but the hotel is new and very nice (although service lacks a good bit of *savoir faire*): singles are 1000 to 1850 pesos ($20 to $37) off-season, 1350 to 2050 pesos ($27 to $41) in-season; doubles are 1450 to 2150 pesos ($29 to $43) off-season, 1850 to 2800 pesos ($37 to $56) in-season. If they're not full or if you're staying for a few days, bargain for a reduction.

A Motel near Caleta and Caletilla

Whether or not you drive to Acapulco, you should consider staying at the **Motel La Jolla** (tel. 748/258-62; in Mexico City, call 566-2377), Costera Aleman and Avenida Lopez Mateos, where a bright and modern double room costs 1400 pesos ($28) off-season, 1700 pesos ($34) in-season. This L-shaped, two-story motel surrounds a swimming pool bordered with coconut palms, and although there is no view of the sea whatsoever, there is a flying-saucer-shaped restaurant serving sandwiches and hamburgers for about 115 pesos ($2.30), other entrees for more. You are near the beaches of Caleta and Caletilla here, although you can't see them.

Acapulco's Budget Hotels
(doubles for $11 to $25 summer, $13 to $30 winter)

It is possible to enjoy this rich man's resort for very little money, if you're willing to do without toll-free reservation lines, wall-to-wall carpeting, and multilingual staff. The budget hotels grouped in the older parts of the city do a steady business with Mexican vacationers and foreign tourists unable or unwilling to pay the vast sums for rooms in the grand style. Sometimes these little hotels and pensions have special treats in store: a completely unexpected luxury such as a swimming pool, or air conditioning, or rooms with a bay view, or a convenient and rock-bottom-priced restaurant just next door, or an especially pleasant and helpful proprietor (did you ever have anything to do with the "proprietor" of a luxury hotel?). However, as these hotels are run on slim budgets, it is essential that you observe the ancient rule of *caveat emptor,* "Let the buyer beware!" Ask to see a room before you sign the registration card, and if the one you see is not satisfactory, ask to see another. If the hotel just won't do, leave it and go in search of another. Whereas the unsatisfactory place might be a week away from a major overhaul, a neighboring hotel might just have had new paint, plumbing, and plaster put in.

While prices in these budget hotels do change a bit from season to season, it is not in drastic leaps such as are made by the giant hotels; and as few of these little places have their own restaurants, it's impossible for them to require you to purchase meals at inflated prices.

I've grouped my choices into three areas: downtown on La Quebrada—which is only minutes from the center of Acapulco; downtown in the area of a street called La Paz—equally convenient; and near Caleta and Caletilla beaches, on the southern side of the peninsula facing La Roqueta Island. None of these locations is far from the public bus routes on Costera Miguel Aleman, and thus the fantastic public beaches on the bay—they're all public beaches, in fact—are a quarter of an hour away from your hotel, on the average. By inexpensive taxi, you're that much closer to the beaches in terms of time.

DOWNTOWN—ON LA QUEBRADA: West of the zócalo and up the hillside to where the famous high-divers do their thing stretches a warren of busy little streets where only the occasional resort-wear shop reminds one that Acapulco lives mainly on visitors. The hotels are simple and cheap—much the same standard, but generally cleaner than the cheap hotels in most other Mexican towns. The one disadvantage to the Quebrada area is that four times each evening big tour buses roar up the hill for the high-divers' act, some leaving their engines running until it's over. The last dive is at 11:30 p.m., so it's not really quiet until midnight. But even so, La Quebrada and neighboring La Paz and Juárez harbor some of the best buys in the city.

The **Hotel Angelita,** Quebrada 37 (tel. 748/357-34), advertises *limpieza absoluta,* or absolute cleanliness, and that's what you'll find in this bright new place. White rooms are adjoined by blue tiled baths, all rooms have ceiling fans, and the sympathetic patron charges 300 pesos ($6) single, 600 pesos ($12) double, 250 pesos ($5) per person for triples and quadruples. If you stay any length of time you get a 10% reduction. Recommended.

The **Casa Amparo** (tel. 748/221-72), Quebrada 69, is a friendly place with lots of greenery and three tiers of rooms, the upper group of which have views of the bay. Service tends to be a bit slow, although pleasant enough; what was once the dining room has now been converted to a row of rather claustrophobic guest rooms, which you'd do well to avoid. Prices are good, at 700 pesos ($14) in summer, 900 pesos ($18) in winter, for a double room. Bargain prices for room and one or two meals are offered.

You'll recognize the **Hotel Mariscal,** Quebrada 35 (tel. 748/200-15), at the bottom of the hill where La Quebrada joins Hidalgo, by its mustard-colored porch and wrought-iron chairs. The 17 rooms here are airy and cool, with comfortable box springs and private baths, although the fluorescent lights and old furniture leave a little something to be desired. Rooms cost 300 pesos ($6) per person in summer; 450 pesos ($9) in winter.

DOWNTOWN—THE LA PAZ AREA: La Paz is one of the streets that runs back into the zócalo, and it, too, is a good area for budget hotels. I like a small hotel called the **Casa Anita,** Azueta 12, corner of La Paz (tel. 748/250-46), a friendly, homey place with ferns growing out of boxes on all the window sills. Fourteen of the 27 rooms have hot water; all have private baths. Price per person is 250 to 350 pesos ($5 to $7), depending on the time of year.

Second place goes to the new **Hotel California,** La Paz 12 (tel. 748/228-93), where the rooms are built around an open paved patio, and all have nice white drapes and sleek Formica furniture (private baths, hot water). Singles here, without meals, are 300 to 400 pesos ($6 to $8); doubles are 400 to 550 pesos ($8 to $11); 100 pesos more ($2) for air conditioning. You'll find the zócalo and the city bus stops only one block away.

An older hotel which has been completely—but completely—redone is the **Hotel Mision** (tel. 748/236-43), Felipe Valle 12. A dusty and none-too-handsome courtyard has been turned into a wonderland of colonial-style tiles, furniture, arches, all centered on an enormous and magnificent mango tree. In the rooms, the tiled washbasin is outside the toilet/shower area, a thoughtful addition. White brick walls, ceiling fans (no air conditioning), and screens are in all rooms, as is constant hot water (so they say). The price is 500 to 700 pesos ($10 to $14) single, 750 to 950 pesos ($15 to $17) double, high for this area, but not for the style of the hotel.

A fine, centrally located budget buy is the **Hotel Colimense,** Iglésias 11 (tel. 748/228-90). All eight rooms are on the second floor and overlook a shaded courtyard supporting such homey features as swings and rocking chairs. Rooms are clean and well screened with ceiling fans to cut the heat. Rates are 250 to 325 pesos ($5 to $6.50) per person.

Other budget hotel owners could take lessons from the owners of the **Hotel Silva,** Juárez 24 (no phone). The rooms, although spartan, are quite clean, equipped with private showers and ceiling fans (but no window screens, alas). Each room has two or three single beds, and rooms are priced at 300 pesos ($6) single, 500 pesos ($10) double, 650 pesos ($13) triple.

NEAR CALETA AND CALETILLA: On the southern reaches of the peninsula, a short walk from Caleta and Caletilla beaches, are a number of older budget hotels popular with Mexican couples and families on vacation. The area is a mixture of squalor and splendor, with a good number of near-palatial homes and also some sympathetic but barely citified peasant dwellings. Advantages here are that most of these hotels are on quiet streets, are near the small beaches, and aren't all that far by bus from the longer stretches of beach, on the bay.

To get to the first several hotels listed below, find the Jai Alai Fronton inland from the beach behind a shady parking lot. Facing the fronton, a road goes up the left side of it—this is Avenida Lopez Mateos, and I'll describe the hotels in order as you ascend the hill.

Three or four persons traveling together might want to consider the cheerful **Hotel Montemar,** across from the fronton (tel. 748/247-76), built in 1968 and run by the pleasant Sra. Gertrudis Alcocer. The hotel is built on the hillside, has a terrace garden and a convent in the background. Nine rooms altogether, one air-conditioned and eight with fans, the latter going for 350 to 500 pesos ($7 to $10) per person. Parking, pool, and kitchen privileges with *agua purificada*. For the air-conditioned room it's a dollar or two more.

The new **Hotel San Antonio** (tel. 748/213-58), to the left of the Jai Alai Fronton on Lopez Mateos, is actually an older hotel that's been completely rebuilt (1980). Now equipped with air conditioning and a swimming pool (still under construction, as of this writing), rooms are rented for 575 pesos ($11.50) per person in summer, 625 pesos ($12.50) per person in winter. The San Antonio is the newest and poshest of the budget hotels in the area.

The 26-room **Motel Caribe,** Lopez Mateos 10 at Ensenada (tel. 748/215-50), with music going constantly in the lobby, has rooms arranged around an open garden. Dark stained doors and slatted windows open off the rooms to terraces: private on one side, public walkways on the other. All rooms have private baths with hot and cold water. Rates are 400 to 650 pesos ($8 to $13) per person; the higher winter price includes a continental breakfast.

The **Posada Caletilla,** Avenida Lopez Mateos 3 (tel. 748/234-27), is a private house with ten rooms, which rent for 200 to 400 pesos ($4 to $8) per person, single or double, all with private baths but no hot water. Sr. and Sra. Elias who run the place (and speak Spanish, English, and French) are thinking of installing water heaters. A really pleasant, simple place.

Now in a slightly different location is an exceptionally good place to stay: facing the Hotel de la Playa between Caleta and Caletilla beaches, take the street to your left up the hill. About 1½ blocks up the hill you'll find the sinuous facade of the **Hotel Belmar** (tel. 748/215-25 or 215-26), an older hotel well kept up and very pleasant. Two small pools and shady patios fill the grassy lawn in front of the hotel. The four-story hotel was built in the '50s, with air conditioning added later. The cool, breezy rooms cost 440 pesos ($8.80) single, 550 pesos double ($11) in summer; 550 pesos ($11) single, 660 pesos ($13.20) double in winter. For 400 pesos ($8) more per person you can have breakfast and dinner each day.

Back toward the center of town on the Costera, across the street from the Motel Las Palmas, is the **Casa de Huespedes Walton** (tel. 748/204-52), Costera Aleman 223. This congenial little pension set back from the busy street is run by a bevy of happy señoras who want everything to go right: signs in the courtyard admonish people, "For the love of God, park correctly and obey the lines!" and "Don't ruin tourism with loud horns and mufflers!'' Rooms at the Casa Walton rent with breakfast and dinner at the reasonable price of 450 pesos ($9) per person in summer, 550 pesos ($11) per person in winter. The small but pleasant Playa Langosta (or Angosta) is only five minutes' walk from your door.

So much for finding a place to stay. Whether you've chosen to bed down in a palace or a pension, your next task is to locate Acapulco's best places to dine. Read on.

Acapulco Bay

Chapter XI

WHERE TO DINE IN ACAPULCO

DINING OUT IN ACAPULCO can be the romantic experience of a lifetime—whether you're clad in a bathing suit and munching a huge hamburger at a beachfront burger place, with that fabulous sand, sunshine, and glorious bay within your view, or whether you're seated at a table high up somewhere overlooking the surf and city lights, with a waiter helping you choose a wine to go with your baby swordfish. But I regret to add that dining in Acapulco can also be disappointing. I was once served a "fresh" fish sauteed in butter, the center of which was still frozen solid. (I complained, the fish was taken away, and reappeared again on our bill at full amount!)

There are several reasons for being careful about where you dine in Acapulco. First, the restaurant clientele here is largely transient (like yourself), and waiters and chefs would much rather cater to steady customers who can appreciate and support their efforts over the years. They know that if you're not fully satisfied, it doesn't matter much because you won't be back again for a year or more anyway. Next, the obligatory "Modified American Plan" which operates in the luxury hotels during the busy winter season robs independent restaurateurs of their top clientele, except at lunchtime—and people are often spending the day on the beach, or don't wish to indulge in a full-course lunch when they know a full-course dinner is not far off. Finally, there is not the element of a large office-worker clientele here (as there is in Mexico City) to encourage the delicious, ubiquitous, and fantastically inexpensive *comidas corridas* (set-price lunches) in the early afternoon. And I think there may be, in certain places, that attitude of "fleece the tourist" which is as old as tourism itself.

These caveats aside, let's get back to that romantic Acapulco dinner. There are some good restaurants in Acapulco which are trustworthy and take pride in their high-quality cuisine and service, and which realize that pleasing you will mean that you'll recommend them to friends when you return home. Service and food quality may sag a little bit even at these places during the off-season summer months, when anticipating the day's clientele (and thus the amount of food to buy) is extremely difficult. To avoid even the slightest disappointment, follow the old rule of never eating in a restaurant that's completely empty during prime meal times—or if you do, realize that you do so as an experiment which may fail (witness our frozen fish, mentioned above).

Mealtimes in Acapulco: Breakfast is anytime from about 6:30 on to about 10:30 a.m., although in the larger hotels the coffee-shop stays open and serves even later, pushing into lunchtime. An *Acapulquen* doesn't usually sit down to lunch before 2 o'clock in the afternoon, and takes his dinner about 8 or 9 o'clock in the evening. As tourists come for a short time, most hotel restaurants adjust their mealtimes (so that you won't have to) and start serving these two meals an hour or so earlier.

Dress: You needn't dress up formally for dinner in the style which is required in colder climates—jacket and tie is hardly ever required in Acapulco. But this does not mean the better restaurants will not enforce a loose dress code based on general presentability. A light jacket with an open-necked shirt, and a pants suit or long but light and summery dress, are quite acceptable. Many people at the large hotels use their Acapulco vacation as an excuse to show off their dashing warm-weather outfits which may be striking, daring, and elegant, but not exactly formal. Men who are undecided can pick up one of the loose, tailless Mexican shirts with pleats or tucks and other decoration which are the fully acceptable "formal wear" in tropical climates such as Mexico and the Philippines (Sr. Presidente Miguel de la Madrid often sports one of these at ceremonious occasions). But these dress tips are important to follow only at the best restaurants or while dining in the top restaurants of the luxury hotels. Everywhere else, an easy resort informality prevails, with beach-front restaurants accepting bathing suits as proper dress during lunchtime.

Here, then, are my choices for dining out in Acapulco, in all price ranges and for all types of food. Each is unique and special purpose in its own way, and different restaurants will cater to your different moods or mealtimes. Remember that it's good to call for reservations at the more expensive restaurants, and that a tax of 10% will be added to your bill.

DELIGHTFUL BUT EXPENSIVE: Want to really do it up right? What about lunch or dinner beside a reflecting pool next to a Moorish pavilion, as ducks glide by and peacocks stalk the grassy sward dotted with exotic, decadent statuary, the whole surrounded by a Moroccan-style crenellated wall? You can swim in the pool after lunch. This could only be **Armando's Taj Mahal,** Costera Aleman 2330 (tel. 4-0393), and while the architecture is definitely more Maghrebian than Uttar Pradeshian, it's still a spellbinding place. Lunch is served from 12:30 to 6 p.m., dinner from 6:30 on, and prices are high: artichokes vinaigrette, seafood soup, or a club sandwich will run 300 to 375 pesos ($6 to $7.50); a "Pepito" (Mexican steak sandwich on a hard roll) is 425 pesos ($8.50). For dinner, you might start with baked oysters, go on to a shrimp dish, or veal scaloppine Marsala or a mixed Mexican plate, and with wine, dessert, and coffee, your bill could easily come to 1500 pesos ($30) per person. I feel sure your meal here will be an unforgettable experience, however.

FOR MEXICAN DISHES: Los Rancheros (tel. 419-08), on the "Carretera Escenica" in Guitarron (the road to Las Brisas and Puerto Marqués), has the best food and service at the most reasonable prices I've found. A western cowboy decor of red tile roofs, rail fences, lassos, and "Wanted" posters surrounds you as you dine on northern Mexican specialties. An immense Mexican combination plate costs 500 pesos ($10). Tortilla soup, *codorniz* (quail, barbecued with potatoes, beans, and salad), barbecued beef with salad, and chili relleno (stuffed pepper) are some of the other delicious choices, or you can dine simply on a pot of beans with onion, epazote, and hot pepper. You'd do well to avoid the fish here, though. Drinks are served, too. Cold beer? It will refrigerate your interior. And now for the extra: if Los Rancheros were in the dusty hills near Fresnillo it would still be worth going to, but instead it's perched on the hillside overlooking the entire Bay of Acapulco, with its lights glistening like phosphorescent jewels at night. Plan to spend about 400 to 650 pesos ($8 to $13) per person here. Los Rancheros is open from 2 to 11 p.m. daily, and it's a bit hard to get to (that must be why it has stayed so good): take a bus to La Base, and then a short taxi ride, or a bus to Puerto Marqués, and hop off at the restaurant; or take a cab from the Diana Circle or from the zócalo.

A Yucatecan restaurant, even on the Pacific coast, is never out of place when it comes to good food, and **Antojitos Mayab** (tel. 228-35) is the place to sample local Yucatán dishes such as suckling pig (cochinita), roasted chicken (pollo pibil), and other regional specialties. Daily special plates cost about 150 to 190 pesos ($3 to $3.80) here, and the food is a welcome change from tacos and enchiladas. The Mayab is on the land side of Costera Aleman near Hornos beach—look for the sign and the thatched roof with tables and chairs set out on a patio in front. The restaurant is open from 9 a.m. until 3 a.m., which means that there are only six hours in every day during which you cannot drop in here for a cold bottle of Yucatecan beer.

ORIENTAL FARE: You can find very palatable Oriental dishes in Acapulco, a fitting reminder that this jet-set resort was once Mexico's premier port for the Far East trade.

Suntory (tel. 480-88), on Costera Aleman at Tte. Maury (across from the Hotel La Palapa near La Base), is a very attractive Japanese restaurant. Simple but elegant, the Suntory has powerful air conditioning, kimono-clad waitresses, a small bar, and a special "Matsu" dinner—a little of everything—for 1400 pesos ($28) complete. You can dine for much less à la carte: sashimi (raw fish), tempura dishes, and lobster salad all cost less than 200 pesos ($4), and teppanyaki steaks cost about 550 pesos ($11). Suntory is open every day for lunch and dinner.

For Chinese meals, look for the illuminated sign on the Costera for the **Restaurant Shangri-La**—you'll see it on the left-hand side just before the Condesa del Mar as you come from the zócalo. Follow the arrow up Calle La Picuda to no. 5, and you will be at the Shangri-La (open 6 to 10:30 p.m. for dinner only, seven days a week). Patio tables (no air conditioning), a lily pond, and garden bridge set the mood, and wonton soup, eggrolls, chicken with almonds, shrimp, fish, and pressed duck fill the bill. You might spend 350 to 550 pesos ($7 to $11) per person complete, if you dine here.

FROM SOUP TO INSANITY: Although it's probably an oversimplification to say that if you've seen one Carlos Anderson restaurant you've seen them all, I couldn't help being struck by the similarity between **Carlos 'n Charlie's** (tel. 400-39), Costera, opposite Las Torres Gemelas Hotel, and Harry's Bar in Cuernavaca or Anderson's Bar & Grill in Mexico City. Same revolutionary posters, same sassy waiters, same ponderous humor in the menu listings ("splash" for seafood, "moo" for beef) . . . well, you get the idea. But the food is good and the place is always packed, which is a good indication that people like what they get for the price they pay. Meals based on meat are in the 350- to 650-peso ($7 to $13) range, seafood the same. Come early and get a seat on the terrace overlooking the sidewalk. While there may be many similarities among Anderson's restaurants, they also have in common the fact that virtually everyone comes away having had a good meal and a good time. Carlos 'n Charlie's is open daily from 6:30 p.m. to midnight; closed Tuesday from May through October.

ON THE BEACH: Blackbeard's (tel. 425-49), on Condesa Beach just before the Hotel Condesa del Mar when you're coming from the zócalo, goes all the way with its pirate motif. Rope and bamboo are simply everywhere, big black barrels serve as tables, various bits of nautical paraphernalia are nailed up wherever there's space, and a half-dozen exquisite ship models dangle from the ceiling. In such a "Yo-ho-ho" place, steak would have to be the specialty, and it shares prime place on the menu with lobster, expensive but delicious. A salad bar laden with "safe" greens and drinks that would make a swashbuckler's grog look weak are other attractions. The crowd here is mostly young and with-it, but by no means made up of beachcombers, as dinner for two, without wine or drinks, will cost about 850 to 1000 pesos ($17 to $20). Blackbeard's is open from 7 p.m. to 1 a.m. daily.

Next to Blackbeard's you'll spot **Mimi's Chili Bar,** the funky, Old West bar daytime annex of Blackbeard's (which is for dinner only). At Mimi's you can pick up a lunchtime bowl of chili, a burger, or a salad, and a cool drink for 250 pesos ($5) or so, even less for just a light snack.

FRENCH RESTAURANTS: For French cuisine, Acapulquines usually visit **Normandie** (tel. 238-68), on Costera Aleman at Malespina, near the Hotel de Gante. The fancy wrought iron-work here makes one immediately think of France (or at least of New Orleans), and the glitter of chandeliers in the dining room makes you think you're anywhere but Acapulco. Diners can sit on the shaded terrace looking onto the Costera, or in the air-conditioned dining room. The manager is French, and makes sure the evening's offerings meet the high standards of the French tradition. You can order the evening's table d'hôte dinner for about 750 pesos ($15.00), plus wine, or choose from the varied menu. Normandie is open from 7 p.m. to midnight.

At **Chez Guillaume** (tel. 412-31), across the street from the Holiday Inn on Costera Aleman, the cuisine is a blend of Mexican and French: Mexican ingredients and French preparation come together in the crema de aguacate glacé (chilled cream of avocado soup). Besides some standard French items such as chateaubriand and duck à l'orange, Chez Guillaume features a few very good and purely Mexican specialties such as carne asada á la Tampiqueña and grilled red snapper, perhaps because of the frequent visits by Mexican tourists staying across the road at the Holiday Inn. Chez Guillaume has both indoor dining rooms and a delightful third-floor terrace lit by glass globe lamps and planted with potted palms and shrubs. The bustle of the street is a satisfying distance below you here, and the soft night air is all around. Note that Chez Guillaume is open only for dinner (which will cost you about 650 pesos—$13—a person, plus wine), from 6:30 p.m. to 12:30 a.m., and that the restaurant is closed on Sunday in summer.

AN OUTDOOR GRILL: In the evening it's pleasant to sit outdoors at the **Restaurant Cocula**, in the complex called El Patio, off Costera Aleman. (There are various branches of Cocula along the Costera, but the one I prefer is right across from the Exelaris Hyatt Continental.) Here you dine in an outdoor patio circle, and grilled fowl and meats are brought from another circle, with a grill, nearby. Another circle serves as the bar. It's quiet here, set well back from the Costera, and prices are moderate for Acapulco: have a steak or a mixed grill, plus a bottle of sidra rosada (Mexican sparkling cider) or wine (try Urbiñon or Los Reyes), and two people will spend less than 1000 pesos ($20) total—that's 500 pesos ($10) apiece.

LOW PRICES IN THE HIGH-PRICE AREA: Even farther east along the Costera, across from La Torre de Acapulco and up from the corner of Lomas del Mar (there's a Denny's here), is **La Tortuga**, a small restaurant with tables outdoors, a friendly Mexican family in attendance, a young clientele, and a cheery atmosphere. Beer and tacos are the most popular items served, but they have sandwiches, pork chops, and fancier items as well. For a light meal, one might pay 100 to 150 pesos ($2 to $3), beverage included; you can spend a dollar or two more if you go fancy.

AMERICAN-STYLE RESTAURANTS: As many of the luxury hotels were inspired by American models, their coffeeshops and restaurants will have many American-style dishes on the menu. Otherwise, Acapulco's Costera Aleman sports a dozen or more American or American-inspired eateries, including—yes, of course—**Colonel Sanders's Kentucky Fried Chicken.** Besides the colonel, you'll find in your progress along the Costera several branches of **Denny's** (there's one in the zócalo, another across the street from the Holiday Inn); a branch or two of the famous Mexican **Sanborn's** chain, selling cosmetics and toiletries, film and newspapers, and all sorts of gifts, besides its familiar American-style fare. A Latin incarnation of MacDonald's called **Doni Burger** is not a bad spot for breakfast as they serve bacon and eggs, hotcakes with syrup, as well as the familiar doughnuts; and coffee refills here, as in most American-style places, are usually free. For a light lunch you can have a seat at **Big Boy** hamburgers, or order a similar munch from **Tastee-Freez. Shakey's Pizza** is here as well.

You may be surprised to find that prices at these restaurants are higher than you expected; although these are often among the cheapest places to eat at home, in Mexico they are places to dine out, and prices are adjusted accordingly (the cheapest place to eat in Mexico is a tiny *lonchería* or *fogata*—literally, a "cookfire"—and not in an air-conditioned, be-Muzaked, clean, and standardized restaurant served by multilingual personnel). But prices are certainly not overly high, and when your digestive system demands something familiar, you can count on these places.

FOR PASTRIES AND COFFEE: The **Pastelería Viena,** just east of the Diana Glorieta on Costera Aleman's inland side, is a tiny Central European haven bedecked with posters of the Tirol and cooled to Alpine freshness by a big air conditioner. In the window and in the pastry cases are various baked delights good at any time of day, although the Viena does serve regular breakfasts (140 pesos, $2.80, for the standard eggs, juice, toast and coffee). Luncheon plates are a hot-weather treat: the special plate (175 pesos, $3.50) holds ham, cheese, egg salad, cole slaw, and little tuna sandwiches. For a light lunch, sandwiches are about half that price. The Viena is open 8:30 a.m. to 11:30 p.m. Monday through Saturday, from 9 a.m. to 10:30 p.m. on Sunday.

DOWNTOWN RESTAURANTS, MODERATE PRICES: Just off the zócalo down Juárez, at no. 19 is the **Picalagua,** one of the nicest restaurants in the area. Iron grillwork separates the tables from the street, and other tables are set back in a tropical garden full of chattering birds. A lamp hangs over every table, and soft Latin music wafts from above. The specialty is seafood, ranging from crayfish and lobster (each served four different ways) to such exotica as baby shark. Most entrees are around 125 to 260 pesos ($2.50 to $5.20), and include turtle, mussels marinara, octopus Veracruzano, or steamed clams. The Picalagua is open daily 8 a.m. to 10:30 p.m. A good breakfast of eggs, bread, coffee, papaya, and frijoles is a mere 80 pesos ($1.60) here.

Also on Juárez, at no. 5, is the **San Carlos,** with a western motif—lots of brick and wood—and food served in pleasant surroundings at chuckwagon prices: charcoal-broiled meats for 90 to 160 pesos ($1.80 to $3.20), fish about the same. A *comida corrida* costs only 115 pesos ($2.30). Service is excellent. The San Carlos is only a few steps from the zócalo.

Mariscos Pipo is a diminutive place that specializes in seafood, and while not dirt cheap gives good value for money. An order of ceviche, which comes with lemon and lots of Saltine crackers, plus a beer, makes a light lunch for 100 pesos ($2). Tuna, octopus, snails, and other delectables come in various combination plates for 150 and 235 pesos ($3 and $4.70). Red snapper is a bit expensive, but almendrado (fish baked with cheese and almonds) is only 185 pesos ($3.70). Tables stand in an airy, vine-draped room off the sidewalk five short blocks from the zócalo. Walk along Costera Aleman west toward Caleta, past the market stalls and down a passageway by the Farmacia Santa Lucía; or walk along Juárez and at the fork in the road, bear left. Legal address of the Pipo (as though any of these streets were marked!) is Almirante Breton 3. Menu in English. Pipo's is open every day from 10 a.m. to 6 p.m.

Very similar to Pipo, but cheaper and a bit closer to the zócalo at the corner of Juárez and Almirante Breton, is **El Amigo Miguel,** a large inside dining room very plainly furnished. Usually it's filled to brimming with seafood lovers taking advantage of the fish at low prices.

Mariscos Milla, at the corner of Azueta and Carranza, might fool you at first into thinking prices are high here. Although the decor is upbeat and pleasant, this doesn't seem to affect the low prices. The kitchen is occupied by a platoon of hard-working señoras who will serve you ceviche (fish cocktail) for a mere 45 pesos (90¢). A delicious meal of fish filet and a beer need cost only 165 pesos ($3.30). Mariscos Milla is open seven days a week from 7 a.m. to 8 p.m. You'll recognize it—an airy corner restaurant—across the street from the Hotel Sacramento, and not far from the Casa Anita.

On the east side of the zócalo is the **Terraza Las Flores,** enter via Calle Juárez, across from Denny's. The menus here are in English, Spanish, and German; the friendly and engaging owner speaks Spanish and English, his son speaks Spanish and German. Glance at the blackboard, which will bear the name and price of the daily special, always a good bargain: chicken soup, "Milanesa Viena" (alias wienerschnitzel), potatoes, salad, dessert, and coffee for 185 pesos ($3.70), for instance. Otherwise, à la carte dinners will cost about 220 to 280 pesos ($4.40 to $5.60) complete if you have meat or fish, a good deal less if you have something like enchiladas. You always seem to find a few exotic (for Acapulco) dishes such as pork and cabbage offered. The Terraza has about two dozen tables on two levels, lots of potted plants, and is open from 11 a.m. to 11 p.m. every day.

ROCK-BOTTOM PRICES: Restaurant **Carmon's** at Juárez 8 is certainly low on the price scale. You don't get so much atmosphere here, for the Carmon is pretty plain, but you don't pay for it either. The *comida corrida* is only 80 pesos ($1.60) for five courses, and the noise from the TV which thrums to itself in a corner costs nothing extra.

Acapulco's lowest prices of all are concentrated along the street named Azueta, near La Paz. *Comidas corridas* at the humble eateries along the way average 60 to 95 pesos ($1.20 to $1.90). Follow Juárez until it meets the Costera Aleman, and tiny hole-in-the-wall cookstands will serve you a four-course lunch for as little as 55 pesos ($1.10). The food will be very simple, but filling.

CALETA–CALETILLA BEACH AREA: The area around Caleta and Caletilla beaches used to be rather down at the heels, but not long ago the municipal authorities pumped lots of money into public facilities here. Now the beaches have nice shady *palapas* and beach chairs, clean sand, and fine palm trees. Three neonative buildings were built to house "Vestidores, Regaderas" (changing rooms, showers and lockers) and restaurants. Little dining places line the outer periphery of the buildings, for which the kitchen work is done at the center (peek around to the kitchen to see boys cutting up fish for the pot).

The best way to find a good meal here is to wander along the rows of restaurants, looking for busy spots where people are eating (and not just sipping drinks). Pore over menus, which will either be displayed or handed to you with a smile on request. Although the restaurants may tend to look all the same, you'll be surprised at the difference in prices. Filete de pescado (fish filet) might be 125 pesos ($2.50) at one place, and 175 pesos ($3.50) at another; beer can cost anywhere from 22 to 34 pesos (44¢ to 68¢).

If you stroll a short distance from the beach in the direction of the Hotel Boca Chica, you'll see the airy raised "patio" which is **Bertha and Bob's** restaurant. The *comida corrida* is quite cheap here, due in part to the fact that it's back from the beach a ways. But the view is fine, and 200 pesos ($4) is hardly a lot to pay for a full lunch.

Below Bertha and Bob's is yet a cheaper restaurant-bar, aptly named **La Fuerza Nuclear** ("The Nuclear Force!").

Chapter XII

ACAPULCO IN THE DAYTIME

WHEN THE SPANISH CONQUISTADORES were prowling Mexico's Pacific Coast in search of gold and converts, they frequently put into Acapulco Bay for shelter from the wind and to replenish their supplies of food and fresh water. Although the mountains and promontories surrounding this breathtakingly beautiful bay did indeed afford the Spaniards some protection from the elements, they soon found that the beginning of summer and the rainy season in May and June brought blustery storms even to the inner reaches of the bay. While there was not much danger, there was a lot of howling wind, thrashing of palm fronds, and dumping of rain. One wonders what they made of the bay then—no doubt they thought it a pretty spot, but hardly worth spending time in as there was little gold to be had.

Half a century ago, a few intrepid outsiders arrived in Acapulco in search of something the Spaniards took for granted: unspoiled natural beauty, year-round warm air and water, low prices, and an easy pace of life. These treasures were theirs for a time, but soon word of Acapulco's beauty spread and the dirt itself became as valuable as gold.

Now it takes a king's ransom to buy a foothold on the virtually perfect beaches which form a crescent around the bay, and the easy pace of life is threatened by the hubbub of cars, motorcycles, airplanes, and overpopulation. But the striking natural beauty and the balmy climate still draw hundreds of thousands of visitors each year.

The king's ransom has to be paid if you want to build on the beach, but the government has sagely set aside *all* of Acapulco's beaches as public property, and so you can wander wherever you want on these golden sands, and no one can tell you that a certain stretch is "reserved" for the guests at this or that hotel or club.

You can, if you like, take an entire day to wander for miles over the wet sand border of the sea from Hornos Beach, just east of the center of town, to Guitarron Beach at the far eastern end of the bay. Little beachfront snackshops, hamburger stands, and informal restaurants will keep you supplied with necessities and treats, and local entrepreneurs will provide for your thrill wishes: you can cruise in a glass-bottomed boat, go deep-sea fishing, soar above the tops of the towering hotels on a parachute pulled by a motorboat, or simply take a sedate motor yacht tour of the bay. Here's all you'll need to know about Acapulco's stretches of sand and things to do during the day.

The Beaches

We'll start our survey of Acapulco's marvelous beaches just east of town with Hornos, and proceed eastward around the bay; then I'll mention the several beaches on the western peninsula; finally, I'll describe a few beaches farther out from the center of things, for which you'll have to travel a bit.

It used to be chic to visit various beaches at various times of day, reasoning that the sun was better on some than others at certain hours, but this elegant habit has gone by the board these days. Usually a swimmer or sunner heads first for the beach closest to his hotel, and later moves on as the spirit leads.

Starting from the docks downtown and the little fortress, the stretches of beach are named Terraplen, Clavelito, Carabali, and Hornos. **Playa Hornos** is the first wide, fine beach, backed by rows and rows of *palapas* (beach shelters made of wooden poles and palm thatch), little restaurants, and gardens.

After Hornos, on the inland side, is the Parque Ignacio M. Altamirano, more popularly called Papagayo Park, a great expanse of greenery and shade good for when the sun's heat becomes overwhelming. The beach along the park front is called **Playa Papagayo.**

Up past the Ritz Acapulco, the Hyatt Continental, and Paraiso/Marriott hotels is **Playa Paraiso,** also called **Playa Pretil.** As you pass the Diana Glorieta, you'll be confronted with the beginnings of **Playa Condesa,** marked by the gigantic Condesa del Mar hotel. **La Redonda** beach is across from the rocky island of the same name, and the seafront here is marked by the Holiday Inn. The crowd here is among the most beautiful and chi-chi due to the proximity of these top hotels, and also because the hillside behind the hotels is a high-class residential section for both *Acapulquens* and sometime visitors and residents.

Out in the surf is El Morro rock, and out of the rock gushes a 200-foot-high spout of water called the **Chorro del Morro** (Morro gusher), laid on by the city fathers just for fun.

The bay curves to the east and south, and the Costera Aleman descends a hill to level ground to continue along Playa Icacos, past the giant Hotel La Palapa. Inland is a new residential quarter, laid out in the best city-planner fashion, to provide for future growth (it's already begun to fill up!).

Icacos Beach is also marked by the impressive bulk of the Exelaris Hyatt Regency, and the beach stretches around the curve to the south and enters the Icacos Naval Base, a Mexican military installation off-limits to casual visitors.

Follow the main road, which becomes the Carretera Escenica ("Scenic Highway"), and leapfrog over the base to **Guitarron Beach,** the least-developed stretch of sand with a fairly steeply rising hill behind it, and few buildings until you come to Las Brisas, the fabulous hilltop resort complex described in Chapter X.

ON THE WESTERN PENINSULA: A short distance south and west of the center of town at the zócalo (main square), along the Costera Aleman, a road turns off to the right and proceeds for 100 yards or so to the western side of the rocky headlands which form Acapulco Bay. Here, nestled between two high and forbidding masses of rock is **Playa Langosta** (or Angosta, "narrow"), a "pocket beach" unknown to many, with few services (although there is a small hotel with a restaurant just across the street from the beach), and thus usually empty. But note: Swimming here depends on the weather, for when you arrive here you are no longer within the protected reaches of Acapulco Bay, and the surf rushing in from the west can be pretty heavy.

The two prime swimming spots, once Acapulco's top beaches, are called **Caleta** and **Caletilla** ("Little Caleta"); *caleta* simply means "cove," or "inlet," which is what these beaches are, but they have the advantage over Playa Langosta of being shielded by La Roqueta Island, south of the peninsula. Caleta and Caletilla are virtually due south of the zócalo, but on the southern side of the peninsula. Because prices in the nearby hotels and restaurants are low, these two watering spots are much favored by budget-wise Mexican families on vacation.

All of the above beaches are connected by dependable if well-worn municipal buses labeled "Caleta Directo" going west and south, "La Base" going east. Taxis are also reasonably priced.

All beaches in Mexico are public property, by law, so feel free to wander.

At Caleta and Caletilla beaches there are convenient "Vestidores" and "Regaderas" (buildings with changing rooms, lockers, and showers), where you'll pay about 50 pesos ($1) for all the services. Other beaches usually have simple changing shelters.

FARTHER OUT: With the booming growth which Acapulco has seen in recent years, beaches to the far west and southeast of the town have come up for development to meet the ever-increasing demand for sand space.

Southeast of the bay, past Las Brisas, the Carretera Escenica continues eastward to the airport, but shortly after passing Las Brisas is a turnoff to the sheltered bay of **Puerto Marqués,** with its Playa Pichilingue, and several miles farther on a completely different area centered on Playa Revolcadero.

The bay of Puerto Marqués is an attractive area in which to bathe. Water is calm, the bay is sheltered, and waterskiing is available (750 pesos—$15—per hour, a fixed union rate). A restaurant here, called Restaurant Marqués, has a good reputation.

Past the bay, there's an open beach called **Revolcadero,** and a fascinating jungle lagoon. Cab fare to Revolcadero is 400 pesos ($8) from the zócalo; you'll have more fun taking a bus to Puerto Marqués and then a canoe through the lagoon to Revolcadero. Canoes, which accommodate four, charge 250 pesos ($5) per boatload. An alternative method is to take the daily boat between Caleta Beach and Puerto Marqués. Departure is at 11 a.m.—return in the late afternoon. Should you be driving to Revolcadero, you'll be charged 10 pesos (20¢) for parking at the beach.

Miles away in the opposite direction is **La Pie de la Cuesta,** about eight miles west of town (buses for "La Pie" leave from near the post office—"Correos," not far from the zócalo—every five or ten minutes), a popular spot from which to watch the sunset—they're big on sunsets in Acapulco—and every sundown the beach is jumping with hammock-swinging sunset aficionados sipping gin-filled coconuts and watching the waves break along the shore. Beware that boys will try to collect money from you to sit under the thatched *palapas* on the public beach—you needn't pay it.

If you drive or take a cab, continue right out along the peninsula, passing the lagoon on your right, until you have almost reached the small airbase at the tip. All the way along, you'll be invited to drive into different sections of beach by various private entrepreneurs, mostly small boys.

Other Things To Do

During the day, it's pleasant to take a walk (early, before it gets too hot) around the zócalo area. Pop into the church, whose big, blue, bulbous spires make it look more like a Russian Orthodox church; and then turn east along the side street going off at right angles. It has no marker, but it's the Calle Carranza and its arcade includes newsstands, shops selling swimsuits, and such-like attractions.

A fabulous view of Acapulco is had by taking a taxi or by driving (no buses) up the hill directly behind the church in the zócalo, following the signs leading to La Mira. The road is good and several people are building magnificent homes up there. In any case, the view is well worth the drive.

TOURS: The quickest and easiest way to learn the layout of Acapulco is to book yourself on a guided tour of the town. Your hotel bell captain or travel desk will be glad to set it all up for you. Here are descriptions of some of the more popular and easily available tours in and around Acapulco, operated by various companies:

The **City Tour** takes up one morning, and includes a drive along the Costera Miguel Aleman, with the major landmarks noted, including a stop for a walk around the Centro Acapulco. A look at La Quebrada, where the divers do their thing, and a spin around the peninsula complete the tour, which costs in the neighborhood of 700 pesos ($14).

Another tour doesn't use a bus at all, but a **glass-bottomed boat,** which tours Acapulco Bay and visits La Roqueta Island, south of the peninsula, for lunch (included in the price). Swimming time finishes up the four-hour tour; cost is about 750 pesos ($15), but remember that this price includes lunch, and in most cases an open bar during the meal.

You can book a day tour to **Taxco** (see Chapter VIII), an 11-hour, all-day affair including almost six hours total on the bus, and an equal amount of time snooping around the picturesque colonial town. Lunch is included in the price of 1750 pesos ($35); note that this tour may run only one day a week, so look into it early on in your stay in Acapulco, and plan accordingly.

Overnight tours to Taxco and even to Mexico City (by air or by bus) are also arranged by local agencies.

While I'm on the subject of tours, note that evening tours to clubs and shows are available—see Chapter XIII.

PAPAGAYO PARK: Acapulco's latest showpiece is beautiful Papagayo Park, near the Paraiso Marriott Hotel on Playa Papagayo. Decades ago, the rambling Hotel Papagayo was built on this spot, but it was torn down in the '70s to make way for this fabulous layout. A regional museum, botanical garden, aviary, open-air theater, aquarium, and restaurants are all set in its garden-like grounds, and traffic has been routed *beneath* the park to preserve the peace.

ACTIVITIES FOR CHILDREN: The beaches, Papagayo Park, the Centro Acapulco, the motor yacht tours of the bay—all these things can be added to the essential hotel swimming-pool time to keep kids happy. But Acapulco has something more. It's the **Centro Internacional de Convivencia Infantil,** or **CICI,** a child's dreamland of activities which include a freshwater swimming pool with wave-making machine, a water slide, a sea-creatures show, and a play island with ships and artificial denizens. CICI is a short distance south of the Centro Acapulco, along the Costera Aleman.

MOTOR YACHTS AND SUCH: Besides the glass-bottomed boat tours mentioned earlier, you can sign up for a cruise on one of the several motor yachts which make a run around the bay, passing all the beaches and hotels on the northern coast and then heading around Punta Bruja (below Las Brisas) to Puerto Marqués. Here the boat stops to give you a chance for a dip in the sea, and then heads off again to pass by La Roqueta Island, around the peninsula to La Quebrada, and then back to the downtown docks via Caleta and Caletilla beaches. The boats making this tour are the motor yachts *Bonanza* and the *Fiesta* (tel. 220-55 or 262-62)̓, or the *Kontiki,* a sailing trimaran (tel. 465-70); you can book through your hotel or a travel agent, or visit the docks just southwest of the zócalo. Price of the 2½-hour bay cruise is about 400 to 700 pesos ($8 to $14), with some drinks included in the price, and live entertainment provided. The morning cruise leaves about 11 a.m. (but you should book the day before, at least), and there is sometimes a late-afternoon cruise as well.

The yacht *Sea Cloud* (tel. 207-85 or 212-17) has similar cruise programs.

For "Lunadas," or moonlight cruises, see the description below in Chapter XIII.

A JUNGLE BOAT TOUR: Want to glide silently into the jungle amid brilliantly colored birds for a look at the wilder shores of Acapulco? Start by taking a bus from the post office ("Correos") downtown, or a taxi, to La Pie de la Questa (described above under "Beaches"), for your destination, the dock of Embarcaciónes Chaix, on La Pie de la Questa Lagoon. From this point, tours of the jungle waterways depart each half hour between 10 a.m. and 12:30 p.m., each tour arriving back at the docks after 4½ hours. If that's too much jungle to take all at once, come for the 4 p.m. afternoon tour, which only lasts 2½ hours, and takes in the tropical sunset.

WATER SPORTS: Aquatic sports are Acapulco's strong point, and there seems to be no interest or thrill that can't be fulfilled here. Take a look:

Scuba Diving

A morning's or afternoon's diving instruction costs between 1000 and 1500 pesos ($20 and $30), depending whether you sign up at an expensive hotel or simply rent the equipment from a shop on Caleta or Caletilla beaches. If you do the latter, be sure to verify the soundness of the equipment and the amount of oxygen in the tanks.

Waterskiing

Various clubs and entrepreneurs dotted along the beaches (or on call by your hotel) will take you out for an hour's run for about 600 to 800 pesos ($12 to $16), using their equipment and boat, of course.

Parachute Rides

If you've never tried this, you've got a fantastic thrill coming. The operators strap you into a parachute harness attached by a tow rope to a fast motorboat, and a few seconds later your feet leave the beach as the specially designed parachute lifts you up toward the rooftops of the giant hotels. Soon you're above them, floating, soaring, with the entire bay and the mountains in view, and although you don't stay up for more than a few minutes, it seems like about a half hour, and you don't forget the thrill once you land with a hop onto the beach again. It looks like a daredevil act, but the operators put people aloft dozens of times each day, with nary a mishap. How they manage to have you land right where they want you, into the arms of the waiting "landing men," is a sight in itself. The thrill is yours for only 550 pesos ($11). You may find yourself doing this every day.

Deep-Sea Fishing

You can book a seat on a boat with all the necessary gear for a day's (seven hours') fishing through any travel agent for about 1750 pesos ($35) per person, a bargain any way you look at it considering what a private boat plus all the gear would cost if you bought them yourself.

Sailboat and Motorboat Rental

Along Hornos and Condesa beaches at various points are little boat-rental places from which you can rent small sailboats or somewhat beat-up motorboats, the price depending a good deal on the amount of business the renters have at that moment and your skill in haggling. A sailboat can cost between 200 and 400 pesos ($4 to $8) for an hour.

GOLF AND TENNIS: Rent clubs and pay your greens fees at the **Acapulco Princess Hotel** (tel. 431-00), or at its sister establishment, the **Pierre Marqués Princess** (tel. 420-00). The latter hotel has *two* 18-hole, par-72 golf courses all its own. Finally, there is Acapulco's own **Club de Golf,** off Costera Aleman (tel. 407-81).

For tennis, sign up for a court at any of the luxury hotels which have courts, but be advised that they may give their own guests preference, even though you must pay a fee to play. Hotels with courts include **El Matador** (tel. 432-90), **Exelaris Hyatt Regency** (tel. 428-28), the **Acapulco Princess** (tel. 431-00), and the **Pierre Marqués Princess** (tel. 420-00). Acapulco also has various private tennis clubs open to the public for a fee. Try the **Club del Mar** (tel. 452-60), **Fragata Yucatán** (tel. 412-25), or the **Villa Vera Racquet Club** (tel. 403-33).

BULLFIGHTS: The bullfight season runs roughly from October to May, with the action starting about 5 or 5:30 p.m. each Sunday. If you've never seen this Spanish-style spectacle, now's your chance. Arrange for tickets in advance through a travel agent or your hotel travel desk. Acapulco's bullring is on the peninsula, near Caleta and Caletilla beaches, behind the old jai alai fronton. Think when you buy your seat—can you stand the sun, or do you want to pay more for a *boleto de sombra,* a seat in the shade?

Do rest up a bit, though, because there's going to be a lot to keep you going—Acapulco rocks at night!

Chapter XIII

ACAPULCO AFTER DARK

THE GLITTERING LIGHTS of Acapulco Bay are the best clue you can find that this town doesn't go to bed early—in fact, it swings all night long. It's as though the crowds lining the beaches during the day were solar powered, storing up megawatts to be expended in dancing and general good times all night, only fading as the sun makes its reappearance.

The variety of evening attractions is rich, from a full assortment of discos and clubs—one for every taste, at least—to the fabled high-divers of La Quebrada. You can even climb aboard a motor yacht for a moonlight cruise which turns into a romantic party-at-sea.

Basically, you can spend as little or as much as you want doing the town in Acapulco. A walk along the beach will cost you nothing, and could hardly be more romantic, even adventurous (you never know who you'll meet). And dinner at a deluxe restaurant, plus a nightclub show, plus some early-morning hours at a disco, can cost upward of $60 a person or more. It's up to you and what you're after.

Although Acapulco is a fine town to be adventurous in, it can be bewildering to the uninitiated, and so to start the rundown of Acapulco nightlife, here is what you'll need to know about nightclub tours.

TOURS AT NIGHT: No need to confront the bewildering and unfamiliar assortment of nightspots in Acapulco without logistical support. Travel agencies in this town organize a number of Acapulco-By-Night tours to help get you started. The standard tour, for instance, costs about 1600 pesos ($32) and takes you to no fewer than three nightclubs in a little over three hours, and the price includes transportation, cover charge, a drink, tips, and a show at each place. For about 2000 pesos ($40) you can sign up for the deluxe night tour, which just about does it all: cocktails and dinner, the Flamenco Dancers at Fort San Diego, the Indian High Flyers show, and the high-divers at La Quebrada, with a drink at each show and all tips—all in one night! The deluxe tour takes close to five hours (but includes dinner, remember). After such an introduction, you'll feel Acapulco is yours.

If this running around seems too ambitious, try the Folklore Evening tour which, for about 1200 pesos ($24), treats you to a buffet dinner, cocktails, and an evening of Mexican folklore from mariachis to *charros* (cowboys).

ACAPULCO'S HIGH-DIVERS: Just below the Hotel El Mirador Calinda's supper club and bar, called La Perla, is the place where Acapulco's famous high-divers do their thing. From a tiny ledge in the craggy rock wall, one youthful diver plunges hundreds of feet into the thrashing surf of La Quebrada—the Gorge. Practice and a long apprenticeship make this breathtaking feat somewhat easier than it looks, but nothing can ever make it easy or really safe. One false start or slip of the foot and the diver ends up on the breakers rather than in the water right next to the rocks. It all happens in an instant, after the diver takes a minute to pray at a small shrine near the diving spot, and so you must be sure to be at La Quebrada on time. (In fact, to get a good vantage point, either in the Hotel El Mirador Calinda or on the observation terrace nearby, you should get to La Quebrada at least 15 minutes before the scheduled time of the dive.) The entire gorge is illuminated with floodlights, and after the successful dive, the diver climbs up the rocks, dripping and smiling, to gather in the gifts and applause of the crowd (a man may be passing the hat or even selling tickets for this purpose on the observation terrace before the dive takes place).

There are four dives each evening of the year, at 8:15, 9:15, 10:30, and 11:30 p.m., and while these times don't change often, it's best to check them before you go—remember, the dive is over in a matter of a few seconds, so you see nothing if you're even a minute late.

To be sure of a good place, try having dinner or a drink in La Perla—see Chapter XI for details.

FOLKLORE EVENINGS: The major hotels often hold special Folklore Evenings, usually on Wednesday, sometimes even several times a week, and for the price of a full buffet dinner you get the meal plus a varied folklore show. The evenings are open to guests of the hotel, and to outsiders, too, but it's a good idea to reserve in advance. Prices for the buffet and show vary with the hotel, but should be in the range of 900 to 1400 pesos ($18 to $28) per person. Perhaps the most deluxe of these Folklore Evenings is the one at the luxurious Pierre Marqués Princess, although you'll need a cab to get to it, unless you have your own car.

Other evenings, each hotel restaurant has its own program of "specials," and one night each week a full steak dinner may be featured at a standard, fairly low, price; another night the feature might be lobster, Italian cuisine, or perhaps a barbecue. Ask around to see what's on the menu of special nights before you make your plans each evening.

A MOONLIGHT CRUISE: The same motorboats which cruise sun-seekers around Acapulco Bay during the day are busy all evening with trips called "Lunadas," or moonlight cruises. Romantic music, a bar, informal dress, and a splendid panorama are all parts of the tour, which begins at 10:30 p.m. Contact the yachts *Fiesta* and *Bonanza* (tel. 220-55 or 262-62), or book your moonlight cruise through a travel agent. The yacht *Sea Cloud* has a similar Lunada program, including a stop at La Roqueta Island for a beach party. Call them at 207-85 or 212-17, or ask a travel agent for current details. Cost for the moonlight cruises is about 400 pesos ($8).

THE CENTRO ACAPULCO: Acapulco now has its own spectacular culture and convention center, called the Centro Acapulco, on the eastern reaches of the bay between Condesa and Icacos beaches. Done with fine and extravagant Mexican taste, the Centro has rolling lawns dotted with a copy of an Olmec head, another of the Quetzalcóatl of Teotihuacan, etc.; you enter up a grand promenade with a central row of pools and high-spouting fountains. Within the gleaming modern building are all the services and diversions one could want: a mariachi bar, a piano bar, a disco, a movie theater, a legitimate theater, a café, a nightclub, several restaurants, and outdoor performance areas. Should you want to buy a stamp, make a phone call, dress a wound, buy a dress, or tape a TV show, all you need is right here. During the day you can stroll around the grounds for free; at night you pay 50 pesos ($1) for admission to the grounds, and all the shows are free, unless you sit at a café table—in which case you pay a minimum. Programs with the center's current offerings are given away around town, at hotel desks and the like, or call 470-50 for latest word.

The **Flying Indians** perform a modern version of an ancient Totonac religious rite which involves whirling around in the air atop a tremendous pole and similar amazing acrobatic feats. Although the ceremony is no longer religious, it is a spectacle worthy of Acapulco, with lots of glitter and thrill thrown in. Shows are held every night of the week, except Sunday, in the Centro Acapulco, which means you have plenty of time for dinner before the show starts.

THE CLUBS: I might almost venture to say that Acapulco is more famous for its nightclubs than it is for its beaches. The problem is that the clubs open and close with revolving-door regularity, making it very difficult for me to make specific recommendations that will be accurate when you arrive. Some general tips will help: every club seems to have a cover charge of about 300 to 400 pesos ($6 to $8), drinks can cost anywhere from 135 to 275 pesos ($2.70 to $5.50), and remember that a 10% tax, and perhaps a service charge of the same magnitude, will be added to your bill. At this rate, margaritas can approach the lofty reaches of 250 pesos ($5) apiece—be careful. Clubs are open, in general, from 10 p.m. to 4 a.m.

Having warned you that things change, here is a rundown on the likely spots for an evening's dancing and drinking:

Armando's Le Club, Costera Aleman 2330 (tel. 403-93), is one of Acapulco's most long-lived discos, having been around (in various incarnations) for the better part of a decade. While its quarters are now more modest than they once were (it used to be housed in the Moorish pavilions of what is now Armando's Taj Mahal—see Chapter XI), it is still a favorite of the famous and the near-famous during the winter season. Go here to be among the established, well-to-do, and well-known.

Baby-O (tel. 474-74), just across the Costera Aleman from Armando's, is the funkiest of Acapulco's discos, where you can order a hamburger or a bottle of mezcal, dance, or jump into a Jacuzzi with your friends. Go here if you're daring, young, and devil-may-care.

The famous and ubiquitous Carlos Anderson, king of Mexican restaurateurs, has opened a very successful club in Acapulco called (it had to be something like this, for sure): **Carlos's Chili**

'n' Dance Hall 'n' Bar 'n' Grill. The mood here is young and lively and good-times-for-all, no serious cooler-than-thou competition, and the funkiness is fun rather than far-out. The cover charge tends to be a slight bit cheaper than at most clubs, too.

For those lucky souls who have carted mammoth suitcases jammed with tremendous wardrobes, there's **UBQ** (tel. 447-77), at Costera Aleman 115. An elegant floodlit facade and a panoramic view of Acapulco Bay (from a disco?) add to the high-class feeling here. Everyone else is going to be very well dressed indeed, and intent on studying your sartorial appeal. It helps to have as part of your outfit a hefty wad of cash.

The disco-bar called, simply, **"9"** (tel. 480-88), Avenida Deportes 110, at the Costera, is Acapulco's self-declared gathering place for the gay crowd, mostly male. Although several other clubs, like **Le Dome** (Costera Aleman 4175, tel. 411-90) are not exclusively gay, as is "9," gay activity is not limited to just one club.

Boccaccio's (tel. 419-01), Costera Aleman 5040, is, like Armando's, one of Acapulco's steadier places when it comes to longevity—but one never knows what will happen here. Right now it's a good and glittery disco drawing a large and general crowd, with lots of distractions and sideshows as well as the disco dance floor.

Besides these "independent" places, most of the large hotels have their own nightclubs which bear the word "disco" in their names, but note that this has become a "buzz" word in club circles, and so an Acapulco "disco," particularly in a hotel, may not have records at all, but in fact a live band.

The lobby bars of the major hotels also have good entertainment in the evenings—the one at the beautiful Condesa del Mar springs to mind first—and anyone can wander in and take in the music. If you take a seat it's expected you'll want a drink, which can come to upward of 250 to 300 pesos ($5 to $6), and which serves as a sort of cover charge. This music is not really for dancing, but rather for early-evening (8 to 10 p.m.) listening and general getting into the Latin mood.

Chapter XIV

TRAVEL TIPS

A Quick-Reference Guide from A to Z

DETAILS, DETAILS! The problem with details in a foreign country is that they're not where you need them when you need them, and so little things like making a telephone call or giving a tip become major problems. In order to help you do away with common travel problems as quickly as possible, here are detailed tips on travel in Mexico, arranged in alphabetical order, all in the right place at the right time.

ABBREVIATIONS: Dept.—apartments; **Apdo.**—post office box; **Av.**—Avenida, **Calz.**—calzada or boulevard. C on faucets stands for *caliente* (hot), and F stands for *fria* (cold). It's not uncommon, however, to see faucets made in the U.S. and marked H and C. Yet because the plumbers don't understand English, the C faucet will be on the left *(caliente)* side, and will dispense *hot* water; the H faucet will be on the right and, in this case, will signify *cold* water.

ALTITUDE: Remember as you stroll around Mexico City that you are now at an altitude of 7240 feet—almost a mile and a half in the sky—and that there is a lot less oxygen in the air here than what you're used to. If you run for a bus and feel dizzy when you sit down, that's the altitude; if you think you're in shape, but all the same you puff and puff getting up Chapultepec hill, that's the altitude. It takes about ten days or so to acquire the extra red blood cells you need to adjust to the scarcity of oxygen.

At Acapulco, there is no such problem, of course. But in summer at this tropical latitude and seaside location, the air is muggy and that, too, makes for heavy breathing. Don't overdo it here, either.

AMERICAN EXPRESS: The Mexico City office is at Hamburgo 75 (tel. 905/533-1680), in the Zona Rosa. It's open for banking, the pickup of clients' mail, and travel advice from 9 a.m. to 2 p.m. and from 4 to 6 p.m. Monday through Friday, and also 9 a.m. to 1 p.m. on Saturday. If it's mail you're going for, remember that they charge 50 pesos ($1) if you have no American Express credit card, travelers check, or tour ticket to prove that you're a client of theirs.

The Acapulco office is at Costera Aleman 709A (tel. 748/410-95).

ART EXHIBITS: In Mexico City, you'll find an open-air show in **Sullivan Park** every Sunday from 9 a.m. to 3 p.m. Sullivan Park is located one block north of Reforma just east of Insurgentes between Sullivan and Villalongin. The Casa del Lago and the Museum of Modern Art in **Chapultepec Park** have galleries which display the works of visiting contemporary Mexican painters. The **Bellas Artes** also has visiting exhibits, national as well as international. You can look over lots of paintings, both amateur and professional, at the Bazar Sabado in San Angel.

Art exhibits are not Acapulco's strong suit, except perhaps in private homes. For what there is, though, you should check at the Centro Acapulco. The government-run **Fonart** craft shop is opposite Hornos Beach, next to the Hotel De Gante.

BANKS (see also Money): Open Monday to Friday from 9 a.m. to 1:30 p.m. Closed weekends (except for Mexico City's Banco del Atlantico, which is open for a short while on Saturday and Sunday). They give you the best peso-dollar rate you'll get anywhere. Most banks have an employee who speaks English. Travelers checks or cash are the surest ways for uncomplicated and fast service. Cashing a personal check in Mexico may delay you for weeks while the bank waits for it to clear. The currency-exchange counter at the airport is open as long as flights are arriving or departing.

BARBERSHOPS: First-class ones charge about 200 to 300 pesos ($4 to $6) for haircuts, same for shaves.

In Acapulco, every big hotel has its own barbershop, but you must expect to pay more in these luxury places.

BOLETRONICO: This is the name of Mexico City's electronic ticket system, similar to the Ticketron outlets known in the U.S. Bullfight tickets, those for the Ballet Folklorico and for other attractions are all on sale in the booths of this municipally run system; the booths are scattered around the city, and your hotel clerk will know which one is most convenient for you. Boletronico is not in use in Acapulco, although it may arrive soon.

BOOKSTORES: In Mexico City, **Sanborn's** and **Woolworth's** always have books in English, as well as magazines and newspapers. So do the **American Bookstore,** Madero 25, off Bolívar (tel. 512-7284), and the **Librería Británica,** Madero 30A (tel. 521-0180). **Central de Publicaciónes–Librería Mizrachi,** Juárez 4 at the corner of Lázaro Cárdenas, has a very fine selection. The **American Benevolent Society's Caza Libros** (tel. 540-5123) at Monte Athos 355, 2½ blocks off of Reforma *west* of Chapultepec Park in the section called Lomas Barrilaco, has used books in Spanish and English, hardback and paperback, plus magazines, records, and prints. All profits go to charity projects of the society.

French and English books and magazines, especially those dealing with Mexico, its history, archeology, and people, are the specialty of the **Cia. Internacional de Publicaciónes,** or Librerías C.I.P. for short. Branches of this firm are located at Serapio Rendon 125 (just off Sullivan Park, near the Hotel Sevilla), at Avenida Madero 30, not far from the House of Tiles; also in Polanco, and in San Angel.

In Acapulco, many hotels have their own bookshops, or the newspaper and tobacco counter sells some paperbacks as well. Sanborn's, downtown on the waterfront a short distance east of the zócalo, has its usual assortment of English-language books and magazines.

BULLFIGHT TICKETS: You can get them through any hotel travel agency. Cheapest tickets are general admission *Sol General;* those on the shady side of the Plaza México cost much more. You can also get to the bullring early, and wait in line. The easiest way to get tickets, however, is to drop by a computerized Boletronico (see above) ticket booth near your hotel in Mexico City.

In Acapulco, it's hardly worth dragging yourself over to the bullring near Caleta Beach for the tickets when your hotel can get them for you. As in Mexico City, tickets in the shade and reserved seats cost more than general admission sun-seat tickets.

BUSES: Mexico has a good, dependable, inexpensive system of intercity buses; intracity routes are also usually quite serviceable. Full information will be found in Chapters II, VIII, and IX.

CAMERAS AND FILM: Both are more expensive than in the States; take full advantage of your 12-roll film allowance. You're permitted to take two cameras into Mexico with you—one for stills and one for movies. If you get caught short, though, major brands of film are readily available in Mexico City and Acapulco. **Sanborn's** carries the full line, as do many hotel tobacco and newsstands.

CAMPING: Yes, camping is fun and easy in Mexico, and fairly inexpensive, considering what you get. There's a small camping area south of Mexico City just off the old road to Cuernavaca, and several others on the periphery as well. In Acapulco, prime areas are the **Acapulco Trailer Park,** at La Pie de la Cuesta; and the **Coloso,** a short distance south of the main Mexico City–Acapulco highway (turn left on the shortcut to San Marcos and Pinotepa Nacional just before beginning to climb the last hill into Acapulco). Fees are in the range of $5 to $8 per night for a camper or trailer, with hookups.

CAR RENTALS: The car-rental business in Mexico is as far flung and well developed as in Europe and the U.S., with the usual problems and procedures. As elsewhere, it's good to reserve your car in advance in Mexico, an easy task when you fly into the country, as most airlines will gladly make the reservations for you. Mexico City and most other Mexican cities of any size have several rental offices representing the various big firms and some smaller ones. Rent-here/leave-there arrangements are usually simple to make.

With a credit card (American Express, VISA, MasterCard, and so forth) rentals are simple if you're over 25, in possession of a valid driver's license, and have your passport or Tourist Card with you. Without a credit card you must leave a cash deposit, usually a big one.

Driving in Mexico City, and especially in and out of it (to

sights a day's drive out of town) is a pretty big hassle, and parking's certainly a problem, so I can't recommend a rental car. But if you have enough people to fill one and to share the cost, and this is your preference, the information below may help you out.

The basic rates for all rental cars and insurance are set by the Mexican government, so the only room for competition between the various companies is in service, special packages, and the like. You can save yourself some money by renting only as much car as you *need:* make sure that the company you select offers the VW Beetle or Datsun—usually the cheapest car—if that will do, and make sure they will have one on hand to rent you. (Sometimes they'll say they do over the phone, but when you arrive at the office the Beetles or Datsuns will be "all booked up" for two weeks, etc.)

Don't underestimate the cost of renting a car. The total amount you'll be out of pocket for a short one-day trip to, say, Cuernavaca (85 kms, or 50 miles, from Mexico City) might be in the range of $40. Take your time when you look over the company's brochure, estimate the distance and time, allowing a generous margin for wrong turns, side trips, etc.—those kilometers are expensive!—and then add up *all* the charges you'll have to pay *before* the clerk starts filling out an order form.

Your completed estimate should look something like this, based on a total of 170 km, for the very cheapest car offered:

Basic daily charge	600	pesos
Kilometers (170 @ 2.40 pesos each)	680	
Full nondeductible insurance	250	
Subtotal	1530	
IVA tax (@ 10%)	153	
Gas (@ 8.01 pesos per liter)	180	
Tolls and parking	150	
Grand Total	2013	pesos
	($40.26)	

This estimate is for Mexico City; in Acapulco a one-day rental would be slightly cheaper as the custom there is to include 200 free kilometers in every rental deal. But longer rentals in Acapulco turn out to be even more expensive than in Mexico City. An average three-day rental in Acapulco might be $140, a few dollars cheaper in Mexico City. For a week, the figures might be $333 for Acapulco, $305 for Mexico City—and these are for the very cheapest car offered, Group A. Add about 15% to these estimates for Group B or C cars (VW Caribe, the Mexican version of the Rabbit, or VW Safari), about 30% for Group D cars (Jeep, Ford Fairmont, VW Bus or Combi). Weekly unlimited-mileage rentals, when offered, still come out to about $40 a day minimum when gas, insurance, and tax are added.

Once you've made up your mind to rent a car, finding a rental office is a snap. Rental desks are set up in the airports, in all major hotels, and in many travel agencies. The large firms like Avis, Hertz, National, and Odin have rental offices on main streets as well.

CREDIT CARDS: Those who swear by life on the little plastic card will be happy to know that all major credit cards are readily accepted in all parts of Mexico. VISA, MasterCard, American Express, and others can be used in all but the cheapest hotels and restaurants, and in many good shops as well. It is particularly good to have a credit card if you plan to rent a car. If you need cash, you can charge a certain amount of pesos against your card, and then pay the amount back on your monthly bill. By the way, you may not see the exact VISA or MasterCard logos in shop windows, but rather their Mexican equivalents: VISA, Carnet, Bancomatico, or Bancomer. Don't worry—your card will work just as well.

CUSTOMS AND DUTY-FREE GOODS: Coming to Mexico, Customs officials are very tolerant as long as you have no drugs (that is, marijuana, cocaine, etc.) or firearms. You're allowed to bring two cartons of cigarettes, or 50 cigars, plus a kilogram (2.2 pounds) of smoking tobacco; the liquor allowance is two bottles of anything, wine or hard liquor.

Returning to the U.S. and Canada, Canadians receive a $150 exemption for goods bought in Mexico, while U.S. citizens or residents are allowed to bring back up to $300, with special exemptions. The exemptions come under a system called the Generalized System of Preferences, which means that certain items brought in from certain countries are duty free, and although you must declare them, they will be deducted from your $300 duty-free allowance. There are some further restrictions and regulations, but in general this means the following items come in duty free: baskets, books, candles, ceramic ware, earthen or stone tableware, artificial flowers, furniture, frames, hats, silver, copper, jade, opals, guitars, drums, flutes, onyx, papier-mâché, piñatas, saddles and harnesses, toys, wood articles, and works of art.

Reentering the U.S., you're allowed by federal law to bring in a carton (200) of cigarettes, *or* 50 cigars, *or* two kilograms (total: 4.4 lbs.) of smoking tobacco, or proportional amounts of these items, plus one liter of alcoholic beverage (wine, beer, or spirits). If you bring larger amounts of these things, you will have to pay federal duty and internal revenue tax. But wait! Your quotas will also be subject to state laws (i.e., of the state in which you reenter the U.S.). The state law may not allow you to bring back *any* liquor, which means *you will have to pour it out*. It's not simply a matter of paying duty, it's a matter of absolute quotas—or no quotas at all—for some states. This liquor quota is most strictly applied at the border posts, less strictly at airports not near the border.

Canadian returning-resident regulations are similar to the U.S. ones: a carton of cigarettes, 50 cigars, two pounds (not kilos) of smoking tobacco, 1.1 liters (40 ounces) of wine or liquor, *or* a case of beer (8.2. liters). All provinces except P.E.I. and the Northwest Territories allow you to bring in more liquor and beer up to two gallons (nine liters) more—but the taxes are quite high.

DENTIST: The American, Canadian, or British consulate (see "Embassies," below) will be able to provide you with names of dentists, as will any of the large hotels.

DEPARTMENT STORES: Woolworth's (Insurgentes Sur 376 and Reforma 99); Sears Roebuck (San Luís Potosí 214); La Ciudad de México (5 de Mayo and Zócalo); Sanborn's (Madero 4, Reforma 45), Niza (at Hamburgo, Reforma 333, Juárez 70, Salamanca 74, Insurgentes at Aguascalientes). And on Calle 20 de Noviembre, in the block south of the zócalo, is Palacio de Hierro, recently under new management and catering to the very posh set, and the less expensive Liverpool. Paris Londres, 16 de Septiembre (near the Zócalo), is a high-quality store.

Acapulco is only now witnessing the appearance of fledgling "department stores," most in the zócalo area.

DOCTORS: American citizens can phone the U.S. Embassy, Reforma 305 (tel. 905/553-3333), for a list of English-speaking physicians. Nationals of other countries should call the appropriate number under "Embassies," below. The **A.B.C. Hospital** (tel. 905/515-8500) is excellent for travelers, though expensive. The majority of the doctors listed through the embassy practice here. It's efficient, bilingual, and staffed by some of the best doctors in Mexico. The hospital is located at Sur 132–136 at the corner of Avenida Observatorio ("Sur 132," believe it or not, is the street name!). You can take the Metro (Line 1) to Observatorio; it's a short taxi ride from there.

In Acapulco, most good hotels always have a competent and dependable doctor on hand who speaks English, or you can call your consulate.

DRIVING IN MEXICO: Should you have occasion to rent a car and drive in Mexico, you'll find that the roads are not quite up to U.S. or Canadian standards, although they're sufficient. Don't plan your driving times as though you were traveling on Interstate highways. Watch for obstacles: flocks of animals, people crossing the roads, donkeys, slow-moving vehicles. It's not a good idea to drive at night in the countryside as road markings are not the best, some vehicles travel with bad reflectors and burnt-out tail lights, and pedestrians are hard to see along the road edge.

Traffic signs are on the European model, with some American signs as well. Speed limits and distances are given in kilometers, of course. The road between Mexico City and Acapulco is fairly well trafficked during the daylight hours.

DRUGS: The Mexican authorities have been encouraged to be zealous with drug offenders or suspected drug offenders. It is not unheard of that people are put in jail and pressured to sign confessions for the mere *suspicion* of having enjoyed a "recreational" drug such as marijuana. Do your best to look as though you don't use prohibited drugs, and then don't use them, too! There is little the American or Canadian authorities can do to help you once you've been arrested, and no matter what you've heard, bribes do not always do the trick. Logical arguments, such as those holding that it's absurd not to smoke pot in Mexico, the Land of Pot-Growing, are of little comfort when you're behind bars.

DRUGSTORES: The word is *farmacia,* and they will sell you just about anything you want, with prescription or without. Most are open every day but Sunday from 9 a.m. to 11 p.m.; the **Farmacia del Caballito,** at Juárez 97 and Reforma in Mexico City is open from 8 a.m. to midnight. The **Sanborn's** chain has a drug counter in many of their establishments.

ELECTRICITY: Despite its continental sympathies in many regards, Mexico operates on American- and Canadian-style electric current: 110–125 volts, 60 cycles, with the standard American flat-prong plugs.

ELEVATORS: The lowest button on the elevator is marked **P.B.** for *planta baja* (ground floor). The first floor above the ground floor is numbered "1" in Mexico.

EMBASSIES AND CONSULATES: In Mexico City, they provide valuable lists of doctors, lawyers, regulations concerning marriages in Mexico, etc. Here's a list:

Canada: In Mexico City, the embassy is at Melchor Ocampo 463–467, at Reforma (tel. 905/533-0610); the Honorary Consulate in Acapulco is in the Hotel El Mirador Calinda at the top of La Quebrada hill at no. 74 (tel. 748/372-91). Hours are 9 a.m. to 1 p.m. and 3 to 5 p.m. weekdays; off-hours, the name of a duty officer is posted on the embassy door.

U.S.A.: In Mexico City, the embassy is at Reforma 305, right next to the Maria Isabel Sheraton Hotel (tel. 905/553-3333). The Honorary Consulate in Acapulco can be reached by dialing 748/219-06.

U.K.: The British Embassy in Mexico City is at Calle Río Lerma 71, at Calle Río Sena (tel. 905/511-4880 or 514-3327). In Acapulco, the honorary consul makes his home in the Hotel Las Brisas on the Carretera Escenica (tel. 748/466-05).

HOLIDAYS, PUBLIC: Several Mexican holidays correspond to major holidays in other countries, or in some cases a purely Mexican holiday may be celebrated on a day which is also a U.S. or Canadian holiday. On all these days, banks, stores, and other businesses are closed:

January 1	New Year's Day
February 5	Constitution Day
March 21	Benito Juárez's Birthday
May 1	Labor Day

May 5	Anniversary of the Battle of Puebla (Cinco de Mayo, 1862)
September 1	President's Message to Congress
September 16	Independence Day
October 12	Columbus Day, or "Day of the Race"
November 20	Mexican Revolution Anniversary
December 25	Christmas Day

HOSPITAL: In Mexico City, it's the **American-British Cowdray (A.B.C.) Hospital,** Calle Sur 136, no. 201, in Colonia Tacubaya (tel. 905/515-8500); for an emergency, call 515-8359. See also "Doctors."

INFORMATION: The **Secretariat of Tourism** in Mexico City, once located right downtown at the intersection of Juárez and Reforma, has moved to Avenida Presidente Masaryk 172, north of Chapultepec Park in the section called Polanco. To replace their handy downtown info booth there is now a special Tourist Information telephone number (the person on the other end will speak English): dial 250-0123.

Acapulco has two tourism offices, one on the way into town on the highway from Mexico City, and the other on Costera Aleman at Hornos Beach (tel. 221-70).

LAUNDRY: All hotels can make some arrangements to have your laundry taken care of. Small laundries can be found on the side streets, but the tourist's best bet in Mexico City is the chain **called Lavianderia Jiffy** (that's "HEE-fee"; tel. 511-6501), with a handy shop one block from the Angel Monument at Tiber and Río Lerma. Open Monday through Saturday, 9 a.m. to 7 p.m. Closed Sunday. English spoken.

LIBRARIES: Mexico City has several libraries of English-language books connected with her diplomatic missions. Check out the Benjamin Franklin (American) Library, on Niza between Londres and Liverpool. The Canadian Library (English and French books and periodicals) is at Melchor Ocampo 481, near the intersection with Reforma, open Monday through Friday from 10:30 a.m. to 1 p.m. and from 2 to 5 p.m. The British Embassy, Consular Section, has British periodicals in the waiting room. See also "Bookstores," above.

MAIL (see also Post Office): For the most reliable and convenient Mexico City mail service, have your letters sent to you c/o the **American Express** office at Hamburgo 75, México D.F. (open Monday through Friday from 9 a.m. to 2 p.m. and 4 to 6 p.m., on Saturday from 9 to 1 p.m.), which will receive and forward mail for you if you are one of their clients (a travel club card or an American Express travelers check is proof). They charge a small fee if you wish them to forward your mail. General delivery is *Lista de Correos* in Mexico, and you pick it up at the Palacio de Correos, or Correo Mayor, corner of Tacuba and Avenida Lázaro Cárdenas. Mail service within Mexico and between Mexico and other countries is highly idiosyncratic.

In Acapulco, *Lista de Correos* mail can be picked up in the post office ("Correos") near the zócalo.

To U.S., airmail postcards or letters cost 4 pesos for 10 grams or a fraction. Within Mexico, postcards cost 2.50 pesos and letters are 4 pesos for 20 grams or fraction, airmail. To Europe the 10-gram air rate is 7 pesos, to Oceania it's 8.50. Unless you don't mind having the postcard you sent to your neighbor arrive a month after *you* get home, send *everything* by airmail, and even then it can take from 10 days to 3 weeks. Special Delivery or Express mail is *Entrega Immediata* in Spanish, and this service costs extra per piece of mail if you're mailing in Mexico.

MONEY (see also Banks): The dollar sign ($) is used to indicate pesos in Mexico. As many establishments dealing with tourists also quote prices in dollars, confusion is cleared up by the use of the abbreviations "Dlls." for dollars, and "m.n." (*moneda nacional*—national currency) for pesos, so "$20.00 m.n." means 20 pesos. Banks often charge a fee for changing travelers checks, or give a rate of exchange below the official daily rate. Hotels usually exchange below the official daily rate as well.

The currency exchange counter at the airport is open as long as there are flights arriving or departing.

If you need to get money from your bank at home, don't try to clear a check through a Mexican bank—it takes too long. Instead, go to the office of **Telegramas Internacionales** (tel. 519-5920), Balderas 14–18, near Colón and just off the west end of the Alameda in Mexico City, between 8 a.m. and midnight any day except Sunday. Have the money remitted to that office, and pick it up about four days later with your passport and Tourist Card. If there's any chance you'll leave Mexico City before the money arrives, try to get cash somewhere else. It takes up to six months for your home bank to track down an unclaimed international money order.

In Acapulco, the Telegraph Office is in the Post Office, down near the zócalo.

MOVIES: Prices in the capital range anywhere from 60 to 80 pesos ($1.20 to $1.60) and up. It's almost impossible to see a movie on Sunday because of the crowds; afternoon shows during the week are easiest to get into, but there still might be a long line waiting for tickets. Whenever possible, buy tickets in advance. Unescorted women should be careful of the theaters they attend and never go to lower-priced theaters without an escort. Times and prices for films are listed in the English-language *The News* and in the Spanish-language *Excelsior.*

NEWSPAPERS: For American travelers in Mexico City, the English-language newspaper *The News* is an excellent buy at 16 pesos, more on Sunday (prices higher in Acapulco). It carries many Stateside columnists as well as newsworthy commentaries, and a calendar of the day's events including concerts, art shows, plays, etc. A Spanish-language paper, *Excelsior,* has a daily partial page in English. Most hotels carry the *Mexico City Daily Bulletin,* a free throw-away sheet in English with a list of events in the city and environs. *Note:* Not all the information is correct (e.g., museum hours). Sanborn's carries many United States papers, usually a day old.

POST OFFICE (see also Mail): The main one in Mexico City is located on the corner of Tacuba and Avenida Lázaro Cárdenas, just east of Bellas Artes; open from 9 a.m. to 11 p.m.; closes at 8 p.m. on weekends. You buy stamps at the windows marked *"estampillas."* On the third floor, they have an interesting philatelic exhibit, which is usually open on weekdays from 9 a.m. to 1 p.m. and on Saturday from 9 a.m. to noon. It's free. Foreign parcels must be taken, *open for inspection,* to the Correo Internacional no. 2, Calle Dr. Andrade and Río de la Loza (Metro: Balderas or Salto del Agua), open Monday through Friday from 8 a.m. to noon. Smart residents *never* have packages mailed *to* them in Mexico. *Lista de correos* is poste restante (general delivery).

Branch post offices are scattered around this mammoth city.

The most convenient ones for readers of this book will be at Arriaga and Mariscal, just north of the Monument to the Revolution; in the railroad office building adjoining Buena Vista Station; at the corner of Londres and Varsovia in the Zona Rosa; and on Calle Río Lerma near the corner with Calle Río Marne.

RADIO STATIONS: Lots of stations in Mexico City, on both AM and FM, all in Spanish. Station XELA, 800 kH AM and 98.5 mH FM, broadcasts classical music, as do several university stations.

SHIPPING: If you want to send things home ahead of you from Mexico City, you can take them already packaged to the **Central de Aduanas,** Dinamarca 83 (tel. 525-7660), which handles them by land, sea, or air. Cheapest is by sea and the minimum weight they'll accept is 10 kilos (22 pounds). Or you can mail things, in which case you'll have to visit the special Customs post office (see above under "Post Office"). Theoretically, you're not supposed to mail anything except books from any other post office except this one, and therefore you may find it more convenient to take your packages to some other Mexican town, where there's only one post office that accepts everything.

SIESTA: Although many shops and other concerns no longer take a long afternoon siesta, there is usually an extended lunch hour during which things are closed. Normal business (but *not* banking!) hours are from 9 a.m. to 2 p.m. and from 4 to 6 p.m. weekdays, with a half day (9 to 1) for offices on Saturday. Shops tend to be open all day Saturday. Most every commercial concern closes on Sunday, of course.

Try to work yourself into the schedule, and take a break between 2 and 4 o'clock each afternoon.

In Acapulco, the siesta is more alive and well, and shops may close at 2 and not reopen until 6 at night, and then stay open from 6 to 8.

SPANISH LESSONS: Three-week courses (three hours daily, five days per week) are offered monthly by the **Mexican North American Institute of Cultural Relations,** Hamburgo 115 and Varsovia 43 (tel. 511-4720) in Mexico City. A course produces excellent results.

SUPERMARKETS: They're all over Mexico now with names like **Sumesa, Gigante, Aurrera,** and are as big as, and bigger than, some of the ones you're used to back home. Outlets of the government's **Conasupo** and **Conasuper** chain can be found everywhere in Mexico.

TAXIS: See the separate sections describing taxis in Chapters II and IX.

TELEGRAMS: Telegramas Internacionales is located at Balderas 14–18, just west of the Alameda (tel. 519-5920), in Mexico City, open 8 a.m. to midnight Monday through Saturday. Telex service is here as well.

In Acapulco, you will find the telegram office inside the Post Office down near the zócalo.

TELEPHONES: Local calls in Mexico cost 20 centavos for three minutes. There are two types of coin phones: in one the slot at the top holds your coin in a gentle grip until your party answers, when it drops; if there's no answer or a busy signal, you can pluck your coin from the slot. The other type is the sort where you insert a coin which disappears into the bowels of the machine, and drops into the cashbox when your call goes through, or into the return slot if it doesn't (after you hang up). This type of phone is often jammed, and your coin won't drop, so that when your party answers you will hear them but they won't hear you. Try from another pay phone.

Long-distance calls in Mexico are as expensive as local calls are cheap. And international long-distance calls tend to be outrageously expensive, unless you are calling collect to the U.S., Canada, or Britain. To find out estimated charges (*tarifas*), and area codes (*claves*) you don't know, dial 07 in Mexico City.

To call the U.S. or Canada collect, dial 96 + area code + number, and tell the *operadora* that you want *una llamada por cobrar* (a collect call), *telefono a telefono* (station-to-station), or *persona a persona* (person-to-person).

If you don't want to call collect, you'll have to go to a *caseta de larga distancia,* or call from your hotel, as it's impracticable to load hundreds of 20-centavo pieces into a pay phone. Your hotel will levy a service charge—perhaps a percentage:—on top of the already exorbitant rate. Ask in advance what they'll add on. At a caseta you pay just the call charge.

From a caseta or hotel, dial 95 + area code + number for the U.S. and Canada, or 98 + area code + number for anywhere else in the world. If you need the international (English-speaking) operator after all, dial 09 in Mexico City. Casetas in Mexico City are at the airport (two), Buenavista Station, Terminal Norte de Autobuses, in the Insurgentes and Merced Metro stations, at Donceles 20, and at Sullivan 143.

To call long distance (abbreviated "lada") within Mexico, dial 91 + area code + number. Mexican area codes/(*claves*) are listed in the front of the telephone directories. For Mexico City, it's 905/; for Acapulco, 748/.

You can save up to 29% by calling in off-peak periods. The cheapest times to call are after 11 p.m. and before 8 a.m. any day, and all day Saturday and Sunday; most expensive times are 8 a.m. to 5 p.m. weekdays.

TIME: Mexico City and Acapulco are on Central Standard Time, in the same time zone as Chicago, Kansas City, Dallas, and New Orleans; but note that in Mexico, Daylight Saving Time is not observed.

TIPPING: 10% to 15% in expensive places, a few pesos for $2-or-under meals. You don't have to tip taxi drivers unless you want to, but there are small services that might be performed unasked which, as a matter of course, are worth a few pesos' tip.

TOILETS, PUBLIC: Public toilets in Mexico may be called *baños, servicios, sanitarios, retretes,* or even *W.C.* After you've asked and found your way there, you pick the right door by the conventional symbol (pipe for men, fan for women, etc.) or by the words *"Hombres"* or *"Caballeros"* for men, *"Mujeres"* or *"Damas"* for women. You may have to leave a tip of a peso or so if there's an attendant.

WATER: Most hotels have decanters or bottles of purified water in the rooms and the snazzier hotels have special taps marked *"Agua Purificada."* Virtually any hotel, restaurant, or bar will bring you purified water if you specifically request it.

NOW, SAVE MONEY ON
ALL YOUR TRAVELS!
Join Arthur Frommer's $15-A-Day Travel Club

Saving money while traveling is never a simple matter, which is why, almost 20 years ago, the **$15-a-Day Travel Club** was formed. Actually, the idea came from readers of the Arthur Frommer Publications who felt that such an organization could bring financial benefits, continuing travel information, and a sense of community to economy-minded travelers all over the world.

In keeping with the money-saving concept, the membership fee is low—$14 (U.S. residents) or $16 (Canadian, Mexican, and foreign residents)—and is immediately exceeded by the value of your benefits which include:

(1) An annual subscription to an 8-page tabloid newspaper *The Wonderful World of Budget Travel* which keeps you up-to-date on fast-breaking developments in low-cost travel in all parts of the world—bringing you the kind of information you'd have to pay over $25 a year to obtain elsewhere. This consumer-conscious publication also provides special services to readers:

Traveler's Directory—a list of members all over the world who are willing to provide hospitality to other members as they pass through their home cities.

Share-a-Trip—requests from members for travel companions who can share costs and help avoid the burdensome single supplement.

Readers Ask . . . Readers Reply—travel questions from members to which other members reply with authentic firsthand information.

(2) The latest edition of any TWO of the books listed on the following page.

(3) A copy of *Arthur Frommer's Guide to New York*.

(4) Your personal membership card which entitles you to purchase through the Club all Arthur Frommer Publications for a third to a half off their regular retail prices during the term of your membership.

So why not join this hardy band of international budgeteers NOW and participate in its exchange of information and hospitality? Simply send U.S. $14 (U.S. residents) or $16 (Canadian, Mexican, and other foreign residents) along with your name and address to: $15-A-Day Travel Club, Inc., 1230 Avenue of the Americas, New York, NY 10020. Remember to specify which *two* of the books in section (2) above you wish to receive in your initial package of members' benefits. Or tear out this page, check off any two books on the opposite side and send it to us with your membership fee.

FROMMER/PASMANTIER PUBLISHERS Date _____
1230 AVE. OF THE AMERICAS, NEW YORK, NY 10020

Friends, please send me the books checked below:

$-A-DAY GUIDES
(In-depth guides to low-cost tourist accommodations and facilities.)

☐ Europe on $20 a Day $9.25
☐ Australia on $20 a Day $7.25
☐ England and Scotland on $25 a Day $7.95
☐ Greece on $20 a Day $7.25
☐ Hawaii on $25 a Day $8.95
☐ Ireland on $25 a Day $6.95
☐ Israel on $25 & $30 a Day $6.95
☐ Mexico on $20 a Day $8.95
☐ New Zealand on $20 & $25 a Day $6.95
☐ New York on $25 a Day $5.95
☐ Scandinavia on $25 a Day $6.95
☐ South America on $25 a Day $6.95
☐ Spain and Morocco (plus the Canary Is.) on $20 a Day $6.95
☐ Washington, D.C. on $25 a Day $7.25

DOLLARWISE GUIDES
(Guides to tourist accommodations and facilities from budget to deluxe,
with emphasis on the medium-priced.)

☐ Egypt $6.95
☐ England & Scotland $7.95
☐ France. $7.95
☐ Germany. $6.25
☐ Italy $6.95
☐ Portugal (incl. Madeira) $7.25

☐ Canada $8.25
☐ Caribbean (incl. Bermuda & the Bahamas) $8.95
☐ California & Las Vegas $7.95
☐ Florida $6.25
☐ New England $6.95
☐ Southeast & New Orleans . . . $6.95

THE ARTHUR FROMMER GUIDES
(Pocket-size guides to tourist accommodations and facilities in all price ranges.)

☐ Amsterdam/Holland $3.95
☐ Athens $3.95
☐ Boston $3.95
☐ Hawaii $3.95
☐ Dublin/Ireland. $3.95
☐ Las Vegas $3.95
☐ Lisbon/Madrid/Costa del Sol . $3.95
☐ London $3.95
☐ Los Angeles $3.95

☐ Mexico City/Acapulco $3.95
☐ Montreal/Quebec City $3.95
☐ New Orleans $3.95
☐ New York $3.95
☐ Paris $3.95
☐ Philadelphia/Atlantic City $3.95
☐ Rome $3.95
☐ San Francisco. $3.95
☐ Washington, D.C. $3.95

SPECIAL EDITIONS

☐ How to Beat the High Cost of Travel $3.95

☐ The Urban Athlete (NYC sports guide for jocks & novices) . . . $6.95

☐ Museums in New York (Incl. historic houses, gardens, & zoos). $7.95

☐ Speak Easy Phrase Book (Fr/Sp/ Ger/It.in one vol.) $4.95

☐ Where to Stay USA (Accommodations from $3 to $25 a night) $6.25

In U.S. include $1 post. & hdlg. for 1st book over $3; 75¢ for books under $3; 25¢ any add'l. book. Outside U.S. $2, $1, and 50¢ respectively.

Enclosed is my check or money order for $_____

NAME _____

ADDRESS _____

CITY _____ STATE _____ ZIP _____